ESKIL FRANCK

Revelation Taught

The Paraclete in the Gospel of John

CWK GLEERUP

Doctoral Dissertation submitted to Uppsala University 1985.

CONIECTANEA BIBLICA
New Testament Series 14

© Eskil Franck
Teol. kand.

Revelation Taught
The Paraclete in the Gospel of John

Abstract
The subject of this dissertation is the concept of the Paraclete and the saying about it in the Gospel of John. The purpose is to avoid a one-sided approach which is dominant in much previous research, i.e., the location of the Paraclete's background in *one* specific area from which its function and meaning is determined. Instead, a multidimensional model is presented where proper proportions are assigned to the forensic aspect, the aspect regarding the farewell-situation, and the didactic aspect, the didactic aspect taken as the dominant with regard to the content.

The validity of this model is then investigated by examining the various functions ascribed to the Paraclete. The presupposition for this examination is that the Paraclete *is* what he *does*, i.e., that his *function*, not *origin*, is of primary importance.

Having confirmed the validity of this model, the investigation goes on to show that there is a 'triad' involved in didactic authority in the Gospel of John, i.e., an interrelation between Jesus, the Paraclete and the Beloved Disciple. The absent Jesus is represented by the Paraclete, who, in turn, is embodied in the Beloved Disciple and legitimates him. The Gospel of John itself, as the result of the Beloved Disciple's activity, is seen in this context as the initial work of the Paraclete.

The next question taken up is that of a possible background and model for such a didactic activity. Scriptural interpretation and exposition in the service of the synagogue is focused upon and the relevance of its 'midrashic attitude' is emphazised. This context suggests a particular official, the Methurgeman, as phenomenologically a possible concrete background for the concrete and personal presentation of the Paraclete. The viability of this proposal follows as the *result* of the investigation and is *not a presupposition* for it.

Eskil Franck, Teologiska Institutionen, Box 1604, S-751 46 Uppsala

Distributor: Liber, S-205 10 Malmö, Sweden
Printed by Wallin & Dalholm, Lund 1985

ISBN 91-40-05114-5

Parentibus
pio animo

CONTENTS

8

1. Introduction

1.1. The problem and the task

The subject of this dissertation is the concept of the Paraclete (henceforth called the P) and the sayings about it in the Gospel of John[1] (henceforth called the GJ). Considering the enormous literature published on the subject,[2] it might seem presumptuous to present a further investigation. As long as the riddle of the P remains in many respects unsolved, however, one is justified to attempt a contribution to the understanding of this crucial issue.[3]

Why, then, is the idea of the P a riddle? The cause is at least twofold.

A. The word παράκλητος is, in biblical literature, found only in John 14-16[4] and in 1 John 2:1. Material upon which one might make direct comparisons is thus missing in the rest of the NT and the LXX.[5] This lack of internal comparative material becomes problematic for both linguistic and history of religion analyses. There is, also, a recognized hiatus[6] between the P's title and its functions in the GJ itself.[7] The title, if it re-

---

[1] 1.14:16-17. 2.14:26. 3.15:26-27. 4.16:7-11. 5.16:12-15.

[2] Rather than presenting here the history of the P-research, I refer to the following up to date surveys: Betz, 1963, 4-35. Blank, 1964, 317-322. Johnston, 1970, 80-118. Woll, 1981, 69-80. A very short survey is recently found in Casurella, 1983, 181 note 53. Casurella also contributes the most detailed survey so far of the interpretation of the P-sayings in the early Church. See also Porsch, 1974, 5-14, where he treats the role of the Spirit in the GJ in the history of research, and 305-317 where the history of research of the P-problem is discussed.

[3] For the enigmatic quality of the P and the continued interest in the P see Schulz, 1957, 143. Thyen, 1971, 343. Riesenfeld, 1972, 266. Leaney, 1972, 152. Müller, 1974, 31. The saying of Kothgasser, 1971, 569, is representative: "Das Problem der Herkunft des Paraklet-Titels bleibt also der weiteren Forschung anheimgestellt".

[4] Kysar, 1975, 234, calls it one of "the fourth evangelist's innovative concepts".

[5] With the exception of Philo there is no extra-biblical evidence during the first century CE (possibly with the exception of the occurence in Didache 5:2. It depends on when one dates the Didache). The word παράκλητος occurs, on the whole, rarely in greek literature. See Grayston, 1981, 74f.

[6] The expression taken from Bornkamm, 1949, 26, and Kothgasser, 1971, 568.

[7] The problem is made clear by Mowinckel, 1933, 118, and Porsch, 1974, 216. An illustration of the confusion is found in Dodd, 1953, 414f. Already in the early Church one has faced the problem. See Casurella, 1983, 142f.

tains the general meaning of secular greek, does not naturally label the functions ascribed to it in the GJ. Thus, one reason (cause A.) why the P remains enigmatic has to do, simply, with text-external and text-internal problems.

B. Much of the scholarly work on the P-problem has attempted to find *one* more or less complete history of religion background for the P and *one* meaning for the functions attached to it in John 14-16. A. is a real difficulty whereas B. is a methodological error. One violates the material of the GJ in general and the P-sayings in particular by restricting them to *one* field of association and meaning.[8] The material of the GJ is so complex from the point of view of literary criticism,[9] concerning background motifs, use of language,[10] and technique of composition, that one must count upon including a broad field of associations in any attempt to understand the figure of the P.[11]

If one tries to do justice to this latter fact one can end up *either* with a procedure of addition[12] which sets the different notions beside one another or adds them to one another and which, thus, results in a variety of meanings to choose from as the situation demands; *or* one can attempt to find the fundamental basis upon which the different notions and meanings are connected.[13] I have choosen to work according to the latter alternative.[14]

It is, thus, unrealistic to imagine a simple resolution to the riddle of the P. Such would ignore the character of the GJ's material and disregard previous research on the subject. Therefore, I intend to go through the material brought forward so far and, rearranging it, give parts of it different priorities and different degrees of relevance. Thus I hope to do justice to already known facts to which there has not been, in my opinion,

---

[8] Cf the statement by Schulz, 1957, 151: "Zu einfach wäre es wohl einer der zur Verfügung stehenden Schemata...absolut zu setzen". Cf also Boice, 1970, 156, where he gives "...a warning against interpreting the spirit's functions in too rigid or too limited a manner". Hill, 1979, 149: "Paraclete - a word which is virtually untranslatable if all its nuances are to be preserved". Finally Isaacs, 1983, 397: "...unduly limited the role of the paraclete in John".

[9] See Brown, 1966-70, I, XXIV-XXXIX.

[10] See recently Richard, 1985.

[11] Stressed by Michaelis, 1947, 147. Or using the terminology of Schulz, 1957, 156: "Die Paraklet-Thematradition zeichnet sich hinsichtlich ihres Ursprunges durch eine Komplexität aus". Cf also Brown, 1967, 118.

[12] Schulz, 1957, 156.

[13] Schulz, 1957, 156: "den tragenden Grund".

[14] Thus I share Schulz' methodological approach but not his conclusion, i.e., that the fundamental basis is the motif of the apocalyptic son of man and his forerunner.

enough attention paid. In doing so one must not only examine each part of the problem separately but also try, at the same time, to present a meaningful integration of the material. By approaching the riddle of the P in this manner I hope to contribute to the understanding of the P's functions and meaning in the GJ's presentation.

1.2. Literary presupposition

One area which remains of great importance to the scholarly work concerning the figure of the P in the GJ is that of literary criticism. The scholars who have paved the way in this regard in modern research are H. Sasse[15] and H. Windisch.[16] Sasse regards chapter 14, on the one hand, and chapters 15-16, on the other, as two variants of the same theme. Chapter 14 is the original, whereas 15-16 are later insertions functioning as a repetition of chapter 14. Windisch, however, regards all five P-sayings as independent of the context. They can, without any difficulty, be lifted out of their context and, thus, can be seen as interpolations. Sasse's thesis has later been taken up by J. Becker,[17] U.B. Müller,[18] and D.B. Woll.[19] These scholars find the original and decisive sayings about the P in 13:31-14:31.[20]

The starting point of the literary critical problem is the identification of the P with the Holy Spirit.[21] This difficulty is, in turn, caused by the question of whether the P-the Spirit is to be construed as a person or as a power. The P is usually seen to represent the personal aspects whereas the Spirit interpreted as a power. One also asks if all the functions of the P shall be derived from the notion $\pi\alpha\varrho\acute{\alpha}\varkappa\lambda\eta\tau os$ itself or if its connection

---

[15] Sasse, 1925, 261-270. On p.263 he refers back to Wellhausen's thesis on the subject.
[16] Windisch, 1927, 111-113.
[17] Becker, 1970.
[18] Müller, 1974, 40.
[19] Woll, 1981, 9-12.
[20] Another way of arranging the different layers of the farewell discourse and the P's place within them is represented by Painter, 1981. According to him the author of the farewell discourse did not bring about one but three versions: 1) 13:31-14:31. 2) 15:1-16:4a. 3) 16:4b-16:33. The three parts represent three different historical stages of the johannine community's development, and the P is in every stage used as an answer of the problem of that stage. A thorough attempt to demonstrate "Grundschrift" and "Redaktion" concerning the whole GJ is made by Langbrandtner, 1977. I hardly see that his conclusions (p.65f) contribute to a better understanding of the P.
[21] See Locker, 1966, 567.

with the Spirit has added anything new.[22] One consequence of a literary critical approach can be the understanding that the P originally was an independent figure which was later combined with the Spirit.[23]

There are obviously similar literary critical problems concerning the presentation of the P as concerning the GJ as a whole.[24] One should neither deny them nor try to explain them away. The question is, however, what role one should attribute to literary critical problems and how much importance one should attach to them when facing the text of the GJ in its present shape. There are three alternatives from which to choose:

1. One can make full use of the literary critical results one has reached and either delete secondary aspects, paying attention only to those which have been found primary or at least more original, or one can rearrange and restructure the text in order to offer a new context for the sayings, thereby creating new meanings. Bultmann's commentary is a good example of such a method. It has, of course, been critizised. A more modest critique of this sort aims at showing that the results can go now one way, now another, and thus do not give reliable answers to the literary questions asked.[25]

2. While admitting the usefulness of the literary critical method, many scholars today reach results quite opposite to those of the previous alternative.[26] They come to a more or less homogeneous understanding of the P-sayings in their contexts and do not accept the different theories of interpolation since the notion that the P-sayings are interpolated from different sources causes such enormous difficulties that it complicates rather than facilitates their interpretation. Their literary critical work results, instead, in the conclusion that the P-sayings have been a part of the context *before* the final redaction.[27] One admits, however, that the sayings enter the text in a remarkably unprepared and immediate way.[28]

---

[22] Windisch, 1927, 124.

[23] Brown, 1967, 113.

[24] A survey of the various major theories is found in Kysar, 1975, 10-81. A somewhat different literary procedure is found in Gryglewicz, 1979. With the help of word statistics he finds four layers in the GJ in its present shape.

[25] Betz, 1963, 10. Cf the resigned statement by Leaney, 1972, 147: "For there is no doubt in my mind that this Gospel is composed of a number of sources, but I really do not know how to delimit them". Cf also Whitacre, 1982, 3, regarding "...the perhaps ultimately impossible task of disentangling the various sources and redactions".

[26] See Schnackenburg, 1977, 285, where representatives of this trend are mentioned. See also Miguens, 1963, 14-44.

[27] Brown, 1967, 114f. Concerning the whole farewell discourse see Wilckens, 1980, 188.

[28] Kothgasser, 1971, 559.

3. The third approach presupposes that the text, in its present shape, functioned as a text among its first readers. It was, then, when it first began to circulate, "in some sense homogenous and coherent".[29] This starting point avoids both the question of whether the sayings were originally independent and the problem of their doubling. This approach asks, rather, what meaning the sayings have *in their present shape* and what kind of connections one can draw between them.[30] It means that even if one, from the literary critical point of view, has reason to regard the P-sayings as interpolations one nevertheless presupposes that they are so well assimilated in their context and are marked by such a stylistic and linguistic unity that it is reasonable to work with them in their present form.[31] Not until this supposition becomes untenable or insufficient in the individual case should the pre-history of the text be included in its explanation.[32]

This third alternative seems to be a reasonable methodological presumption, and I agree with it. Thus, this study is primarily syncronic. It is, at the same time, open to relevant comparative material in contemporary literature. In other words, the investigation is primarily syncronic taking both text-internal and text-external considerations into account.

1.3. Methodological procedure

Ones methodological procedure is dependant upon the questions one wishes to answer.[33] Much of the P research has aimed at recovering the background material (ideas as well as concrete figures) upon which the author of GJ may have relied. The natural starting point for such a procedure is to focus upon the word παράκλητος, ask for its etymology and profane greek field of usage and, from that perspective, search for relevant history of religion material in the OT, Judaism, Qumran writings,

---

[29] Olsson, 1974, 6. Cf Porsch, 1974, 217: "Dennoch haben die Sprüche selbstverständlich auch in ihrem jetzigen Kontext eine Funktion und sind vom Verfasser (bzw. Red.) mit einer bestimmten Absicht gerade an ihrer jetzigen Stelle 'eingefügt' worden... Aufgabe der Exegese muss es sein, ihre Funktion im heutigen Kontext und damit die wahrscheinliche Absicht des Verfassers (bzw. Red.) zu bestimmen. Welche Vorstellungen leiteten ihn, welche Ziele verfolgte er mit ihrer 'einfügung'?" See also Dunn, 1983, 316f; de Jonge, 1979, 106: "...start where every scholar should start: the present Gospel as a literary product with a (more or less) consistent theology of its own".
[30] Cf Thüsing, 1960, 142; Locker, 1966, 568; Porsch, 1974, 220.
[31] Carrez, 1981, 323.
[32] Olsson, 1974, 6.
[33] Brown, 1967, 115, gives some examples.

Mandeism, etc. One then returns to the johannine material and adapts the background ideas to the P's tasks and functions even though one, in the end, is forced to admit the existence of a discrepancy between the P's title and functions.[34] This description of the method is, indeed, a sweeping generalization. Nonetheless, it illustrates its essential weakness. The answer to the question concerning the origin of a motif or concept says nothing about its characteristics or meaning in an certain context. Many odd answers to the riddle of the P have been reached through the use of this method and are still published.[35] In the best case they manage to focus upon only one facet of the P's prism.[36]

If one, however, inquires into the *function* and *meaning* of the P on the basis of the present shape of the P-sayings, one is led in another direction. This notion is, of course, not new. Sasse[37] pointed out that starting with the word παράκλητος and associations attached to it leads one astray. Rather, one should examine the relevant texts from their own point of

---

[34] The statement of Bornkamm, 1949, 12, is symptomatic even if it is unconscious: "Aber woher stammt und was bedeutet die Gestalt des zweiten Gesandten?" Cf also the title of the article of Leaney, 1972: "The Historical Background and Theological Meaning of the Paraclete". Mowinckel, 1933, 98, expresses this method explicitly in a critical examination of the methodological approach of Windisch, 1927, and Asting, 1931: "So muss es auch hinsichtlich der Vorstellung von dem Parakleten das Richtige sein, zuerst die entsprechenden jüdischen Vorstellungen zu ermitteln und in ihrem Zusammenhang zu verstehen. Erst dann wird das, was dem Christentum eigentümlich ist, klarhervortreten und voll verständlich werden, und erst dann kann man die Frage nach dem Ursprung der johanneischen Vorstellung mit Hoffnung und Erfolg in Angriff nehmen". Cf also Mowinckel's statement on p.118, note 75: "Das Problem des Parakleten is somit kein lexikographisches, auch kein im engeren Sinne exegetisches, sondern ein religionsgeschichtliches".

[35] See, e.g., Shafaat, 1981.

[36] Attempts to demonstrate origin and parallels should meet the double test found in Michaelis, 1947, 150, (in that particular case intended for Bultmann's solution). Michaelis, however, leaves no room for the ambiguity of the GJ which seems to be a weakness.

[37] Sasse, 1925, 261. I share Sasse's methodological approach but not his conclusions concerning literary considerations. A similar intention is later found in Johnston, 1970, 87. An elucidating example of where one can land up if one only focuses upon the word παράκλητος and ignores the functions ascribed to the P is found in Billerbeck, 1922ff, II, 560-562. He starts from the word παράκλητος which he assigns a forensic meaning. He goes on to say that the rabbis took over this word through the transcription $p^e raqlēṭ$. This word has a more common synonym, $s^e nēgōr$, which also is a transcription of the greek word συνήγορος The Spirit is never rendered with $p^e raqlēṭ$ by the rabbis but with $s^e nēgōr$ and then in the function as an advocate. Billerbeck's conclusion is that "die Vorstellung vom HeiligenGeist als einem Fürsprecher Israels innerhalb der Synagoge nicht unbekannt gewesen ist, wenn sich auch die Bezeichnung desselben als $p^e raqlēṭ$ nicht nachweisen lässt".

view. The correct point of departure is to find the unique characteristics of the johannine P in the GJ's own description of him.[38] The analysis of the P-sayings themselves is consequently of great importance, not a very original conclusion. Nevertheless, it is one which has been often overlooked.[39] In analyzing the P-sayings one can approach the context in two different ways:

1. One can start in the P-sayings and then move forwards and backwards in the GJ, allowing the whole gradually to shed more light upon the sayings.

2. One can start in the GJ as a whole and then move towards the more immediate contexts of the sayings.

I intend to follow both approachs beginning with the latter alternative. In using both procedures one avoids limiting the P only to *one* function, meaning, or background. I hope to show that the P-sayings have their place within a 'multidimensional model' and, in this way, do justice to the ambiguous character of the GJ. (Chapter 2).

When I have reached the P-sayings themselves (Chapter 3), I shall concentrate upon an analysis of the functions ascribed to the P. They are of primary interest concerning the P's role and meaning in the GJ's presentation and take precedence over a possible lexical or history of religion explanation.[40] The P *is* what he *does*. I then widen the context circles concerning the P's functions to include the entire GJ and, finally, to include other relevant contemporary writings.

Through this approach I hope to demonstrate the general didactic character of the P's functions. Didactic connotes here the formation of tradition, revelation, and prophecy. In order to further describe this aspect which is basic to the GJ I shall (Chapter 4) give an account of the 'didactic triad' in the GJ: Jesus - the P - the BD and, in the process, indicate that the P functions also as the guarantor of the trustworthiness of the tradition found in the GJ.

In chapter 5 I investigate the question as to the type of didactics the functions of the P express. The answer to this question is given through an inquiry into the background against which such a description of the P's didactic activity should be seen. The circles are widened here and the history of religion question is touched upon, especially in regard to the service of the synagogue. The history of religion question is further

[38] Brown, 1967, 126.
[39] Davies, 1953, 35. Porsch, 1974, 5.
[40] Michaels, 1975, 245. See also Mussner, 1961, 59; Johnston, 1970, 87.

developed in chapter 6, where I review the possibility that the Methurge-man of the synagogal service serves as a concrete background figure for the P.

The advantage of such a procedure is that it does justice to the P-say-ings in their literary context in the GJ as it now stands and, at the same time, anchors the notion of the P in its immediate context according to the functions ascribed to it in the P-sayings. Secondarily, the P-sayings are also related to relevant contemporary literature and are, still taking the point of departure in the analysis of the texts, linked to a possible history of religion background.[41]

The *function* and the *meaning* of the P (within the framework of the lite-rary context) are the primary concerns of this method, the *origin* of the concept of the P remains a secondary issue.

---

[41] This method, in a way, chooses the best of the three alternatives Riesenfeld, 1972, 266, outlines and merges it into a, if not completely covering, 'new covering' method. My methodological conclusions come close to the ones presented by Porsch, 1974, 216f.

2. The multidimensional model

2.1. Introductory

This chapter approaches the P from perspective of the Gospel of John(GJ) as a whole as well as, of course, from the vantage point of more specific textual contexts. This approach gives rise to three 'dimensions' in my exposition. By including these dimensions, the treatment of 'the announced one' will embrace more of the expectations and needs of the receivers of the GJ than possible in a narrower fixation either on the P as a title or on the P's functions. These dimensions are not equally significant in relation to the P. Each of the them contributes a varying degree of exactitude to the meaning of the johannine conception of the P. This variation is found in the movement from the wider to the narrower contexts from the P-sayings' point of view. My exposition follows this movement. It begins with the GJ as a whole which, as I will show, is characterized by the forensic dimension although, as also shall be made clear, the forensic ideas are more or less explicitly connected to specific P-sayings as well. It then goes on to the narrower context of ch.13-17, the farewell-speech, which focuses upon questions of comfort and legitimate succession, and ends up with the the P-sayings themselves, seen from a didactic point of view. Thus we will have reached down to the immediate contexts of the P-sayings and can move from the analysis of more general associations to the specific johannine texts which describe the actual functions of the P, i.e., the P-sayings themselves.

2.2. The overall forensic dimension

2.2.1. The title παράκλητος

If, for the present, we leave aside the earlier mentioned hiatus between the P as a title and his functions and concentrate on the title itself, we move naturally into the field of forensics. παράκλητος belongs, in the secular environment, to the legal sphere. There is a fairly broad agreement among scholars on this issue, even if opinions vary about the degree to which it belongs to the forensic world in a technical sense.[1] There is no need to go into a more detailed discussion concerning the exact role the word παράκλητος played in this regard. It is sufficient here to indicate how the lexical meaning has been used in the previous johannine P-research. Two main lines can be seen. I propose a third alternative.

2.2.2. The treatment of the background meaning
The first line

This line establishes a forensic meaning and applies it to the P in the GJ.[2] Various ways of resolving the obvious discrepancy between the title and the functions of the P have been attempted. Mowinckel makes a distinction between form and content. The title refers to the form and originates in the intertestamental jewish notion of the Spirit as a witness, intercessor, and accuser, whereas the contents of the P's activity are christian-johannine. The 'content' of the P refers, thus, to an inspirator and

---

[1] See e.g. Liddell-Scott, 1968, 1313; Bauer, 1958, col. 1226f; Behm, 1967, 803; Betz, 1963, 1; Porsch, 1974, 227f.

   A recent exception from this unity of opinion is the contribution of Grayston, 1981. He goes through all known occurrences from the fourth century BC till the third century CE to show that παράκλητος did not get its meaning from legal activities but was a more general term, occasionally used in legal contexts with the meaning 'supporter' or 'sponsor'. It should , however, be an embarrassing fact for Grayston that all the earliest instances occur in legal contexts. Grayston would translate παράκλητος with 'sponsor' or 'patron', a translation he finds suitable for the P-sayings in GJ. If many scholars overly stress the forensic connection, Grayston seems to undervalue it. However, I appreciate his opening the door to a meaning of the word less fixed in the forensic sphere.

   Docent J-F Kindstrand, at the Institute for Classical Philology, University of Uppsala, has helped me in judging Graystons article.

   Grayston's survey of the research concerning this matter is worth noting: 67-70.

[2] One of the most clear presentations of this line is the one by Mowinckel, 1933, 118f. It becomes even clearer in his presentation as he realizes the difficulty concerning the relation title-function. "Das berechtigt aber nicht dazu, den Wortsinn des Titels ändern zu wollen." Mowinckel combines this opinion with the generally Jewish background he wants to ascribe to the P-motive and lets this motive be completely coloured by the Jewish judicial system. Johansson, 1940, 257, is on the same line as Mowinckel but has not very much more to contribute than Mowinckel concerning the johannine P.

   Bornkamm, 1949, 26, chooses the middle course. He is of the opinion that the word παράκλητος has been divested of its original forensic "Anschauungsgehalt" and received new contents of meaning. But, at the same time, it belongs to the legal sphere in a special context, namely through the fact that it is ascribed the same functions as the son of man-the judge of the world according to the apocalyptics and the NT.

   See also Holwerda, 1959, 64; Leaney, 1972, 55; Trites, 1977, 81 and 117ff.

revealer.[3] Other scholars regard some sayings as forensic and thereby allow title and function to remain more or less together.[4]

Another way of solving this problem is to stress that the P is the advocate of Christ and not of the disciples.[5] In this way the correspondence title-function becomes closer. As the spirit of revelation and the witness of Christ, the P defends Christ to the disciples and to the world. If the P is understood to be the advocate of the disciples, it becomes more difficult to explain why he teaches, reminds, and guides the same disciples. This way of arguing is correct only under the condition that one sticks to a pronounced forensic meaning.

This consistent forensic way of looking at the matter is, for several reasons, unsatisfying:

a. It makes too much out of the forensic meaning of $\pi\alpha\varrho\acute{\alpha}\varkappa\lambda\eta\tau\sigma\varsigma$ in a technical sense. The comparative textual material does not, actually, support such an interpretation.

b. The actual discord between title and function is, therefore, more strongly stressed than it need be.

c. It excludes other possibilities of association, for example, with $\pi\alpha\varrho\alpha\varkappa\alpha\lambda\epsilon\tilde{\iota}\nu$-$\pi\alpha\varrho\acute{\alpha}\varkappa\lambda\eta\sigma\iota\varsigma$. See further under 2.3. and 2.4.

The interpretation of the P-sayings demands a greater flexibility than a purely forensic understanding will allow.

2.2.3. The treatment of the background meaning
The second line

The second line of approach is to clearly admit the legal background of $\pi\alpha\varrho\acute{\alpha}\varkappa\lambda\eta\tau\sigma\varsigma$ but to minimize this background's importance for the understanding of the functions themselves.[6] This is done by selecting another association for the word $\pi\alpha\varrho\acute{\alpha}\varkappa\lambda\eta\tau\sigma\varsigma$ or the verb $\pi\alpha\varrho\alpha\varkappa\alpha\lambda\epsilon\tilde{\iota}\nu$, and

---

[3] Mowinckel, 1933, 128f; Cf Leaney, 1972, 153: "a Jewish conception represented by an exclusively Greek word".

[4] Johnston, 1970, 141-144; Moule, 1967, 91, describes it in a falling scale: The description of the P as a lawyer a) does not violate the literal meaning of the word, b) does fullest justice to 16:8-11, c) gives in any case good meaning to 15:26f., and d) does not run counter to the other sayings.

[5] Boice, 1970, 153. This thought is also to be found in Mowinckel, 1933, 128, and in Brown, 1967, 116. Cf the objection of Porsch, 1974, 321, from the perspective of 15:26: when the P gives witness about Jesus in front of the disciples he is, at the same time, both advocate and helper.

[6] A polemical argumentation against Mowinckel and Johansson is to be found in Barrett, 1950, 11. See also Brown, 1967, 116f, and Locker, 1966, 566, who also question the forensic situation in 16:8-11.

to try to prove the priority of that association.[7] The same criticism given before can also be made here, i.e., the result becomes too one-sided. One association alone is not able to throw light over the whole range of meanings represented by the five P-sayings.

2.2.4. The treatment of the background meaning
A third line

I propose a third line of approach which combines aspects of the two previous ones. First, the basic forensic meaning of the word παράκλητος should be kept intact. It seems unlikely that the author of the GJ would bring into his exposition a word to which the readers-listeners[8] could not spontaneously apply the everyday meaning. This implies that the GJ relies upon a non-technical description of the function of the P in the society of that time as a compositional-technical-pedagogical means of drawing the attention of the readers-listeners to a more specific and important phenomenon.[9] In such a sense the forensic aspect is applicable to the P and the P-sayings.[10]

If one, then, relates the word παράκλητος primarily to a forensic context, one should ask why such an association has been choosen when the P's activity is not, at least not primarily, forensic. In all likelihood more suitable labels could have been choosen, such as teacher, preacher, or revealer.[11] It also seems probable that such titles would have caused less

---

[7] One example of such an association is found in Riesenfeld, 1972. He refers (p.268) to "a specific use of παρακαλεῖν in the Septuagint" best represented by the understanding of the Wisdom's function, especially in Prov.8:4ff where it means "comfort". παράκλητος in the GJ "has in this case been usurped regardless of its juridical meaning in literary Greek and filled with a signification equivalent to the participle ὁ παρακαλῶν, he who comforts" (p.273).

[8] It deserves to be noticed that the written gospels were primarily meant to be communicated through reading aloud (particularly in the services) and not through private reading. See Hengel, 1984, 33-37.

[9] One could make a comparison with the modern pedagogics of advertising. There one speaks about "eyecatchers", i.e., striking sayings and pictures, striking because they contain associations to something well known and of everyday character but which are used in sensational way. The similarity to the function of the parables in the gospels is obvious.

[10] Concerning the saying in 16:8-11, which comes closest to the legal sphere, see 3.4. The attempt of Betz, 1963, 137-158, to try to find Hebrew-Aramaic equivalents with clear forensic connections becomes, in the light of a possible application of the everyday meaning of the word, unnecessary or even misdirected.

[11] This observation is made by Boice, 1970, 155.

misunderstanding. One can see, for example, that in 1 John 2:27 the description of τὸ χρίσμα is similar to the description of the P. Both the P and τὸ χρίσμα are pseudonyms for the Spirit, yet τὸ χρίσμα seems a more natural description than the P of the Spirit's functions.

It is my thesis, then, that at the same time, paradoxically, as the word παράκλητος in its immediate context causes a hiatus between title and function, it fulfills the task of orientating the P-sayings in the GJ, seen as a whole. *Hiatus in the microstructure becomes coherence in the macrostructure.* This is possible on account of the legal structure which runs throughout the GJ,[12] from the opening-scene (1:19-28) when John the Baptist is questioned by the men sent out by the Jews through the interrogations with Jesus concerning his testimony (5:31-40; 8:13-19) to the dramatic trial before Pilate.[13] The background of the exposition of the GJ is a court procedure. This does not, however, only involve the proceedings against the earthly Jesus but also the broader and deeper litigation between the world and God. One could call it a "theological process".[14] I do not allege that the process motif dominates the GJ. Such an understanding of the compositional features of the GJ would be incompatible with the ambiguity of the GJ to which I have already called attention. Rather I should like to point out this motif's importance within the web of motifs that binds together the GJ. For my study it is not necessary to analyze in detail the different pericopes and sayings which create the forensic milieu in the

[12] Holwerda, 1959, 64. Cf Trites, 1977, 78: "The Fourth Gospel...presents a sustained use of juridical metaphors." Harvey, 1976, has attempted a complete grip on the GJ from this perspective. It is no wonder that the P receives a dominating forensic impress.

[13] Brown, 1967, 116. Cf Leaney,1972, 155: court motif. Cf also the statement of Büchsel, 1926, 498: "Jesu Streitreden an die Juden sind bei Johannes beinah weniger Lehrreden als Streitreden, Prozessreden". Note 6: "Vgl. besonders 5:31-47; 8:12-20; 10:34-39; 12:44-50 und die ausführliche Zeugenvernehmung in cap.9".

[14] Kothgasser, 1972, 4f. Cf Meeks, 1967, 65: "...the whole gospel suggests an extended court process between God and the world". See also note 1 and the litterature mentioned there, particularly the article of Preiss, 1954, which is quoted by other scholars. Preiss maintains the same thesis as my study, i.e., the problem of the GJ can not be solved only from one point of view. Instead, it concerns several themes which are intervowen. The point where these themes converge is the person of Jesus. The GJ is therefore in a real sense christocentric. Preiss wants, however, to stress one aspect particularly which, according to him, offers "a more coherent system of ideas", i.e., the juridical one. In many ways the argument of Preiss is convincing. But in relation to the P the reasoning becomes one-sided as only those sayings which fit into this juridical notion are treated. Concerning the P, Preiss makes the same mistake he wanted to avoid, namely, to solve the problem of the johannine riddle from only one point of view. Cf also Betz, 1963, 120-123, and Porsch, 1974, 222. Trites, 1977, 79: "John is concerned to prove a case".

GJ.[15] It might, however, be of some interest to indicate statistically the range of legal terms found in the GJ.[16] Such a statistical procedure has no proof value, but it places the word παράκλητος within a conceptional framework where it becomes natural and can thereby be related to the context as a whole.

The farewell-discourse does not represent an exception in this respect. There also one finds the forensic frame of reference. The hatred and persecution-motif in 15:18-25, which terminates in the saying regarding P as a witness, can be said to belong to this frame, just as does the saying in 16:2 concerning excommunication from the synagogue. Whether this excommunication was to be effected in a formal court process in the synagogue court (bēth dīn), or through the mob taking the decision in its own hands, or both, would be difficult to determine and not of importance here. It is probable, however, that the last mentioned alternative is intended.[17] This prediction of excommunication is followed by the P-saying which has the most obvious forensic association, 16:8-11. In this way the forensic dimension and the next dimension I shall describe (the farewell-discourse in 2.3.) overlap. Thus one must be weary of defining too sharply the lines between the different dimensions.

2.2.5. Summary

The forensic παράκλητος, as a title, functions in the GJ by connecting the presentation of the Holy Spirit to one of the motifs which runs through the gospel, i.e., the court-process motive. The associative character of this relation does not primarily concern the contents of the concept

---

[15] Cf Meeks, 1967, 305, and Boice, 1970, 155.

[16] The following statistics are built on Morgenthaler, 1958. The numbers state the occurrence in the GJ, the numbers within brackets the occurrence in the entire NT. A word can, of course, be present in a non-forensic context. Sharp borderlines here are difficult to draw. One must count upon an associative pattern which goes beyond what is found in the immediate context.

αἰτία 3(20), ἀρνεῖσθαι 4(32), ἐλέγχειν 3(17), καταλαμβάνειν 2(13), κατηγορεῖν 2(22), κατηγορία 1(3), κρίμα 1(27), κρίσις 19(114), κρίνειν 11(47), λιθάζειν 4(8), μαρτυρεῖν 33(76), μαρτυρία 14(37), ὁμολογεῖν 4(26), πιάζειν 8(12), σταυροῦν 11(46), τίτλος 2(2). Cf the enumeration in Trites, 1977, 80f.

[17] The two parallell passages ἀποσυναγώγους ποιήσουσιν ὑμᾶς and πᾶς ὁ ἀποκτείνας ὑμᾶς point in this direction.

of the P but is rather found in technique of composition.[18] The fact that this compositional-technical feature enters some of the descriptions of the P's functions[19] does not justify the notion that it leaves a mark on the meaning of all the sayings.[20] Such a character is instead given by the two following dimensions. They also explain why precisely the juridical word παράκλητος has been choosen.

2.3. The farewell-discourse

2.3.1. The background in jewish texts

The fact that the P-sayings are a part of the farewell-discourse (ch.13-17) has drawn little attention in previous research and then only to answer the question how the continous presence of Jesus will be effected.[21] It is, of course, quite legitimate to ask this question but, at the same time, the place of the P-sayings must be studied in terms of form criticism. The P-sayings are elements of the genre 'farewell-discourses'. The one who has lately shed light upon this question is U.B.Müller.[22] Referring to the work of Bultmann, Betz, and Bornkamm, Müller claims that these scholars make a methodological error by pursuing a history of religion approach without taking form criticism into consideration. Analogies between religious historical phenomena can only, with some certainty, be genealogically related to each other if such phenomena are expressed in a form

[18] As distinguished from 1 John 2:1 where the case is the opposite. Cf the statement in Porsch, 1974, 321, about the purpose in the GJ calling the Spirit ὁ παράκλητος: "um spezifische und wesentliche Aspekten seines Wirkens in einer forensischen Situation besser zum Ausdruck bringen zu können". Porsch seems, however, to place greater forensic meaning on some of the P-sayings than I am prepared to do, based on the associations I have proposed.

[19] μαρτυρεῖν, ἐλέγχειν. Cf Porsch, 1974, 305.

[20] I share the view of Porsch, 1974, 224, that the author of the final GJ has made a "Transposition" from the public-legal life, yet I have difficulties in seeing the aim of this transposition to be "das Innere des Menschen". The relation between the P and the disciples is mirrored just as much on the external level, i.e., in worship and teaching.

[21] Woll, 1981, 18 and 32f. Woll's own thesis is, that the problem treated in the farewell-discourse isn't "eschatological, historical, or hermeneutical distance from the Son to be overcome, but the opposite, an illegitimate collapsing of hierarchical distance between Son and followers". It is difficult for me to understand why one must contrast these two alternatives.

[22] Müller, 1974.See also Becker, 1981, 440-446.

of language which indicates consistency.[23] Müller's own course of action
is to study those jewish texts which deal with the problems surrounding
the death of an important person when his work is to be overtaken by
someone else. Müller does not limit his study to the literary farewell-
discourse genre, but also includes texts which describe a farewell-situation
and 'make a theme' of this situation, even though the farewell-discourse
genre does not formally exist.[24] Even if his terminological ambivalence
is problematic, Müller's way of arguing is convincing.[25] He sees four different ways of treating the farewell-situation in the texts with which he
works.[26]

The first category which is not relevant to the farewell-discourse in the
GJ concerns a dying patriarch's sayings about the future in which he as-
sures his descendents salvation after their apostasy from God and conversion to him.[27]

The second category concerns the exhortation of a dying man to a right
conduct of life.[28] Through the remembrance of and obedience to this exhortation the survivors insure that God's promises to Abraham and his
seed are fulfilled. Müller sees certain resemblances here to the farewell-
discourse in the GJ, but the relevant Jewish texts do not distinguish any
individual to carry on the tasks (e.g., the task of exhortation, which is
of special interest to the P-sayings) of the dying one after his death.

The third category, in contrast to the two previous ones, is characterized by the existence of a certain instrument through which the work of
the dying man will be carried on. This instrument is not an individual
but consists of the written remains of the dying one, including the scrip-

[23] Müller, 1974, 38f. On p.39, note 32, Müller points out how "stepmotherly" the P-con-
ception has been approached from the perspective of the farewell-discourse as a literary
genre.
[24] Müller, 1974, 52: "...auch solche Texte heranziehen, bei denen zwar die Abschiedssitua-
tion...themathisiert wird, ohne dass die Gattung 'Abshiedsrede' direkt vorliegt." Cf also
the article by Bergman, 1979.
[25] A serious objection against Müller, according to my argument in 1.2., is that he limits
the P-texts in the GJ to 13:31-14:31. Ch.15-16 are, according to Müller, secondary, and
the P-texts within these chapters "können keine Beweiskraft für Kap.14 und die ursprüng-
liche Parakletvorstellung haben" (p.36f). My objection to Müller does not prevent me
from applying his results to the P-texts in ch.15-16. Cf the critique of Müller in Wilckens,
1980, 189f.
[26] Müller, 1974, 52-65.
[27] A detailed presentaion is found in Becker, 1970(b), 172-177.
[28] Jub.21:36. 36:5. 1 En.91:3.

tures he has inherited from earlier generations.[29] Of special importance in this case are two texts, 4 Ezra 14 and syrBar 77ff.

4 Ezra 14 describes how Ezra's activity, after his death, will be taken over by the scriptures he dictated. The scriptures, as did Ezra himself, shall reprove the people, comfort the lowly ones, and instruct those that are wise (14:13). This is made possible through Ezra's gift of the Holy Spirit. What he dictated is impressed with knowledge and wisdom. A comparison with the P-sayings is, according to Müller, inevitable. The books of Ezra and the P guarantee the continuity of the works of Ezra and Jesus, respectively, after their deaths. The task of both successors is to exhort, comfort, and teach. The similarity , however, goes further. The books of Ezra can not only be paralleled with the P-figure. Through the writing of the GJ, that which was the intended task of the P according to 14:26 - to remind the disciples of the words and work of Jesus - is carried out. Thus, through this book, the continous effect of the words of Jesus is insured, as was Ezra's words through the compilation of the Ezra tradition.

There is also in syrBar 77 a farewell-situation. Before Baruch departs from the people, he will send them a letter of doctrine which serves the purpose of comforting. The basic form of this farewell-discourse corresponds to the one in John 13:31-14:31 (announcement of removal, exhortation, and giving of promise). The letter of Baruch to the people in exile shall, together with the law, guarantee continuity after his own removal, as well as after the removal of the prophets.

Not only is the question of continuity solved in this way, but also the authoritative status of these writings is reinforced. When Ezra leaves 94 writings behind (24 canonical books of the OT and 70 noncanonical writings) they receive the status of inspired writings. In this way the farewell-discourse legitimates pseudepigraphic authorship in that the anonymous writer lets the authority of the dying man in the past stand behind the writing of his own book. This also has its applications to the GJ material. The anonymous writer of the GJ legitimates his writing by pointing at its extraordinary origin, partly as a manifestation of the activity of the Spirit and partly as a result of the activity of a holy man in the past.[30] I shall return to this third farewell-situation in a moment, but I shall first give an account of Müller's fourth category.

This fourth category is distinguished by the fact that the person who goes away appoints a successor. There are important examples of such

---

[29] Ass.Mos.10:11. Slav.En.33:5ff. 36:1. 47:1-3, 54. 66:7.
[30] See further in ch. 4.

in the OT, i.e., Moses-Joshua,[31] and Elijah-Elisha.[32] In both cases, especially the latter, it is important that the successor becomes a bearer of the Spirit. Indeed, the continuity is guaranted precisely through the inheritance of the Spirit from the predecessor. The case is the same in jewish intertestamental literature.[33] If one compares the relationship Moses-Joshua with the relation between Jesus and the P, one discovers a great resemblance. In both cases the continuity consists in the taking over of the functions of Jesus among the disciples now left behind. There are also similarities concerning the equipment of the Spirit. Joshua receives the Spirit while the P is the Spirit.

Summing up, one notices two primary similarities between the OT-writings which describe a farewell-situation and the farewell-discourse in the GJ. The first convergence is found in the formal elements in the johannine farewell-discourse and in the farewell-discourses in the jewish texts: both textgroups speak of the departure of a great personality. Both exhort, comfort, and give promises - especially about something special which will insure the continuity in the future. The second resemblance is the role of the Spirit in the question of continuity. In jewish texts the Spirit becomes a guarantor of continuity either through inspired persons as successors or through inspired writings. In the GJ the continuity is primarily guaranted through the fact that the Spirit takes the place of Jesus and, secondarily, because the GJ itself is the work of the same Spirit.

2.3.2. The linguistic connection

The preceeding paragraph indicates that the johannine farewell-discourse and its sayings about the Spirit have a correspondance in the OT and jewish texts. The question remains whether there are linguistic grounds to associate the concept of the P and the 'farewell-discourse' in terms similar to the relationship between the P and the forensic dimension discussed in 2.2. I think I can reply to that question in the affirmative, even if such an answer rests less on a watertight argument than on a reasonable assumption.

The starting-point is the word $\pi\alpha\varrho\acute{\alpha}\varkappa\lambda\eta\tau\sigma\varsigma$, which as a verbal adjective used as a noun not only has an active meaning but is equivalent to the

---

[31] Num.27:18. Deut.31ff.
[32] 2 Kgs.2:9f and 15f.
[33] Lib.Ant.19-20. Ass.Mos.1. syrBar.44-56.

active participle.[34] Taking such a point of departure, the way is open to the semantic field made up by the verb παρακαλεῖν in its entirety, including its derivate παράκλησις. Such a linguistic interpretation is certainly not indisputable but nevertheless probable. The arguments *against* it are mainly as follows:

a. In philology it is considered a mistake to derive from the verb the noun which reflects an independent meaning, since the verb and the noun have usually evolved quite separately.[35] This argument is correct in principle but can be applied too strictly. In the GJ we are dealing with a use of language which is so free, associative, and creative, that it is legitimate to set aside this principle in the light of such conditions. I shall elaborate in a moment.

b. One starts from the simple fact that neither the verb παρακαλεῖν nor its derivate παράκλησις exist in the GJ.[36] To appropriate an association common to these words for the P would, therefore, be either difficult or impossible. This kind of argumentum e silentio seems too narrow. The frame of reference can not be limited to just the writing being investigated. It is in the nature of an association to go beyond the selfevident and immediately demonstrable. One must also take into account the frame of reference implied by the milieu of the receivers. It is, parenthetically, this method one adopts when, adducing the profane greek usage, the P is given a clearly forensic meaning. Also in this case there is a lack of sufficient proof, as the word παράκλητος is not found in the rest of the NT (with the exception of 1 John 2:1) or in the LXX. Again, turning back to the former case, one can not say anything certain. If, however, one takes into account the christian usage of language in the Early Church as it is found in the NT, one often finds both παρακαλεῖν and παράκλησις used in a sense which is relevant for my study. I shall develop this point later.

c. The third and weakest argument moves in a circle. The function and

---

[34] παρακαλῶν. So e.g. Porsch, 1974, 227; Müller, 1974, 63. Cf alsoLemonnyer, 1927, 299. For him παράκλητος in this way becomes a nomen agentis to παρακαλεῖν while παράκλησις becomes a nomen actionis. To assign παράκλητος an active meaning dates from Origin. See Casurella, 1983, 4f.

[35] Holwerda, 1959, 36.

[36] Michaelis, 1947, 148; Kothgasser, 1971, 569; Grayston, 1979, 29. Cf Schmitz, 1967, V, 793, where he tries to explain the johannine absence of παρακαλεῖν-παράκλησις. The explanation is said to be that the synoptic pericopes concerning petition for help before Jesus are missing in the GJ. This may be one cause but presumably not the only one.

meaning of the P in the GJ excludes any connection to[37] As the P obviously stands for an intercessor in a forensic sense, any affinity to the verb and its derivates is impossible. The situation becomes closed and one excludes the chance that other possibilities might shed light upon the P-problem. The subsequent argumentation will show if this critique is valid.

I myself draw the conclusion that there are no methodological obstacles against letting the verb $\pi\alpha\rho\alpha\kappa\alpha\lambda\epsilon\tilde{\iota}\nu$ and its derivates, especially the active participle and the noun $\pi\alpha\rho\acute{\alpha}\kappa\lambda\eta\sigma\iota\varsigma$, shed light upon the function and meaning of the P.[38]

2.3.3. $\pi\alpha\rho\acute{\alpha}\kappa\lambda\eta\tau\sigma\varsigma$-$\pi\alpha\rho\alpha\kappa\alpha\lambda\epsilon\tilde{\iota}\nu$

We now turn to the previously mentioned question regarding the actual relationship between $\pi\alpha\rho\acute{\alpha}\kappa\lambda\eta\tau\sigma\varsigma$ and $\pi\alpha\rho\alpha\kappa\alpha\lambda\epsilon\tilde{\iota}\nu$. The semantic field of the verb $\pi\alpha\rho\alpha\kappa\alpha\lambda\epsilon\tilde{\iota}\nu$ is relatively broad. It embraces "comfort, encourage, reprove, exhort, teach, and preach".[39]

In general, the comfort-motif is well suited to embrace the entire picture of the farewell-discourse in the GJ.[40] It is possible to go into more detail and see a closer technical connection between $\pi\alpha\rho\acute{\alpha}\kappa\lambda\eta\tau\sigma\varsigma$ and $\pi\alpha\rho\alpha\kappa\alpha\lambda\epsilon\tilde{\iota}\nu$ in farewell-situations. This is Müller's approach.[41] He does not succeed in proving his hypothesis either, but it is so probable that it is here accepted. He shows that the tasks of many of those instruments (persons, books, etc.) which in the farewell-situation are thought to guarantee continuity, are to comfort, exhort, and teach, precisely the contents of $\pi\alpha\rho\alpha\kappa\alpha\lambda\epsilon\tilde{\iota}\nu$. Certainly the objection could be raised that one does not encounter the greek verb in the jewish farewell-texts but only in its latin or syric equivalents, in that the greek witnesses are no longer existant. It is, however, very probable that $\pi\alpha\rho\alpha\kappa\alpha\lambda\epsilon\tilde{\iota}\nu$ stood behind the way of expressing the function in farewell-situations. This assumption is strengthened by the fact that $\pi\alpha\rho\alpha\kappa\alpha\lambda\epsilon\tilde{\iota}\nu$ in the LXX has a similar range of usage. This is not least valid in eschatological contexts. It is obvious that the translators emphasized the motive of comfort within an

---

[37] $\pi\alpha\rho\alpha\kappa\alpha\lambda\epsilon\tilde{\iota}\nu$-$\pi\alpha\rho\acute{\alpha}\kappa\lambda\eta\sigma\iota\varsigma$. Büchsel, 1926, 498, note 8.
[38] Cf also the argumentation in Müller, 1974, 63.
[39] Grayston, 1979, 27; Bauer, 1958, col.1223ff; Liddell-Scott, 1968, 1311.
[40] Brown, 1967, 118.
[41] Müller, 1974, 54-56, 61-65.

eschatological perspective.[42] $\pi\alpha\varrho\alpha\varkappa\alpha\lambda\epsilon\tilde{\iota}\nu$ thereby became the equivalent of *nācham*.[43]

It can also be shown that an aim of jewish teaching was to comfort. Such was the case in the sermon of the jewish synagogue in NT times.[44] A previous style of preaching, primarily instructive, had evolved into a more edifying discourse. This latter mode of preaching included an eschatological introduction as an important element. The edifying and instructive discourse ended with a word of comfort, a $\lambda\acute{o}\gamma os$ $\pi\alpha\varrho\alpha\varkappa\lambda\acute{\eta}$-$\sigma\epsilon\omega s$. Hence the act of comforting is not an isolated event but finds its practical application in preaching.

2.3.4. Concluding remarks

I have drawn attention to similarities which exist between farewell-situations in jewish literature and the farewell-discourse in the GJ. I have also supported the view that a relationship can be established between them if one accepts that $\pi\alpha\varrho\alpha\varkappa\alpha\lambda\epsilon\tilde{\iota}\nu$, not only etymologically but also semantically, can shed light upon the P. The meaning of $\pi\alpha\varrho\alpha\varkappa\alpha\lambda\epsilon\tilde{\iota}\nu$ which has the greatest relevance here is 'comfort', an interpretation which finds support both in the LXX and the synagogue sermon. The objection can be raised that the comforting is not explicitly mentioned in the johannine farewell-discourse and is, therefore, supplied. Such an addition, however, would be very natural,[45] as indicated in the discussion concerning the forensic dimension in 2.2., although it is most obvious in the case of the farewell-discourse. The author of the GJ wishes to give a further field of association to the P than the forensic one, i.e., the farewell-situation with its implied themes and terms. This reliance on known and documented farewell-situations would appear to serve primarily as a background for the johannine exposition: Jesus is departing just like so many 'fathers' in the history of the Jews. Those for whom he is responsible, the disciples, will not, however, be $\dot{o}\varrho\varphi\alpha\nuo\acute{\iota}$. The reassurance is given that Jesus and his father have seen to the preservation of continuity. This comfort will be realized through the P who will remain with the disciples forever. The fact that comforting is not explicitly mentioned should, however, restrict the idea of comfort from dominating to the point that $\pi\alpha\varrho\acute{\alpha}\varkappa\lambda\eta\tau os$ is translated by 'comforter' in the GJ.[46]

---

[42] Riesenfeld, 1972, 269.

[43] Davies, 1953, 35-38; Schmitz, 1967, V, 777.

[44] For the following information see Elbogen, 1913, 196; Dugmore, 1964, 8.

[45] Cf Brown, 1967, 118.

[46] Cf Bacon, 1917: "The other comforter".

The bridge from the farewell-dimension to the most immediate context of the P-sayings is found in those functions which are ascribed to farewell-situations in Jewish texts: exhortation, reproving, guiding, and teaching. The comfort given consists in all of these activities. One encounters also here a certain overlapping which makes the discernment of sharp borderlines impossible.

2.4. The didactic dimension

2.4.1. Introductory

A rudimentary investigation of the functions of the P will indicate his activity to be characterized by didactic-proclaiming-teaching.[47] It is this observation which has caused the hiatus title-function. I have in 2.2 and 2.3. tried to eliminate this discrepancy partly by doing justice to the forensic aspect of the title and partly by establishing a new field of association for the title. I now go on to show that the latter procedure is also of help for the understanding of the didactic-proclaiming-teaching function. The starting point is the same as the conclusion in 2.3.2: παρα-καλεῖν-παράκλησις can be used to explain the role of the P as expressed in the P-sayings. The comparative texts drawn upon come from early christian literature.

2.4.2. παρακαλεῖν-παράκλησις in the NT

παρακαλεῖν in the NT has several meanings: call, invite, ask for help, plead, make an inquiry, comfort, exhort, reprove, etc. [48] Many of these meanings are general. A special kind of usage which I wish to call attention to occurs when παρακαλεῖν-παράκλησις are connected with the language dealing with teaching and preaching.[49] Their involvement in

[47] The verbs expressing the functions are: ἀναγγέλλειν, διδάσκειν, ἐλέγχειν, λαλεῖν, μαρτυρεῖν, ὁδηγεῖν, ὑπομιμνῄσκειν. See further ch.3.

[48] Besides Bauer, 1958, παρακαλεῖν, see also Grayston, 1979, 28.

[49] Grayston, 1979, 28. Bjerkelund, 1967, is in this case not of much use: a) He deals only with Paul, not with Acts or the other letters. b) He works only with the verb, not with the noun παράκλησις. c) He is interested in those sentences introduced by παρακαλῶ and presenting such characteristics that there is reason to speak of a sentence category of its own in Paul. See p.13.

However, Bjerkelund investigates the usage of both the verb and the noun as a whole in the NT, which is of interest to my study. See pp.24-34. His conclusions confirm my own results.

this part of the semantic field must not be characterized in such a technical way that both words became termini technici. In some passages it would not be unjust to describe the usage as technical,[50] but usually the meaning of both words leans toward the didactic. In most cases one can translate with 'exhort-exhortation' or 'comfort'. These are the most frequent meanings in Acts and the epistles.[51] One must remember that neither such exhortation nor comforting occurred in isolation from some kind of teaching. They were probably components of an overall didactic context. That context could very generally be characterized as teaching-proclamation-preaching.[52]

2.4.3. παρακαλεῖν-παράκλησις as teaching-preaching in the NT

The first evidence for such a context is Acts 13:15. Paul visites a synagogue service in Antioch in Pisidia. After the reading from the Scriptures the head of the synagogue invites anyone who might want to say a λόγος παρακλήσεως to the people to do so.[53] Paul takes the opportunity and speaks to the people. What follows could hardly be characterized as 'exhortation' or 'comfort' in a narrow sense, but more generally as teaching-proclamation-preaching. It is also not, as are most of the exhortation-comfort passages (as can be seen in the pauline letters), directed to the christian community but is a missionary message directed to Jews and proselytes. It is difficult to make an exact comparison between this λόγος παρακλήσεως and the type of synagogal exhortation touched upon in 2.3.3. It can be observed, however, that both have their natural home within the synagogue's sermon tradition as the ending word of comfort. Paul, it seems according to the exposition of Luke, appropriated and adapted the form for the christian mission. It seems justified to call this speech in Acts "un midrash homiletique".[54]

Once more λόγος παρακλήσεως is mentioned in the NT. I am referring to the self characterization of the letter to the Hebrews in Hebr.13:22. This passage does not reflect the meaning 'comfort' I mentioned in 2.3.3.

---

[50] For example Acts 13:15.
[51] The gospels are here left aside. The usage in them is mainly within the general field: call, plead, etc.
[52] Cf Bjerkelund, 1967, 195 note 11.
[53] It should be noticed that this is one of the best records of the function of preaching in the jewish synagogue in NT times. Cf Bjerkelund, 1967, 31.
[54] Dumais, 1976, 87. See also Hartman, 1963-64, 120-134, and Cothenet, 1977, 91f.

The verb ἀνέχεσθαι makes such a meaning less probable. If the narrower meaning 'exhort' is intended, then v.22 must refer only to ch.12-13 with their unmistakable exhortations. As the rest of the letter is of a more general teaching-character such an understanding of ch.12-13 seems unjustified. The λόγος of 13:22, in the singular, could as well be interpreted as a reference to the entire letter. The succeeding phrase διὰ βραχέων ἐπέστειλα ὑμῖν is also in favour of this reading. That ἐπιστέλλειν would refer only to the exhortations in ch.12-13 is very unlikely. Thus, if this λόγος παρακλήσεως refers to the entire letter it has to be given a meaning that can include all parts of the letter, its doctrine regarding faith, exhortation, and comfort. Such a meaning is found within the field teaching-proclamation-preaching.[55]

One passage in Paul which points in the same direction is 1 Tess.2:3f. There is no juxtaposition of the words λόγος παρακλήσεως yet γάρ in v.3 refers to verses 1 and 2 where Paul speaks about his success in his missionary work and the proclamation of the gospel in Thessalonica. The παράκλησις which follows this γάρ summarizes, in one word, his proclamation of the gospel. Both 'exhortation' and 'comfort' are too narrow to render παράκλησις in this context. The more general preaching-proclamation-teaching is more adequate.[56] παράκλησις has the same edifying character of proclamation in Acts 9:31. [57] The growth (ἐπληθύνετο), in the christian congregation is here seen to be the result of παράκλησις. It is worth noting that the Holy Spirit is specified as the one who acts through the paraclese. The step from ἡ παράκλησις τοῦ ἁγίου πνεύματος to ὁ παράκλητος, τὸ πνεῦμα τὸ ἅγιον in John 14:25 does not seem very large.

In 1 Tim.4:13 παράκλησις stands between ἀνάγνωσις and διδασκαλία as one of the three main tasks of Timothy. Such positioning suggests a more general meaning than exhortation or comfort. In order to differentiate the paraclese from the διδασκαλία, it is best to render it by 'proclamation' or 'proclaiming'. This interpretation is supported by the three-

---

[55] Sometimes the letter to the Hebrews has been characterized as a 'homilia'. Bacon, 1917, 275: "pulpit oratory"; Michel, 1960, 4: "die erste vollständige urchristliche Predigt". Nissilä, 1979, 6: "zugesandte Ermahnungsrede".

For me it is not necessary to discuss the literary genre of Hebr. in a technical sense, i.e., artletter, epistle, or real letter. For me the important thing is the character of its contents.

[56] Cf Müller, 1974, 63f; Bjerkelund, 1967, 26f.

[57] Cf Lemonnyer, 1927, where Acts 9:31 plays a dominate role in his argument.

fold formula which indicates three didactic elements in the service.[58] The borderlines among the elements are not sharp, as seen from Tit.1:9, where the instrument for παρακαλεῖν becomes διδασκαλία. One also finds an aspect of proclamation in 2 Cor.5:20. God proclaims his message through his messengers. Here too it becomes reductionistic to render παρακαλεῖν by 'exhort'. It concerns, rather, a proclamation concerning the foundations of the christian message. The usage in 6:1, on the other hand, comes closer to 'exhort'.

2.4.4. παρακαλεῖν-παράκλησις and prophecy

I have already called attention to the relationship the Spirit-the paraclese in Acts 9:31. A special aspect of this relationship concerns the connections between prophecy and the paraclese. In the previously mentioned passage concerning the letter from the apostolic council (Acts 15:32), Jude and Silas, in their capacity as prophets, perform an activity which is described by the verb παρακαλεῖν. Also here we encounter the broader meaning preach-proclaim-teach. The juxtaposition διὰ λόγου πολλοῦ παρεκάλεσαν is similar to the expression λόγος παρακλήσεως. The juxtaposition is not a technical expression here, but one could imagine it as such if the combinations λόγος-παρακαλεῖν and λόγος-παράκλησις express proclamation-preaching in a broader sense.

The prophetic speech in Acts reflects the idea of the Early Church, that through the pouring out of the Spirit it became the new bearer of prophecy which God had promised to renew. [59] The new preaching was filled by the Spirit and thus powerfully active. In addition to 15:32 παρακαλεῖν turns up in one other prophetic context, 2:40.[60] Together with διαμαρτύρεσθαι it designates the speech Peter made on the first Whitsunday. [61] The speech is both teaching, challenging, and prophetic. A notable argument which supports the correspondence between prophecy and paraclese is the interpretation of the name Barnabbas in Acts 4:36. Here παράκλησις corresponds to nāvi' and would thus stand for prophetic

---

[58] Brox, 1969, 180: "technisch-liturgischen Bedeutungszusammenhang". See also Kelly, 1963, 105, who makes a comparison with Acts 13:15. ἀνάγνωσις refers to the reading of the law and the prophets, and παράκλησις refers to "the exposition and application of Scripture". Jeremias, 1981, 34, refers also to Acts 13:15 as well as to Hebr. 13:22.

[59] The reference to the Joel prophecy in Acts 2:17f is an indication of this notion.

[60] Boring, 1978, 119.

[61] Cf 1 Peter 5:12 where the juxtaposition of παρακαλεῖν-ἐπιμαρτύρεσθαι summarizes the activity of the author in this letter.

teaching rather than comfort as it is rendered in most translations.[62] Regarding comfort, the hebrew equivalent to παρακαλεῖν is *nācham* as mentioned in 2.3.3.

In 1 Cor.14 παρακαλεῖν-παράκλησις' ground in prophecy finds its most significant expression. The thesis of the superiority of prophecy as a charisma is here defended, particularily in relation to speaking in tongues. In v.3 Paul states that prophecy has a public character that sets it apart from speaking in tongues which, according to v.22, nobody can understand because it consists of secrets and aims at God or, according to v.4, serves only the edification of the speaking person himself. The contents of prophecy are described by three terms: οἰκοδομή, παράκλησις and παραμυθία. The meanings of the first and third terms seem clear. οἰκοδομή stands generally for speech that is edifying for the congregation. It thereby refers to consolidation which is evidenced by a reference to the congregation (vv.4, 5 and 12), in contrast to individual edification. By παραμυθία is meant an encouraging and comforting address.

The question remains as to the meaning of παράκλησις in 1 Cor.14:3, situated as it is between οἰκοδομή and παραμυθία. The juxtapositions of terms makes it clear that the speech intends to get results. A similar intention can be traced in 1 Thess.2:12 : παρακαλοῦντες καὶ παραμυθούμενοι...εἰς τὸ περιπατεῖν... That παράκλησις is synonymous with παραμυθία expressing the aspect of comfort seems less probable. They rather express different aspects of a real οἰκοδομή, although the difference is not very great. If οἰκοδομή is a dominating term[63] and the two following ones explications of οἰκοδομή, then παράκλησις could be seen to represent the challenging side, παραμυθία the encouraging one.[64] Challenging and edifying prophetic preaching would then be a suitable definition of παράκλησις in this context.[65]

In 14:31 the verb παρακαλεῖν is directly related to the act of prophecy and expresses, together with μανθάνειν, the purpose of that activity. In contrast to 14:3, there is here a synonymous relationship between the verbs. μανθάνειν means to learn, to acquire knowledge.[66] As παρακα-

---

[62] Cf Bacon, 1917, 275.

[63] See Conzelmann, 1981, 285. I do not, however, share his view that "die beiden Vokabeln (παράκλησις, παραμυθία) hier praktisch synonym sind".

[64] This could be compared with the later pair of conceptions: law and gospel.

[65] Cf Grudem, 1982, 183, who stresses the general, loosely defined character of παράκλησις here. He does not manage, however, to make any distinction between παράκλησις and παραμυθία.

[66] Expresses the passive counterpart of διδάσκειν. Cf 1 Tim. 2:11f.

λεῖν here expresses the purpose of prophetic activity in general, a special aspect of the verb can not be intended, i.e., expressing the comforting or exhorting. Such would also imply a constriction and reduction of 14:3. Instead, a more general meaning must be implied, i.e., teach, preach. In its passive form in this context the verb thus stands for 'getting edifying education'.

It is difficult to demonstrate the specific meaning of παρακαλεῖν-παράκλησις in prophetic contexts. If a distinction is to be made, one might say that in prophetic contexts these words are often explicitly connected to the Spirit as a spontaneous gift. This is an important aspect in relation to the P-sayings. One further comment can be made. The performance of the paraclese in a prophetic context seems to be possible for every person in the congregation while this task in other contexts is performed by persons with a special vocation. The latter can be said about Paul (1 Thess.2:3) and Timothy (1 Tim.6:2) not to mention God Father and Christ.[67] The previously mentioned summary of the pentecostal speech in Acts 2:40 has to be regarded as a borderline case. Peter, if any, could be called an 'office-bearer'. Yet the paraclese is so determined by this particular pouring out of the Spirit, that it is difficult to connect the prophetic function too closely to Peter as an office-bearer.

2.4.5. Summary

I have tried to show that within the extensive range of usage παρακαλεῖν-παράκλησις have in the NT, there is one area which includes teaching-proclamation-preaching.[68] There is evidence of such in both missionary preaching as well as in the internal teaching of the congregations. The proclamation is of a challenging sort, intended to effect the listeners. The preaching can be prophetic as well as non-prophetic, can be performed by appointed and/or 'sent out' speakers, or by ordinary members of the congregation. The Spirit stands often, explicitly or implicitly, in the background as the cause of this kind of proclamation.

[67] 2 Cor.1:3-7. Cf Acts 15:32, where Jude and Silas, as messengers, perform prophetic paraclese. It is unclear, however, whether it is their prophetic status or their occasional function (their prophetic charisma as member of the congregation) which is to be stressed. The question hangs on what the second καί in v.32 refers to. Does it mean that they, in addition to being messengers, were also prophets? Or is the intention to stress their equality with those in the congregation who were considered to have the prophetic gift?

[68] My argumentation has, on several points, been influenced by Asting, 1931. His contribution is little known because it is in Norwegian. Cf Müller, 1974, 65 note 85, who refers to Asting indirectly, presumably because of the language problem.

2.4.6. The relevance for the concept of the P

The functions ascribed to the P, elucidated by the way παρακαλεῖν-
παράκλησις are used above, places the P within a didactic field of associations within the conceptual framework of the Early Church.[69] The P
can, thus, be described as the Spirit of christian paraclese, i.e., the Spirit
of christian proclamation.[70] It is therefore justified to translate παράκλητος with teacher or preacher.[71] Such translations are as reasonable as many others, both established and more tentative.

By so encircling the P's field of associations we have reached the point
from which we can investigate whether or not the conclusions concerning
the composition as a whole are valid while, at the same time, we are in
a position to analyze the P-sayings in their immediate contexts.

[69] The NT as a witness in this respect is a *practical* starting point and does *not* imply a
principal priority.
[70] Barrett, 1950, 14.
[71] Asting, 1931, 92; Müller, 1974, 64. Cf Snaith, 1945-46, 50: "Convincer, i.e. , He who
convinces men of the things of God, and accomplishes in them a change of heart".

3. The functions of the P according to the P-sayings

3.1. Introductory

In the preceding chapter I have tried to show that it is possible to explain the exposition of the P in the GJ by postulating three dimensions which, in turn, liberate the interpretation of the P from the dangers inherent in one-sided models of explanation. This investigation concerned itself with a general characterization of the P in the GJ. It is therefore necessary to go one step further and determine if the conclusions remain valid in the analysis of the individual P-sayings.

The primary presupposition of this chapter is the same as I stated in ch.1: the P *is* what he *does*. The functions ascribed to the P clarify the role he plays according to the exposition of the GJ. The present task is to analyze each P-saying and determine the elements of those functions. Consequently, I ignore other problems - in themselves of importance to the understanding of the text - which need not be solved in order to clarify the functions of the P.

One additional introductory comment should be made. Each P-saying is made to stand on its own feet. The answer to the question concerning the function of the P is sought in the individual P-sayings without relying on other texts for assistence. Not until this procedure becomes insufficient the discussion is widened and then primarily to the GJ as a whole. A synchronic analysis of the GJ reveals a certain affinity between different parts, passages, and expressions within the GJ. Although the immediate context is decisive, this affinity should be taken into consideration. Extra-johannine texts, on the other hand, can indicate a background, against which the exposition of the GJ becomes clearer.

3.2. The first P-saying - 14:16-17

3.2.1. Introductory

This saying both introduces and presents the P. This description of the P is marked by two attributes: ἄλλος παράκλητος and τὸ πνεῦμα τῆς

38

ἀληθείας. They indicate the dependence of the P on and closeness to Jesus, the role of the P as the one who replaces Jesus and as the one who will continue his activity as revealer. Hence, in a strict sense, this saying does not ascribe a function to the P but states in what *capacity* and on whose *authority* he will function.

3.2.2. The two attributes of the P

Concerning the first attribute, ἄλλος παράκλητος, I follow the tradition which interprets it non-pleonastically, i.e., 'another P'. The first P would then be Jesus himself. The pleonastic interpretation, 'another one, i.e., a Paraclete', which Michaelis[1] argued, seems unwarranted. There is no evidence of a further pleonastic use of ἄλλος in the GJ, in spite of the fact that this word occurs often (34 times). In addition, the fact that there is no earlier mention of another P in the GJ argues against a pleonastic interpretation. ἄλλος παράκλητος introduces, it is true, a new and problematic term, yet one loses rather than gains by using a pleonastic interpretation to solve the problem. παράκλητος will stand even more isolated and without references. If one, instead, lets the expression point to another P, one who remained previously unmentioned, it becomes possible to make further comparisons. The reference in Haacker[2] to Deut.18:15 seems relevant. Here Moses promises "a prophet like me", although Moses was never himself described in the Pentateuch as a prophet. In both cases - Deut. and the GJ - the designation comes at the announcement of a successor. Jesus thus appears to be the unmentioned P to which the first P-saying refers. In 4.2. I will return to the consequences of this identification.

The second reference, τὸ πνεῦμα τῆς ἀληθείας, also strengthens this idea of a comparison to Jesus. It is hardly a coincidence that this expression is used in close proximity to the saying of Jesus in which he characterizes himself as the truth.[3] The P is the Spirit which relates to the truth as it is revealed in the person of Jesus. The appropriateness of this interpretation becomes more evident in the last P-saying in 16:13a. In that passage the Spirit of truth will guide the disciples in all the truth, which is the total meaning of the revelation in Jesus. To explain the expression

[1] Michaelis, 1947, 152f.
[2] Haacker, 1972, 218.
[3] Most commentators do not even mention this fact. Barrett, 1978, 463, does mention it but does not draw any conclusion from it. Cf, however, the description in Schneider, 1978, 262: "...der Geist der Wahrheit, der die Jünger in der Wahrheit Jesu erhält."

by referring to the view of the Spirit in the Qumran-sect[4] is to find an explanation which lies too far afield from the GJ, as Brown[5] and Barrett[6] have justly pointed out.

The question remains how the Spirit relates to this truth, i.e., how the genitive construction is to be understood. One can understand it as a subjective genitive, which makes the saying almost "essential or ontological":[7] the Spirit is dependent on truth. One can also treat it as an objective genitive.[8] The meaning is then 'the Spirit which communicates truth'. I see no reason, however, for making a choice between these alternatives.[9] On the contrary, the ambiguity of the saying does justice to both aspects of the mediator function which is characteristic for the P. He is able to communicate the truth just because he is part of it. It is this ambiguity, this double sidedness, that the explication in 16:13b expresses: "He will not speak of his own...but what he hears... ".

My interpretation of the two attributes given in 14:16-17 corresponds to the two most important intentions of the farewell-discourse genre (see 2.2.), i.e., to preserve the continuity in the performance of tasks and to legitimate the succession, so that the successor is able to act by order of the predecessor and according to his will.

3.2.3. The persons subjected to the activity of the P

A continuity of tasks does not entail identity in all respects. Such is the case concerning the persons subjected to the activity of the P. Jesus was sent for the sake of the world (3:16f) while the P serves the disciples. The reason for this accommodation is the world's repudiation of the revelation in Jesus.[10] Only the disciples have received Jesus in faith and understood who he is (17:25). In the same manner, the disciples are the only ones

---

[4] Betz, 1963, 147-158.

[5] Brown, 1967, 126.

[6] Barrett, 1978, 463. See also Müller, 1974, 34.

[7] The expressions are taken from Brown, 1966-70, II, 639. He is, however, against such a description.

[8] Brown, 1966-70, II, 639, and Barrett, 1978, 463, choose this interpretation and reject the subjective one. According to Barrett, 1950, 14, the notion 'the Spirit of truth' then becomes equivalent with 'the Spirit of Christian proclamation'. Interpreted in this way the expression is in line with my argumentation in 2.4. and parallels the conclusions in 2.4.6. The didactic function of the P is thereby marked.

[9] Both interpretations go back to ancient times, to the Early Church. See Casurella, 1983, 38 and 45.

[10] There is a kind of correlation between 1:10f (ὁ κόσμος αὐτὸν οὐκ ἔγνω ...οὐ παρέλαβον) and 14:17 (οὐ δύναται λαβεῖν ὅτι οὐ...γινώσκει). Cf Bultmann, 1950, 476f.

who can recognize and understand the continous revelation mediated by the P. This involves a setting apart of the disciples as the true people of God, those among whom the promises of God will be realized. That the P will be with and in the disciples is probably an allusion to the OT thought that God is with his people and, in the new covenant, will come closer to them and be within them.[11] It is worth noting that in Jeremiah[12] this promise is connected with the accomplishments of the law, the obedience to the commendments, and the true knowledge of God. One can trace the same idea in the first P-saying. The obedience of the disciples to the commendments of Jesus is followed by the promise of the P being with and in them. Against this background it is possible - already in this introductory presentation of P - to see a leaning towards the didactic in the description of the tasks and functions of the P. The quotation in 6:45 indicates that the thought of divine education was of interest also in another context in the GJ.

Though the P is a gift to the disciples, it is important to stress that he is not without a certain relationship to the world. What the P does has relevance for the world, as I show later (see especially 3.5. and 3.6.). The *effects* of the activity of the P also concern the world. It is *the gift as such* that only falls to the lot of the disciples.

3.2.4. Concluding remarks

The presentation of the P in the first P-saying establishes his christological origins which renders him authority and benefits the disciples. The knowledge of Jesus' death will not place them in a more disadvantageous position than they were when he was physically present. On the contrary, they can not experience the fullness of God's promises before the P arrives. The first saying does not specify how the P will realize this fullness. That will be dealt with in the following sayings.

[11] Fully treated by Malatesta, 1978. Concerning the εἶναι ἐν-expression se 30f and 54f. Concerning a broader field of association of the covenant thinking in the farewell discourse in the GJ see Hartman, 1979, 147, who claims to "bring in more material for the assessment of these features, also adding new nuances to the field of association..."
[12] Jer.31:33f.

3.3. The second P-saying - 14:25f

3.3.1. Introductory

That the P has a didactic function is firmly established in the second saying, where διδάσκειν is the first verb to express his function. Thus, the
hiatus between the lexical meaning of the P's title and his actual function
becomes apparent. It seems strange, therefore, to allow the lexical meaning, i.e., the forensic, to dominate and determine the role of the P. Teaching is, of course, not a very important task of forensics. Thus, a more
careful analysis is required to judge how far and in what way διδάσκειν
is representative of the functions of the P.

3.3.2. The context

V.25 rounds off the previous exposition. How far back this exposition reaches is difficult to say. The phrase ταῦτα λελάληκα occurs in the GJ for
the first time here. It reappears later several times[13] in a way which indicates that it does not function as a delimitation in the immediate context
but rather summarizes Jesus' discourse with his disciples.[14] Judging from
14:25 the summary is meant to embrace the entire earthly fellowship of
Jesus with his disciples. παρ'ὑμῖν μένων is an indication of this. The fact
that v.26 is adversatively linked with v.25 then becomes clear. When Jesus
leaves his disciples and the world he will be succeeded by the P-the Holy
Spirit who, in turn, will carry out his functions.[15] The Father is, namely,
going to send this P 'in my place', the best rendering of ἐν τῷ ὀνόματί
μου.[16] The predicates of the P - διδάσκειν, ὑπομιμνήσκειν - in the future
tense, corresponds to λελάληκα. The latter refers to the concluded discourse of Jesus while the former concerns the time during which Jesus
is invisible to the disciples.

The structure of this saying is similar to the structure of the concluding
P-saying in 16:13ff. In both cases the P-promise is articulated in terms of
what Jesus has said and what he wants to say. Both sayings as well function as 'resting plateaus' in the exposition, before a new theme is introduced.

---

[13] 15:11. 16:1, 4, 6, 25, 33.
[14] See Olsson, 1974, 268.
[15] This is the only P-saying in which the P is explicitly presented as τὸ πνεῦμα τὸ ἅγιον.
[16] Brown, 1966-70, II, 653; Barrett, 1978, 467 and his reference to Mk.13:6.

3.3.3. The teaching function

3.3.3.1. In the P-saying itself
The functions of the P are here twofold: to teach and to remind, expressed
by the verbs διδάσκειν and ὑπομιμνῄσκειν. διδάσκειν is, for once, constructed with an object, πάντα. Otherwise διδάσκειν, in the synoptics
as well in the GJ (as distinguished from the profane-Greek usage and the
usage in intertestamental Judaism), stands in the absolute position, a
construction which refers to the person of Jesus marking him as the
Teacher with a capital 'T'.[17] It is this construction that justifies the description of διδάσκειν as a verb of revelation and Jesus as the revealer.[18]
Expressed more sharply, the important thing is not what Jesus instructs
but *that* he delivers divine teaching.

The teaching of the P also includes the mediation of revelation. In the
reference to the P in 14:26, the verb's object is also the object of ὑπομιμνῄσκειν. The P, as a revealer, is not independent but rather completes
the task of Jesus. This becomes obvious with the second part of the saying
and especially in the relative clause ἅ εἶπον ὑμῖν. It is reasonable to suppose that this second part is an explanation of the first. In doing so καί
functions as a καί-explicativum.[19] The latter part then becomes a description of the contents of the former. This teaching consists of the deepened remembrance of all that Jesus said during his earthly life.

3.3.3.2. Teaching in the GJ
The above mentioned teaching-revelation originates from the Father (8:
28) and is mediated by Jesus who is the Teacher in the GJ. The teaching
function is so pronnounced that at the final trial of Jesus this function,
and the contents of his teaching, becomes the focus of the high priest's
interrogation (18:19f).

With the exception of one passage (9:34) the Father, the Son, or the
P are the subjects of διδάσκειν in the GJ.[20] The Father is the one who
gives the Son insights into the hidden reality. Similarily as the Son mediates this knowledge, the P becomes the last link in the 'revelation chain'
in order to clarify what remains obscure or incomplete in the earthly life
of Jesus and in his absence.

[17] Rengstorf, 1964, 140f; Mussner, 1961, 59.
[18] Cf Olsson, 1974, 269; Kothgasser, 1971, 588.
[19] Schnackenburg, 1965ff., III, 95. See also Miguens, 1963, 204 note 89.
[20] The Father: 8:28. The Son: 6:59. 7:14, 28, 35. 8:2, 20. 18:20. The P: 14:26.

It is worth noting, however, that in the GJ the teaching of Jesus often is said to take place in the synagogue or at the temple.[21] It then becomes reasonable to imagine that much of Jesus' teaching is pictured against the background of the teaching which was performed at these institutions.[22] Jesus is thereby cast in the role of a teacher similar to that of the synoptics,[23] and the character of his teaching becomes open and public.[24]

3.3.3.3. Comparative material

A. Early christian literature.

Other texts in the early christian literature are pertinent to the understanding of the teaching function of the P-saying in three respects:

a. In 1 John 2:27 the Spirit, called τὸ χρίσμα, is seen as the only teaching authority to which one should adhere. The affinity with the P-saying in the GJ is evident, even if the differences are also obvious. In 1 John the forensic aspect is missing,[25] and the internal teaching of the Spirit is more heavily stressed than in the GJ.

If 1 John 2:27 stresses the value of teaching for inward knowledge one finds, in Hermas Sim.9:25, the reception of the Holy Spirit to be the prerequisite for teaching the word of God.[26]

b. Teaching is treated in quite another way in the Pastorals.[27] The function itself is similar to the one found in the GJ. The difference concerns the carrier of the function. In the Pastorals there is little mention of the Holy Spirit and nothing is said concerning its teaching function. This function is held by persons who are found to be reliable (2 Tim.2:2). They

---

[21] 6:59.7:14. 7:28. 8:20. 18:20.

[22] Rengstorf, 1964, 139 and 145.

[23] See, e.g., the use of καθίζειν in 8:2. Cf Lk.4:20 and Mt.5:1.

[24] 7:26ff. 18:20.

[25] Notice that this is the only only context where παράκλητος occurs outside the GJ in the NT. Here (2:1) Jesus acts as P with a clearly forensic function. He is our intercessor. The forensic and the didactic functions are thus strictly separated. This is an indication that it is not usual in the johannine tradition to let terms with didactic contents stand for forensic functions.

[26] ...οἱ κερύξαντες εἰς ὅλον τὸν κόσμον καὶ οἱ διδάξαντες σεμνῶς καὶ ἀγνῶς τὸν λόγον τοῦ κυρίου...παρέλαβον τὸ πνεῦμα τὸ ἅγιον. This saying adapts the promise given in John 14:26, that the P shall teach the disciples everything.

[27] The Pastorals are of interest because the notion of teaching is basic to and frequent in them. It is the same concerning many other functions ascribed to the P. See Michaels, 1975, 249. I will turn back to this theme in the treatment of each P-saying.

are entrusted a fixed task to preserve and promote ἡ διδασκαλία in contrast to those who deal with ἑτεροδιδασκαλεῖν.[28]

c. In Acts the practical mission work itself corresponds to the teaching function of the P-saying in the GJ. There is no interest in the interpretation and teaching of "all that I have told you" (John 14:26). Rather, the teaching in Acts is subsumed by the Christ-kerygma itself.[29]

B. Philo.

The presentation of the teaching function in Philo places this P-function in a wider context.

a. The subjects which act in this regard are often 'heavy' subjects, i.e., God,[30] the interpreting word of God,[31] the Scripture,[32] the law,[33] Moses,[34] or δόγμα.[35] Only he who is the source of all knowledge is able to give knowledge and guidance to others.[36] Real teaching, however, does not focus on the knowledge of the teacher but on the needs of those who are taught.[37] Such can be compared with John 14:18, where the P is necessary for the disciples.

b. In two passages of Philo teaching is combined with the motif of remembering in order to gain real knowledge.[38] Learning is an extended process which Philo compares with the eating habits of ruminating animals. One can not utilize (συλλαβέσθαι) everything at once. One must repeat the knowledge. The memory then works like glue (κόλλα) for the gained knowledge (νοήματα). The juxtaposition διδάσκειν-ὑπομιμνήσκειν could be illustrated in this context (cf 3.3.3.1.).

---

[28] The character of the teaching is indicated by the relationship to παραγγέλλειν (1 Tim.4:11) and παρακαλεῖν (1 Tim.6:2). To say that these two occurences are parts of "ethical" contexts (Rengstorf, 1964, 147) seems to be an exaggeration. One could say, on the other hand, that they signify a challenging teaching and preaching.

[29] πάντα ἃ εἶπον ὑμῖν in John 14:26 corresponds to τὰ περὶ τοῦ Ἰησοῦ in Acts 18:25 and 28:31. (Cf Hebr 5:12 where a similar missionary teaching is hinted). This teaching may also originate in the Spirit. Apollo (18:25) is expressly said to teach ζέων τῷ πνεύματι. It is also of some interest that the teaching of Apollo is related to the synagogue. Teaching, inspired by the Spirit in the context of the synagogue, seems to have been possible in the early church in other traditions than the johannine.

[30] Leg.All., II, 85.

[31] ὁ ὑποφήτης λόγος. De Mut.Nom.18.

[32] Quis rerum 207.

[33] De Post.Abel et Caini 132.

[34] De Migr.Abr.8. De Mut.Nom.32, 220, 236.

[35] Leg.All., III, 1. The Scripture passage, Gen.3:8, is brought in here as a δόγμα with a teaching function.

[36] De Migr.Abr.42.

[37] De Post.Abel et Caini 140-142.

[38] De Post.Abel et Caini 148. De Spec.Leg.IV, 107.

Philo, as a representative of certain greek speaking circles at this time, expresses thus the thought that teaching is of an almost revelatory kind and that it is appropriated through repetition.

3.3.3.4. Concluding remarks

The P mediates information from Jesus that the disciples no longer are able to directly receive on account of his physical absence. It is therefore natural to see basic similarities in the teaching-function of Jesus and the P. Their teaching is revelation, i.e., authoritative knowledge originating in the Father. The GJ shares such interest in and need of revelatory knowledge with the relevant comparative literature.[39] On the other hand, it is distinctive of the johannine tradition to give to the Spirit a dominate role.

At this point in the discussion it is impossible to determine the exact context in which the P's teaching took place. The second P-saying states only that he is going to teach. One receives, however, some clues in this matter from three other factors. The teaching of the Jews took place, according to the GJ, in the synagogue, a fact which is supported by other sources. Philo's description of the synagogue as a διδασκαλεῖα, a place for education, indicates that such was the case.[40] Much of Jesus' teaching activity took place, according to the GJ, in the synagogue or at the temple. Furthermore, the johannine community had its origin in the synagogue.[41] Against such a background it is not unreasonable to think of the teaching activity of the P as related to the teaching which occurred in the synagogue.

In spite of the fact that we have arrived at a somewhat elusive understanding of the teaching function, we can say that it is a fundamental characteristic of the P in the GJ. In order to arrive at a more precise understanding it is necessary investigate the second function of the P displayed in this saying, i.e., the reminding.

---

[39] In addition to the mentioned literature, see also LXX, e.g. Ps.24(25):4, 5, 9. The relevance of this psalm in this context depends on the mention of several functions closely related to the P's: μαρτυρεῖν (μαρτυρία v.10), μένειν (ὑπομένειν v.5, 21), ὑπομιμνῄσκειν (μιμνῄσκεσθαι v.6, 7) and especially ὁδηγεῖν v.5. The last mentioned function is often seen as a background to the corresponding P-function in 16:13.

[40] Hegstad, 1977, 30.

[41] John 16:2.

3.3.4. The reminding-function

3.3.4.1. Introductory
The teaching and reminding functions are seen to be parallel to one another in the second P-saying. The tense, person, and object of the verbs
are the same. The reminding-function, however, is modified by the relative clause ἃ εἶπον ὑμῖν. This relative clause could, of course, also be
assigned to the first motif, teaching, but it stands closer to the second.
This clause leaves its mark on the reminding-function of the P, while the
reminding, in turn, leaves its mark on the teaching. καί functions in the
latter case explicatively, as I have mentioned earlier (3.3.3.1.). Teaching
is, thus, modified by reminding which, in turn, is modified by the relative
clause. If one wants to express the difference in function represented in
the saying, one could say that the former and broader aspect indicates
the *representative* function of the P while the latter indicates an *interpretative*
function. The P has inherited the teaching-function from Jesus, while the
reminding-function is something unique for the P in relation to Jesus.
One could express it in a simpler manner: P will teach through the remembrance of Jesus' teaching.

　　To better comprehend the reminding-function one must go beyond the
P-saying itself and consider the matter in its wider context. It appears that
the reminding-function is very important for the understanding of the
GJ.[42] If one wishes to fathom this function in 14:26 one must investigate
the whole semantic field connected with the remembering and reminding
expressions in the GJ.

3.3.4.2. The remembering-reminding sayings in the GJ
The sayings are of two kinds:
　　a. Sayings of promise and prediction. The second P-saying in 14:26 belongs to this group, as well as the saying which deals with the relation
of the servant to his master in 15:20, and the prelude to the fourth P-
saying in 16:4. Just as in 14:26, the predictions in 15:20 and 16:4 are related to the discourse of Jesus. In 16:4 the choice of words is the same: ταῦτα
λελάληκα ὑμῖν. The stress in 15:20 and in 16:4 is not, however, on the
reminding activity of the P, but on the disciples' own capacity to remember. This can be seen from the objects: the more general πάντα and the
more limited αὐτῶν. There is reason to question whether the sayings in
15:20 and 16:4 are to be seen as manifestations of the general reminding-

---

[42] Dahl, 1948, 94.

task of the P (14:26), or if the remembering-function of the disciples is independent of the P. Even if the stress is on the disciples in 15:20 and 16:4 it seems clear that this activity is included within the sphere of the P. 16:4, in its context of persecution, is framed between 15:26 and 16:7 where the role of the P is emphasized. There is no mention of the reminding-function of the P in these passages, but the disciples' dependence on him is evident. 15:20 has a similar hatred-persecution context as that in 16:4. The effect of framing can not be adduced as an argument , in that the distance between the sayings is too great. The conclusion regarding 16:4 may also be applicable to 15:20, namely, that in order to remember the words of Jesus the disciples are dependent on the reminding-activity of the P. Also 15:20 stands after 14:26. It is not unnatural, therefore, to make an association with the latter passage.

Thus, if this remembering (and being reminded) in 15:20 and 16:4 can be seen as an activity influenced by the P, light is shed upon the reminding-function of the P. It is not only a stage in intellectual understanding, but also produces results in concrete situations. In this case, the remembrance prepares the disciples for the hatred and the sorrow they will experience (16:6).

b. Reminding and interpretation. That the reminding-function aims at practical results becomes evident from the 'remembering-passages' in John where the verb μιμνῄσκεσθαι is used (2:17, 22, and 12:16). These passages say much concerning the process of interpretation after the death and resurrection of Jesus. The growth of the tradition of the GJ consists mainly in remembering, in the attempt to determine what happened in what seemed to happen, and to perceive the real meaning in what had been said by Jesus. The act of reflection had two objects: the words of Jesus and the Scriptures.[43] Their convergence in 2:22 shows not only that Jesus is to be understood in terms of the Scriptures,[44] but also that the words of Jesus are on the same authoritative level as the Scriptures. The Scriptures confirm the words of Jesus, legitimating them as true revelation. Consequently, the disciples can rightly have both ἡ γραφή and ὁ λόγος ὃν εἶπεν ὁ Ἰησοῦς as equal bases of their faith. Furthermore, the attention paid earlier only to the Scriptures can now also be given to the words of Jesus. The words of Jesus can be said to be the new Scrip-

---

[43] Woll, 1981, 98, remarks that the GJ never lets Jesus quote directly from the Scriptures but lets the disciples remember the Scriptures as an explanation of the words and acts of Jesus (2:17;12:15f).
[44] For example, 5:39.

tures, i.e., the new authority, because Jesus has fulfilled the Scriptures completely. I will deal with the consequence of this identification in ch.5. For the moment it is sufficient to state that the reminding-function of the P (through the disciples' activity in 2:17, 22, and 12:16) is meant neither to retain the exact wording of the historical Jesus,[45] nor to present any vaticinia ex eventu,[46] but to penetrate deeper into the deeds of Jesus and the experiences the disciples had during their time together. This function can be formulated in many ways.[47] Not only are certain passages in the GJ the result of the reminding-activity of the P, but the entire GJ can be seen as such.[48] It is characteristic of the GJ, as distinguished from the synoptics,[49] to acknowledge itself as a result of a post-easter process of reflection.

Thus, the P, as the cause and executor of this reminding-activity, functions as an interpreting mediator of tradition. As such he has an intermediary position, making possible the necessary communication both between the earthly Jesus and the disciples and the heavenly Christ and the disciples. What Jesus said then and what he means now are held together through remembrance. This intermediary position includes also a teaching-function, one which intends to make the disciples understand the words of Jesus. The teaching therefore becomes directed towards results, such as "... neu erkannte, neu verstandene Christusoffenbarung und das in ihrer Totalität".[50]

[45] Locker, 1966, 571, however, means that the reminding-function of the P guarantees that the words of Jesus are not lost. To remind means: "etwas in Gedächtnis rufen, einen an etwas denken machen, und zwar in Bezug auf Einzelheiten, Fakten, Worte".

[46] Carson, 1982, 81, distinguishes correctly between 'vaticinium ex eventu' and 'interpretatio ex eventu'.

[47] For example Brown, 1967, 129: "re-presentation in a living manner". Kuhl, 1967, 154: "eine in die Tiefe und die Breite wachsende Einsicht in Gestalt und Sendung des Gottgesandten". Mussner, 1961, 60: "beinahe die Bedeutung des Joh γινώσκειν ... vertiefte Einsicht in Wort und Werk Jesu". Kothgasser, 1971, 591f, (following Schlier,): 1. Vergegenwärtigen 2. Auslegung 3.Erfahren lassen.

[48] Cf 2.3.1. and Sasse, 1925, 274.

[49] Lk.24:6 and 8 deal with a remembering-function occuring at a certain occasion and concerns the resurrection itself. John 2:22 and 12:16 are also caused by a certain situation but refer to happenings and utterances during the earthly life of Jesus in a way that indicates a conscious process of reflection. The placing of 2:14-22 (compared with the synoptics), the development of this pericope, and its conclusion are the most obvious evidences of this process.

[50] Kothgasser, 1972, 33. But to admit this and, at the same time, to say that this is far from being "neue Offenbarung" is, in my opinion, a laboured distinction.

3.3.4.3. Comparative material

It is quite natural that the community's need to turn back and remember increases with the distance from the life, death, and resurrection of Jesus. Thus, one finds more references to this theme in later periods of the Early Church. Not infrequently, the objects of remembrance are advanced one generation, so that the interest does not primarily concern the words of Jesus but those of the apostles, e.g. in Jud.v.17, or similarly in 1 Cor.11:2 where Paul's congregation adheres to the traditions he brought them. Being reminded of the words of the apostles in Jud.v.17 is meant as a preparation for the events to come.[51] Remembering predictions and discerning their fullfillment makes one capable of interpreting the present. This, it seems to me, is primarily a prophetic task. The type of reasoning reflected in Jude is similar to the one expressed in the GJ (16:4).[52]

The other aspect of remembrance in the GJ, remembrance as an act of reflection, is also found in traditions outside the GJ, e.g., Jud.v.5. and 2 Peter 1:12f. In a style reminiscent of the LXX, the author of Jude refers to the deeds of God in the past, especially the exodus events. The function of this reference is to actualize (v.8-15) the events. A similar intention can be seen in 2 Peter 1:12f. The context is, in this case, interesting as the author himself acknowledges it to be a farewell-situation. The reason for both reminding and keeping the congregation awake is that the author shall soon die. The resemblance to the farewell-discourse in the GJ is obvious. The difference, however, is that the role of the Spirit is completely lacking in 2 Peter 1:12f. The author is the one who reminds, and those who remember are the receivers. I have earlier (2.3.1.) pointed out that the authors of the pseudepigraphic literature have other means than the Spirit to secure the continuance of their personal tradition insuring that their writings are accepted as legitimate. So is, presumably, also the case concerning 2 Peter.

The apostolic fathers give, in many respects, a similar picture regard-

---

[51] Cf Schelkle, 1961, 166: "Die Leser dürfen...nicht erstaunt sein".

[52] Another text, reflecting a similar correspondance, is found in the Pastorals, 2 Tim.2:14. Timothy is exhorted to recall suffering, salvation, and other aspects of living with Christ to which Christians are called. Such recall becomes here, together with the proclamation (διαμαρτύρεσθαι), part of Timothy's general task as an official of the congregation: to ὀρθοτομεῖν τὸν λόγον τῆς ἀληθείας. The comparison with the P is of interest here concerning both the functions and who is going to perform them. Timothy, not the Spirit, is the one acting. The Spirit is, however, indirectly part of the context through the laying on of hands mentioned in 1 Tim.4:14 and 2 Tim.1:6 (Cf Dibelius-Conzelmann, 1972, 70.), as well as the agent of the inspiration in 2 Tim.1:14.

ing remembrance as an act of intepretation and reflection. One example may suffice: Barn.12:2. 'To remind' comes close to 'to clarify in order to understand'.[53] The interesting thing here is that God becomes the agent by acting indirectly in two respects: a. Moses is the tool through which God speaks. b.In the discourse with Moses God is represented by the Spirit. It is worth noting that all this takes place within the old covenant. It is as if the process of remembrance, interpretation, and adaption has been moved back, in order to function as did the events of the old covenant.

The structure of thought (to be reminded, to remember, to interpret) is, however, already to be found in the OT-tradition. Rememberance is an important part of the relationship between God and the people in the OT. God remembers, above all, the covenant he has made with his people.[54] When God in this way remembers his people, he also acts accordingly. Inversely, it is also an important moment in the religious life of the people to remember God and his gifts to them.[55] One finds especially in Deuteronomy - which in fact is a farewell-discourse - a remembrance-theology.[56] This remembrance deals in particular with the Exodus events. The purpose of these memories is to promote obedience and confidence and dispel disobedience and 'murmuring'.[57]

3.3.4.4. Concluding remarks

Relative to the P, 'to remind' means to interpret. The objects for interpretation are the words and deeds of Jesus. The purpose of interpretation

---

[53] The text is: $\H{\iota}\nu\alpha$ $\H{\upsilon}\pi o\mu\nu\H{\eta}\sigma\eta$ $\alpha\H{\upsilon}\tauo\H{\upsilon}s$ $\pi o\lambda\epsilon\mu o\upsilon\mu\acute{\epsilon}\nu o\upsilon s$, $\H{o}\tau\iota$ $\delta\iota\grave{\alpha}$ $\tau\grave{\alpha}s$ $\grave{\alpha}\mu\alpha\varrho\tau\acute{\iota}\alpha s$ $\alpha\H{\upsilon}\tau\H{\omega}\nu$ $\pi\alpha\varrho\epsilon$-$\delta\acute{o}\vartheta\eta\sigma\alpha\nu$ $\epsilon\H{\iota}s$ $\vartheta\acute{\alpha}\nu\alpha\tauo\nu$.

[54] Gen.9:15f. Ex.2:24.6:5. Lev.26:42. Ps.105(104):8. Ps. 106(105):45. Ez.16:60. 2 Mack.1:2.

[55] Num.15:39f. Deut.8:2.

[56] Michel, 1967, 675.

[57] Three other examples are Sap.12:2, 18:22, and 4 Macc.18:10-19. The last mentioned passage is an example of how the trajectory of reflection over tradition and the Scriptures evolved. The husband of the mother of the seven children has, according to her, taught from the law and the prophets. In doing so he has read from the Scriptures, spoken, taught, glorified, reminded, sung, quoted, and confirmed. Three of these functions are the same as P's, i.e., teaching, glorification, and remembrance. In Sap.18:22 the reminding explicitly concerns the covenant ($\delta\iota\alpha\vartheta\H{\eta}\varkappa\alpha s$ $\H{\upsilon}\pi o\mu\nu\H{\eta}\sigma\alpha s$). Concerning these texts see Forestell, 1975, 164. One could also mention the title $\acute{o}$ $\H{\upsilon}\pi o\mu\iota\mu\nu\H{\eta}\sigma\varkappa\omega\nu$ in 1 King.4:3 (LXX:3 King 4:3). The exact role of this official of Salomon is much discussed. A good summary of that discussion is found in Mettinger, 1971, 52-62. Two things may be said similar to the conclusions concerning the reminding-function of the P: his basic function is as a royal herald, proclaiming royal decrees and he is sometimes to be found in juridical contexts. It is, however, impossible to make any further comparisons with the.

is to understand the meaning of the revelation in Jesus, and to do so in a way that corresponds to the jewish way of using the primary contemporaneous source of revelation: the Scriptures. The purpose is also to actualize the words and deeds of Jesus, so that the disciples can regard their situation as both foreseen and predicted by Jesus. This actualization should result in readiness of action and obedience.

The P's function as interpreter also comes close to the functions of the mediators of tradition, a fact mirrored in those sayings in the GJ which deal explicitly with interpretations based on remembrance which, in turn, have given rise to the thought that the entire GJ is a literary result of the P's reminding-function.

Corresponding functions can be seen in relevant comparative materials from early christian literature and the LXX. One can find examples of reminding-remembering functions that promote obedience, preparedness of action, deepened reflection, and actualization. Such remembrance reflects, in certain cases, a proclamation-teaching of a challenging and penetrating kind.

Clear differences between the GJ and the compared literaure have also been observed. The most important difference lies in the subject of the reminding activity. Outside of the GJ the Spirit is nowhere mentioned as the one acting directly. Elsewhere it is a question of a human activity. In the Early Church, such a development reflects a shaping of the religious life by appointed officials and institutions.

Hence the P, as an interpreting mediator of tradition, while having a profile of his own in the GJ, also has many points of contact with other chrisian and pre-christian traditions. He is presented in an unique way within a specific context.

3.4. The third P-saying - 15:26

3.4.1. Introductory

In the third P-saying, the P is given the function of witnessing about Jesus. This function is a special concern of the GJ.[58] The verb μαρτυρεῖν occurs 76 times in the NT. 33 are to be found in the GJ.

Witnessing is often assigned a forensic meaning or is thought of against a forensic background,[59] particularly the jewish judicial system.[60] It is

[58] Concerning a detailed treatment see Boice, 1970.
[59] For example Meeks, 1967, 306; Porsch, 1974, 226; Trites, 1977, 78-127.
[60] For example Mowinckel, 1933, especially 103; Betz, 1963, 73-82.

an indisputable fact that the word μαρτυρεῖν has a forensic meaning in many profane contexts.[61] It is, however, equally evident that this verb, in non-Biblical Greek, developed in a non-forensic direction and gradually received a broader meaning so that it could mean either a testimony of actual events and experiences in general or indicate the author's opinions. An important exponent for the latter kind of usage is Epictetos.[62] In his writings the philosopher has an important role as a witness for the truth. It is my task to indicate which field of usage comes closest to the witnessing represented in John 15:26.

3.4.2. The context

15:26 is inbedded in the hatred-persecution context which begins in 15:18 and reaches its climax in the fourth P-saying in 16:8-11.[63] This material deals with the question of how the world perceives Jesus and acts against him and the disciples. It sees but does not beleive (6:36). Instead, it sees and hates (15:24). The hatred is groundless (δωρεάν 15:25). When the P is introduced into the discussion (v.26) he could have been presented as a pure comfort and help to the disciples in times of difficulties. Instead, the P is ascribed a function which is orientated towards the world, both in this passage and in 16:8-11. In the former case the world receives information about Jesus, in the latter about itself. Yet the disciples are also brought into this activity. They are the ones to whom Jesus will send the P from the Father. This fact has to be taken into account when one judges the degree of the disciples' independence from the P in v.27. Seen linguistically, the function of the disciples is something more than the P's, but the nearness of the P to the disciples is represented in v.26 in such a way that it is impossible to separate the one activity from the other.[64] The task of both the P and of the disciples (to witness about Jesus) becomes an answer to the basic lack of understanding the world shows Jesus and the disciples which, in turn, results in hatred and persecution.

In order to investigate the witnessing-function I shall answer three questions: a) *Who* is witnessing in the GJ as a whole. b) *What* are the *contents* of this witnessing? c) *What* is the *purpose* of the witnessing?

---

[61] Strathmann, 1967, 476ff; Trites, 1977, 8ff.

[62] Strathmann, 1967, 479ff.

[63] It might be helpful to make a tradition-historical comparison here. See the excursus in 3.8.

[64] Cf Brown, 1966-70, II, 689; Cf also Mt.10:20.

3.4.3. Witnessing in the GJ

μαρτυρεῖν occurs in many different syntactic constructions in the GJ.[65] The most common construction is the one found in the third P-saying: μαρτυρεῖν περί τινος. This construction contributes to the answer of a. and b. above. Let me start with b. and the contents of this witnessing.

The usual object of μαρτυρεῖν is Jesus or circumlocutions referring to him, i.e., the light (1:7f), or the word (1:15). The other objects are man (2:25), the world (7:7), and the evil (18:23). Of the last three, 2:25 is of interest. In 25b the result of the witnessing leads to knowledge (a knowledge Jesus did not need!). This use reflects a broader field of meaning than the purely forensic one, which I referred to in 3.4.1. If one turns to 18:23, however, the context of 18:23 is clearly forensic. Similar forensic contexts can be discerned in occurences where Jesus is the object, especially 5:31ff, 8:13f, and 8:18, where the forensic aspect is a part of the temple centred teaching of 7:14-8:20 (note the use of διδάσκειν in both 7:14 and 8:20). The question in 8:13f and 8:20 is, which witness is valid and authoritative? The truth of the witness is at stake. The common denominator for the witness about Jesus is the true knowledge about him.

The answer of question a. (concerning the subject of μαρτυρεῖν) is more differentiated. It can be John the Baptist (1:7f;1:15), Jesus himself (5:31ff;8:13f; 8:18), the deeds of Jesus (10:25), the Father (5:37;8:18) or the Scriptures (5:39). Also, of course, the P in 15:26 and the disciples in 15:27 (περί in v.27 has to be supplied from v.26). All of the subjects are important, so important that they - from the juridical point of view - are seen to be invulnerable and cannot be contradicted. The question is if such self-evident dignity breaks the forensic frame. They do not only give valid testimony concerning Jesus, but they also impart Knowledge, with a capital 'K', of a revelatory character. Such witness is intimately connected with pretentions to truth in the GJ (e.g. 18:37;21:24). Thus, the subjects' dignity gives to μαρτυρεῖν, constructed with περί, a didactic content which approaches revelation.[66] When the P appears in this context his

---

[65] a. In absolute position; b. + περί; c. + dat.; d + ὅτι-clause.

[66] The movement away from the strict forensic function can also be illustrated by two other occurences of μαρτυρεῖν in the GJ. In 1:32 the verb, parallelled with λέγειν, almost becomes a verbum dicendi. The contents of the subsequent saying and the summarizing conclusion in v.34 might be characterized as 'preaching'. The verb acquires almost prophetic features in 13:21. Jesus becomes deeply troubled, witnesses, and announces that he is going to be betrayed. A legal function can not be traced here. In a roundabout way (among others Rev.19:1 where ἡ μαρτυρία τοῦ Ἰησοῦ is equal with τὸ πνεῦμα τῆς προφητείας) Michaels, 1975, 246f, means that μαρτυρεῖν, which does not have any self-evident connection with prophecy in the GJ, contributes to an understanding of the P's activity as prophetic.

authority becomes clear. After the removal of Jesus from the world the P alone will serve the function that other subjects served during the earthly life of Jesus. The disciples provide only the concrete means of assistance.

Let us now turn to the third question (concerning the purpose of the witnessing). According to Brown[67] the witnessing in 15:26f is directed "contra mundum". The purpose is to bring the world before the court and to judge it. I can hardly see that such a view is supported by 15:26f or corresponds to the GJ on the whole.

Schnackenburg[68] argues somewhat differently. Instead of "contra mundum" he speaks of "Zeugnis an die Adresse der Welt". He stresses the forensic aspect as "ein überführendes, den Unglauben der Welt entlarvendes Zeugnis", but says that this aspect becomes clear first in 16:8-11. He can not exclude "eine gewisse Ambivalenz des Bezeugens". There is, also, a slight possibility "dass die Menschen das Wort der Jünger annehmen". The disciples, who had accompanied Jesus from the beginning, are added as witnesses in 15:27. It shows, as I see it, that the witnessing of the P has a wider purpose than that of being of comfort and help to the disciples.

It should be noted that in 15:26 witnessing is construed as an activity in itself. There is no mention of any purpose or eventual result. It is true that 15:26f is a part of the passage which also includes 16:8-11, where a purpose vis-a-vis the world is given. One cannot, however, determine the purpose of 16:8-11 and then say that the purpose in 15:26f is the same.[69] Nor is it justified to let the backward-pointing ταῦτα λελάληκα in 16:1 refer exclusively to the P-saying in 15:26f. As I have pointed out earlier (3.2.1.), the expression ταῦτα λελάληκα summarizes a long passage rather than a particular saying. In this case the expression can refer to either 15:12-27,[70] since the earlier ταῦτα λελάληκα is in 15:11, or rather 15:18-27, since these verses form a natural entity. The purpose of the speech as stated in 16:1b (that the disciples shall not fall) corresponds well to the contents of 15:18-27. This, however, does not prevent the ἵνα-clause

---

[67] Brown, 1966-70, II, 699f.

[68] Schnackenburg, 1965ff., III, 136.

[69] Brown's argument - partly also Schnackenburg's - presupposes that one has given ἐλέγχειν a strictly forensic meaning in order to be able to give μαρτυρεῖν a corresponding meaning. If one (as I shall try to do in 3.5.2.) is able to demonstrate that ἐλέγχειν also has a broader meaning than the strictly forensic one, the argument is untenable also concerning μαρτυρεῖν.

[70] So Brown, 1966-70, II, 690, and Bultmann, 1950, 428. Barrett, 1978, 484. Cf Lindars, 1972, 497, from v.20 onwards.

in 16:1b from a secondary application to the material which follows.

Just as the P's activity is directed towards two addressees, a. the disciples and b. the world, so also is the witnessing concerned with the same twofold categories.

a. Witnessing about Jesus is meant to maintain and strengthen the belief of the disciples. In 19:35 the witnessing concerns a certain event in the earthly life of Jesus: his death on the cross. The purpose is clearly mentioned by a ἵνα-clause. Such is also the case in the first ending of the GJ (20:30f). Together with the other ending (21:24) they show that the gospel itself is meant to be seen as a witness about Jesus which strengthens the faith of the disciples. From this perspective the GJ can be seen as edifying teaching.

b. The witnessing towards the world is explicitly mentioned in one saying. The task of John the Baptist, according to 1:7, was to witness about the light so that all would hear the message and believe. Two additional passages indicate results of the witnessing in such a way that its intention can be discerned. The activity of the Samaritan woman in 4:39 (modified by the participle μαρτυρούσης) results in many people coming to faith. The witnessing is parallel with Jesus' own teaching in 4:41. 3:32f. describes, in a peculiar way, how witnessing can result in two attitudes, either in the rejection or the reception of the witness.[71] Witnessing is open to both the positive and the negative reactions. The reaction here and elsewhere (3:11) in the GJ is, however, predominantly negative. If, on the other hand, the rejection of the witness is seen as the only potential reation, it would mean that they were the last generation of disciples and that no new disciples could be won. There is nothing in the GJ to indicate such a conclusion. The witnessing of the disciples in 15:27 points rather in the opposite direction, as does the eschatological perspective of the GJ.[72] Also the missionology one finds hinted at in 10:16 supports the notion of a continuing possibility to affirm the witness about Jesus. This thought is directly mentioned in 17:20.

The possibility to affirm or deny the truth in Jesus, so typical for the GJ, involves also the thought of judgement. Thus one can say that the forensic aspect is built into the proclamation about Jesus, even if the verb μαρτυρεῖν is used. One could illustrate this by the passage in 3:16-18. The primary purpose of the sending of Jesus is salvation, not judgement. A judgement, however, is pronounced automatically when someone rejects Jesus. Thus, the primary purpose is to create faith, but the result

---

[71] No one accepts his message. But whoever accepts his message...

[72] From a somewhat different angle, see 4.5.

56

can be denial and judgement. This implies that the one who witnesses about Jesus might be a 'catalyt' and participate, unawares, in a forensic act.

This seems to be the meaning of the function ascribed to the P in 15:26. In the absence of Jesus his task is to reveal, together with the disciples, an actual, living, and authoritative knowledge about Jesus, which provokes a response in people.[73] When people reject the witness of the P they are automatically judged. The purpose is not to judge, but it can be the result. The further role of the P, in this context, will be treated in the analysis of the fourth P-saying.

Thus it becomes evident that the witness of the P has two functions. It serves primarily to awaken and strengthen faith through teaching and, secondarily, it judges a rejection of such witness.[74] Consequently, witnessing has been placed within two of the dimensions I posited in ch. 2, i.e., the didactic and the forensic.

3.4.4. Comparative Material

In that witnessing seems to be presented in somewhat particular terms in the GJ there is reason to look briefly at the relevant comparative material.

The letters of John are similar to the GJ in this respect. It is only in 1 John 5:6f that one finds the Spirit as an explicit subject. Just as in John 15:26 Jesus is the 'content' of the witnessing. The purpose of the sayings in 1 John 5 seems to be somewhat different than in John 15:26. They are mainly concerned with strengthening the faith of the disciples (v.13) and not with reinforcing a positive approach towards the world.

In Acts, Luke speaks often of witnessing as important to the proclamation of the gospel. The resurrection is the starting point for the understanding of the life and work of Jesus (Acts 1:22. Cf 10:40-43). Its function is to bring people face to face with the decision: belief or unbelief. Acts stresses positive reception more than the GJ. There is, however, no principal difference between them in this respect. Witnessing includes the possibility of responding in both ways. The question of which response becomes dominant is dependent on time, place, and theological purpose.

[73] Cf the statement of Sasse, 1925, 272: "Die μαρτυρία des Parakleten ist...ein Kerygma, eine μαρτυρία περὶ Ἰησοῦ im evangelistischen Sinne".
[74] Cf Preiss, 1954, 15. Except for 4:44 and 13:21 "both verb and noun connote an act that is at the same time religious and juridical..."

The use in Philo[75] confirms the notion that μαρτυρεῖν can reflect a meaning which is primarily didactic. The forensic aspect merely imparts authority and credibility to the argument. Consequently, there is reason to weigh the forensic and the didactic aspects similarly as does the P-saying in 15:26. In several contexts witnessing reveals a teaching built upon the interpretation of the Scriptures.[76] Witnessing also has prophetic overtones in several passages,[77] at times clearly expressing the notion of inspiration.[78] Often witnessing seems to be construed as revelatory.

3.4.5. Summary

I have indicated that the witness function of the P, compositionally, belongs within the forensic dimension of the GJ. The forensic dimension alone, however, does not give a satisfactory explanation of this function. Witnessing in the GJ gives knowledge about Jesus and thus, primarily, helps and comforts the disciples in difficult times and situations, yet it also serves to give the world the opportunity to know Jesus and thereby come to faith. The fact that most people reject the witness is, so to say, the inescapable reverse side of the coin. That reverse side implies an act of judgement.

Witnessing is thus part of a didactic activity which can assume the character of revelation. As such it is an authoritative and trustworthy teaching, at times emanating from God or his Spirit, at times from those who through personal experience are capable of bearing valid witness.

---

[75] How differently Philo may be judged can be seen when one compares Strathmann, 1967, 489, with Trites, 1977, 6.

Strathmann: "There is in Philo not even the first impulse towards a specific use along the lines found in primitive Christianity." Trites: "...he (Philo) serves as a bridge between the Greek and Hebrew worlds and helps one to see the links between the Old and New Testament ideas of witness".

[76] The dominate use in Philo consists of the reference to the Scriptures in general and certain passages in particular as proofs of drawn conclusions. (Trites, 1977, 63f). The subjects are usually 'heavy'. Moses is the dominating one. Others are ὁ χρησμός, ὁ ἱερὸς λόγος, ὁ θεῖος λόγος, τὸ χρησθὲν λόγιον, τὸ θεσπισθὲν λόγιον, ὁ θεός, ὁ θεσπέσιος ἀνήρ, τις τῶν παλαιῶν, τις τῶν πάλαι προφητῶν.

[77] De Abr.262. De Vita Mosis II, 263.

[78] De Confus.Ling.44. De Somniis, II, 172.

3.5. The fourth P-saying - 16:7-11

3.5.1. Introductory

The fourth P-saying is, on the whole, the most problematic. It contains several difficulties which have always plagued interpreters. Recently Carson[79] has presented a survey of the problems as well as recent attempts to solve them. He also presents one of his own. His opening remark refers to awkwardness of the situation: "None of the interpretations offered so far is entirely free from difficulty; and the one about to be presented does not escape this curse either".[80] The problems are such that the solution of one sheds light upon the others. In spite of this, I concentrate on the problem that is central to my discussion and deal with the others only in so far as they contribute to the inquiry concerning the meaning of the

---

[79] Carson, 1979. I shall not review Carson's entire article but bring forward here five points which summarize the problems inherent in the fourth saying.

a. What does ἐλέγχειν περι stand for in this context? Convict, accuse, convince, expose? This is the primary question for my investigation.

b. How are the ὅτι-clauses in vv.9-11 tobe understood? Explanatory concerning the meaning of ἁμαρτία, δικαιοσύνη, and κρίσις? Causal as introductions to the adverbial clauses modifying the verb?

c. How to explain 2nd person plural in θεωρεῖτε (v.10) instead of an expected 3rd person singular or plural?

d. What do the three nouns ἁμαρτία, δικαιοσύνη, κρίσις mean in this context? Furthermore the important question: does δικαιοσύνη refer to the righteousness of the world, of Christ or to righteousness in general?

e. Finally, the most difficult question: how to make the different pieces fit together in an homogeneous way? Most interpretations, in other respects acceptable, result in "a significant built-in discontinuity".

For the moment I just wish to comment on point e. from a methdolocical point of view. Carson is very anxious to avoid "a logical discontinuity insensitive to the structure" in order to do justice to "the integrity of the structure" or "formal identity of structure". He can also express the issue as follows: "Maintenance of the symmetry is a necessary condition for a reasonable interpretation." His ambition is laudable, but I am not sure that he hits the point on the head. I have earlier argued against unambiguous interpretations in the GJ. The text is often ambiguous. The linguistic expressions are not always very sharp or absolute. I refer, for example, to the use of ἵνα and ὅτι. It is not always possible to define them in an unambiguous way. By this I want to say that the concern for "symmetry or formal identity of the structure" in the GJ is not of any value in itself. The question of symmetry must be subordinated to other arguments as an explanation of the text. Doing so runs the risk of treating the text arbitrarily. That risk has to be taken, however. The force of the individual arguments has to be decisive.

[80] Carson, 1979, 547.

P's function in this text containing the verb ἐλέγχειν. Henceforth I shall refer to ἐλέγχειν as the 'e-function' in order to keep the meaning open, not 'locking' it in to early.

3.5.2. Determination of the function

The e-function is the P-function which has the most obvious forensic background.[81] The verb, however, is not only used in forensic contexts in profane Greek, but has a broader meaning,[82] finding application also in educational contexts. The question concerning the P is how one should construe his e-function. Later on I will show that it should include meanings like 'proclaim in a judging and reproving way'. One can, in advance of the argument, generalize and say that the e-function of the P is somewhere on the scale forensic-didactic. The previous scholarly discussions have also pointed in this direction.[83]

What one decides in this matter depends largely on how one reads the context, especially how one answers the question *for whom* is this e-function intended? Is it meant for the disciples or the world? One could say that the alternatives forensic-didactic correlate with the alternatives for the disciples-for the world. The more one stresses 'the disciples' as the beneficiary of the P's activity, the more the forensic side will be stressed. And on the contrary, the more the activity of the P towards the world is emphasized, the more relevant is the didactic side.

V.8 shows that the P's e-function is directed towards the world. V.7,

[81] Lidell-Scott, 1968, 531: "cross-examine, question, accuse, test, bring to the proof, refute, confute". Kothgasser, 1792, 13, draws the conclusion: "Es handelt sich eindeutig um ein forensisches Tun des Parakleten, das somit dem ursprünglichen Sinn des Titels παράκλητος eigentlich am ehesten gerecht wird".

[82] Lidell-Scott, 1968, 531: "put to right, correct, get to the better of, expose".

[83] In the forensic direction: For example Blank, 1964, 335, 399; Brown, 1966-70, II, 704-714; Boice, 1970, 155f; Kothgasser, 1972, 13.

In the didactic direction: For example Sasse, 1925, 273f; Windisch, 1927, 119f; Asting, 1931, 95f; Büchsel, 1964, 474; Locker, 1966, 566.

Partly a combination of both:Bornkamm, 1949, 21; Müller, 1974, 70; Forestell, 1975, 168ff: "The context is more than forensic." Schnackenburg, 1965ff., III, 146, interprets the activity of the P in a forensic way as a court-process not because of the meaning of the verb itself but because of the notions sin, righteousness and judgement connected to it. The verb itself might, according to Schnackenburg, have "recht unterschiedliche Bedeutungen". Cf also Lindars, 1970, 280f, who wants to interpret the saying in a forensic way but says that the e-function "lost its pejorative sense". The e-function is "so broad in its range of meanings that it can be taken as neutral here, requiring the additional words with περί to specify the nuance".

on the other hand, indicates that the disciples are the ones who will benefit from the coming of the P. One can combine these aspects and say that
the P will be of use to the disciples when he calls the world to account.
If so, one could refer either to the final eschatological judgement[84] or to
some kind of earthly court procedure. There is nothing in the text, however, that points to the final eschatological judgement. That judgement
is reserved for the Son, according to 5:27ff. If, on the other hand, it was
a matter of an earthly court-procedure, one must presuppose that it
would have been possible to carry through real punishments. There is,
however, no indication of such a possibility in the text. Finally, it can be
of no use to the disciples only to *threaten* the world by pronouncing judgement upon it. Such would presuppose that the world always accepted this
judgement. There is no indication of this in the text, nor any suggestion
of the results of the punishment.[85]

The relationship between the disciples (v.7) and the world (v.8) must
be approached in a different manner. The first observation one can make
is that there is no mention of the result of the P's activity towards the
world in vv.8-11. This does not, however, seem to reduce the usefulness
of his activity among the disciples.

The e-function seems, as was the case concerning witnessing (see
3.4.3), to engender two reactions. The world either accepts the message
or rejects it. If one assumes such a correspondence one can conclude that
there are features common to both reactions. Both of them refer to some
sort of preaching. In the case of witnessing, it was a preaching about Jesus. The e-function implies a preaching which proclaims to the world that
the rejection of Jesus incurs disastrous consequences (v.11). The consequences of such an attitude toward Jesus are definite and irrevocable, as
the P proclaims. The attitude in itself is not irrevocable, however. The

[84] So Dodd, 1953, 414, who, according to his emphasizing of realized eschatology in the
GJ states: "Thus the coming of Christ after his death, which for the disciples means the
attainment of eternal life, means for the world the Last Judgement. As this coming is
mediated for them by the Spirit, so the Last Judgement also is mediated by the Spirit".
[85] Cf Berrouard, 1949, 365ff, and de La Potterie, 1965, 101ff. Both of them locate the e-
function in the heart of the disciples as a purely inner process which convinces them that
the world is mistaken and that they have choosen the right side. He who is the subject
of this e-activity does not need to be present. Concerning the criticism of this view see
Carson, 1979, 551f.

openness of vv.8-11 justify such a conclusion.[86] The P is going to give correct information about the consequences of the rejection of Jesus, yet will leave the door open for the possibility of changing this attitude.[87]

Seen from this perspective, the benefit gained by the disciples upon the arrival of the P becomes clearer. The P will help them expose the consequences of rejection for the world. The results of this preaching are obedience or disobedience. It is difficult, however, to draw the same conclusion from this text as I did concerning witnessing, i.e., that it aims primarily at making the world answer in the affirmative. The context in 16:1-11 indicates that the author/receivers should not harbour any illusions. It does not seem appropriate, however, to use the P-saying in 14:17 to indicate that the world will not be convinced by the *activity* of the P.[88] That the world is unable to understand and receive the P is one thing. That the world can be influenced by the activity of the P, especially when it is carried out by the disciples, is something quite different.

Summarizing the argument up to this point, one might say that the e-function of the P is characterized by preaching judgement and punishment.[89] Thus one, instead of opposing forensic and didactic, can see them

---

[86] Blank, 1964, 335, seems quite definite when he says that it is here a question of a critical, forensic event. The P continues the judging activity of the Son of man. The presupposition is that the choice has already been made by the world. There is no turning back.

Mowinckel, 1933, 105, has a far more nuanced picture of the situation: "Ob der Betreffende sich durch die ἐλέγξις innerlich überzeugen und bekehren lässt oder nicht, darüber wird mit dem betreffenden Worte nichts gesagt: er kann sich überzeugen, warnen und bekehren lassen, er kann auch den Tadel in den Wind schlagen". Cf the conclusion of Painter, 1981, 539: "According to John 16:7-11 the Paraclete mediates the challenge of the revelation in Jesus to the world. The teaching is wholly optimistic about the outcome, possibly suggesting the rapid conversion of the world."

The basic aim of the e-function is well defined by Büchsel, 1964, 474: "to show someone his sin and to summon him to repentance...to point away from sin to repentance".

[87] My conclusion is close to that of Lindars, 1970, 281: "he will expose the world for a verdict one way or the other". Ibid. page 284: "The Paraclete will condemn the world in so far as it does not believe; on the other hand he will acquit it where there is belief; thus in one way or the other a decision will be made wherever the Spirit is active in the world".

[88] So Brown, 1966-70, II, 711.

[89] Windisch, 1927, 119f. The three notions sin, righteousness, and judgement are, according to Windisch, the basic motifs of the prophetic and apostolic preaching about judgement. Note 1 on page 120 presents the textual proofs for this thesis.

Cf Asting, 1931, 95f. According to Asting the three notions are three stages in the missionary preaching. Cf also Bammel, 1973, 203, to whom the three notions almost correspond to τὰ βαρύτερα τοῦ νόμου in Judaism. They are often described in a similar threefold way.

as two interwoven dimensions in a similar way as was the case concerning witnessing in 3.4. and as was argued in ch.2. The forensic dimension here dominates more than in the other P-sayings. That does not mean that the principal point is not applicable here as before, i.e., that the forensic dimension operates mainly on the compositional level of the GJ, while the didactic dimension expresses the real function. Also, the third dimension mentioned in ch.2, the one caused by the farewell-situation, is evident here. The usefulness of both Jesus' removal and the giving of his testament is clearly pictured in vv.5-7. All three dimensions are thus interwoven in the fourth P-saying in a unique way.

3.5.3. Comparative material

3.5.3.1. In the GJ

The distance to a preaching of judgement is not so far removed from the e-function of 3:20. The passage deals with the judgement which is an automatic consequence of a rejection of the light. Vv. 20 and 21 reflect a parallel construction with the exception of the ἵνα-clause in v.20.[90] Both verses give information; in the former of a negative and judging kind, in the latter of a positive and encouraging kind.

A construction using ἐλέγχειν, similar to that of 16:8, is found in 8:46. The text is concerned with the contrast truth-lies and those who represent them. The passage is difficult,[91] yet it is clear that the e-function stands

---

[90] If one imagines a hypothetical corresponding ἵνα-clause in v.19, it would, in all probability, show that the evil deeds are made ἐν τῷ ἄρχοντι τοῦ κόσμου τούτου (16:11) or, as some manuscripts in connection with v.19 testify, that they are πονερά.

[91] The saying can be interpreted in two ways:

a. A sin committed by Jesus would be a criterion of his untruthfulness. ἐλέγχειν would then mean "to accuse of".

b. Both in 16:8 and 8:46 ἁμαρτία is in indefinite form, a fact that has made Bultmann state that it is not a reference to any particular sin but to the notion as such. (Bultmann, 1950, 433). It is similar concerning the other two notions of 16:8-11: δικαιοσύνη and κρίσις. (See also Schnackenburg, 1965ff., II, 290, note 2.) 8:46 would then concern an incorrect understanding on Jesus' part, which would strengthen the fact that Jesus does not speak the truth. ἐλέγχειν would then mean "correct concerning", a meaning appropriate to the verb.

To choose between the two alternatives is not easy. As Schnackenburg, 1965ff., II, 290, has shown it is difficult to understand the passage as referring to "eine einzelne Sünde" of Jesus or primarily to "die moralische Sündlosigkeit" of him. In such a case the jews could have shown easily, from their perspective, his disregard for the sabbath (15:16;9:16).

for a critical and judging activity. This activity is not identical with the one in 16:8, but does not present a notion contrary to it.

3.5.3.2. *Extra-johannine texts*

A critical, judging activity, placed in a teaching context with the intention to lead to conversion and faith, or to protect faith, is reflected in several early christian sayings outside the GJ.

In the Church-discipline logion in Mt.18:15, the response to the one who has sinned is described by ἐλέγχειν. If the erring man listens, i.e., obeys that which is spoken to him, the one acting has won his brother. It is the aim of the e-function which is important, to win back one who has sinned. The purpose is thus not to effect a judgement leading to rejection, an action taken only in the third stage (v.19) when the erring one does not obey even the reprimand of the entire congregation.

A positive result of the e-function can be seen in 1 Cor.14:24. As a result of prophetic activity which takes place in the common service, the unbeliever (who enters the service) is 'uncovered', bows down and worships God. This result is caused by a preaching of a searching and judging kind,[92] intimately connected with christian prophecy.[93] Thus 1 Cor.14 shows that the e-function is related to prophetic and spiritual activity.

I have earlier pointed out that several of the P's functions have correspondences in the Pastorals. This is certainly the case concerning the e-function. Above all I wish to call attention to 2 Tim.4:2. In his exhortation to Timothy, the author of the letter instructs him to perform certain preaching activities. The tasks converge in the proclamation of the word. One must always be alert and, when the doctrine and the faith of individual christians are threatened, present a preaching described by three terms, ἐλέγχειν, ἐπιτιμεῖν, and παρακαλεῖν. The purpose is to preserve those who remain in the faith as proclaimed. It seems quite clear that

In their eyes this makes him a sinner. On the other hand, the alternative concerning an incorrect understanding of sin is not natural to the context. As the argument deals with actions and their relation to truth, an intellectual interpretation of v.46 becomes somewhat artificial. I have to agree with Bultmann,1950, 244f, when he describes the whole thing as an "eigentümliche Doppeldeutigkeit". The question in v.46 is not meant to supply a criterion in order to judge the blamelessness of Jesus and consequently his pretentions to truth, but to vindicate the revelation of Jesus. The sinlessness does not characterize the personality of Jesus but his word of revelation (cf 7:18).
[92] Müller, 1974, 70.
[93] Boring, 1978, 119.

the e-function belongs within a preaching context.[94] The absence of the Spirit is worth noting. His position is assumed by a permanent official.

I have indicated the uncovering effect of the e-function in 1 Cor.14:24. Ign.Phil.7:1 shows such to be almost revelatory. The Spirit is the one who τὰ κρυπτὰ ἐλέγχει. There is nothing in the text indicating a final eschatological perspective. One should, therefore, assume that the function was performed among living people, especially among the adversaries of Ignatius.[95] There is no mention of how this function was performed, but it is reasonable to relate it to Ignatius' own preaching. ἐν οἷς ἐλάλησα indicates that such a reading of the passage is possible.

That the e-function in some way represented internal exhortation or exhortatory preaching is indicated by Didache 15:3 and by the similar sayings in Didache 4:3 and Barn.19:4.

The LXX also shows that aspects other than the forensic are represented by the e-function. Indeed, the forensic usage is actually rare.[96] In the LXX, the e-function is intimately connected with education and teaching, especially God's teaching and the education of his people.[97] The exhortation is sometimes expressed negatively, expressing what one should no longer do.[98] It can also be expressed positively, as the means to faith.[99]

One text which is ignored in the commentaries but worth noting (not only concerning the e-function but also concerning the whole fourth P-saying) is Sap.1. In this text there are striking similarities to the concept found in John 16:7-11.[100] There is reason to ask if these similarities are

[94] The conclusions concerning 2 Tim.4:2 are confirmed by Tit.1:9 and 13. The e-function is an important part of the preaching task of the leader of the congregation. It is also important to notice that the e-function in v.13 is seen in a positive light. It shows that this function does not necessarily have a negative effect upon those subjected to the function. This is rarely said concerning the P-saying in John 16:8.

[95] Cf Grant, 1966, 104f: "Ignatius recalls an occasion at Philadelphia when he was obviously prophesying in the Spirit".

[96] Ps.50(49):21f is an example of such a use.

[97] Büchsel, 1964, 473f. This feature can be seen through the not unusual combination παιδεύειν-ἐλέγχειν. E.g. Ps.94(93):10. Sir.18:13 (+ διδάσκειν). Cf also Prov.15:12 and Hab.1:12.

[98] Sir.19:14.

[99] Wis.12:2.

[100] ἐλέγχειν: Sap.1:3,5,8; John 16:8. τὸ πνεῦμα: Sap.1:5 (ἅγιον), 6,7 (κυρίου). John 16:7 (the P). ἁμαρτία: Sap.1:4. John 16:8,9. δικαιοσύνη: Sap.1:1. John 16:8. ἀπιστεῖν: Sap.1:2. John 16:9 (οὐ πιστεύειν). πληροῦν: Sap.1:7. John 16:6. κρίνειν: Sap.1:1. John 16:8 and 11 (κρίσις), 11. Furthermore, in regard to the context of the third P-saying: μάρτυς: Sap.1:6. John 15:26 (μαρτυρεῖν). Cf Riesenfeld, 1972, 273: "It would certainly be worth while to scrutinize more thoroughly the use of the terms such as ἀλήθεια, δόξα, εἰρήνη,

accidental, or if the concepts are deliberately transferred into the context of John 16. I doubt the latter. The comparison might show, however, that both texts in some respect reflect the same literary tradition.

3.5.4. Summary

The analysis of the e-function in John 16:7-11 has shown that it can be placed within the forensic-didactic dimensions of a clearly defined fare-well context. The forensic dimension does not dominate in the way many interpreters have posited. Instead, the forensic language affords a structure through which the notion of the P can be linked linguistically with his activity.

Within this structure one finds the actual didactic function which, while expressing judgement, corrects and criticizes in order to effect a reconsideration on the part of the receivers.

Examples from the relevant comparative material show that this is not a contrived interpretation of the e-function. It seems as if the forensic dimension of the e-function has long been over-emphasized and, becoming the traditional interpretation, it has been passed on from scholar to scholar without much support in the texts. In this respect the traditional treatment of the e-function is similar to the traditional treatment of the P.

These conclusions concerning the e-function in 16:7-11 are made without resolving all the problems of interpretation connected with the fourth P-saying.

3.6. The fifth P-saying - 16:12-15

3.6.1. Introductory

The last P-saying reflects the most functions of the P. He will guide in all truth, speak, preach, and glorify. In addition, he will both listen to Jesus and receive from him important means to realize such functions.

The saying rounds off the P-sayings group. Linguistically ($\dot{\varepsilon}\varkappa\varepsilon\tilde{\iota}\nu o\varsigma$ refers back to v.8) it is connected with the fourth saying, vv.7-11. At the same time, however, it is natural to let the $\dot{\varepsilon}\tau\iota$ $\pi o\lambda\lambda\acute{\alpha}$ in v.12 refer to both

---

$\pi\nu\varepsilon\tilde{\upsilon}\mu\alpha$ in wisdom texts...and then trace influences upon the *wording* (my underlining) of the Last Discourse of the Gospel of John". It lies, however, outside the lines of my work to do such an investigation.

what Jesus has said and the functions attributed to the P earlier in the farewell-discourse.[101]

As in the previous sayings, the activity of the P is seen against the backround of the disciples' needs. In the other sayings, such needs have been their loneliness (ὀρφανοί 14:18), their need of deepened knowledge(14:25f), their exposed position because of the hatred of the world (15:18-26), and their sorrow before the removal of Jesus (16:6). The last circumstance results from their basic inability to receive and embrace the entire revelation in one moment βαστάζειν ἄρτι). The P will respond to all the needs of the disciples, giving assistance where the disciples have shown their own insufficiency. -

3.6.2. The structure of the saying

The relations among the functions attributed to the P establishes a hierarchy. Guiding in all truth and glorifying enjoy dominant and somewhat overlapping positions as they function parallel to one another. The guiding is said to be done vis-a-vis the disciples (ὑμᾶς), whereas the glorifying is said to be done vis-a-vis Jesus (ἐμέ). Both functions are explicated in expressions dealing with subordinated functions. The guiding will be carried out through the speaking what the P hears and and the preaching of the things to come, whereas the glorifying will be realized through preaching. This last mentioned function is not independent, but rather takes up and modifies the preaching of the things to come. The listening and taking functions are subordinated and inseparable parts of the explicative functions speaking and preaching (in the latter case). Thus the structure of this P-saying can be displayed as follows:

A. ἐκεῖνος ὁδηγήσει ἐν τῇ ἀληθείᾳ πάσῃ ὑμᾶς

γὰρ { λαλήσει ὅσα ἀκούσει (οὐ λαλήσει ἀφ'ἑαυτοῦ)
      { ἀναγγελεῖ τὰ ἐρχόμενα

B. ἐκεῖνος δοξάζει ἐμὲ ὅτι ἀναγγελεῖ — ἐκ τοῦ ἐμοῦ { λήμψεται
                                                      { λαμβάνει

---

[101] Cf Dodd, 1953, 415: "These verses (16:12-15) form a short *coda* to the monologue..."(ch 15-16:15).

If one focuses on what the P is actually supposed to do it is better, however, to view the structure from another angle and see how the speaking and preaching, with their elucidating attributes, result in actual guiding and glorifying. The structure then looks as follows:

A. λαλήσει ὅσα ἀκούσει $\left.\right\}$ ⟶ ἐκεῖνος ὁδηγήσει ὑμᾶς
   ἀναγγελεῖ τὰ ἒρχομενα

B. ἀναγγελεῖ (ἐκ τοῦ ἐμοῦ $\genfrac{}{}{0pt}{}{λήμψεται)}{λαμβάνει)}$ ⟶ ἐκεῖνος δοξάϚει ἐμέ

My presentation of the P's functions in this saying will be based on this latter way of displaying the structure of the text.

3.6.3. The speech-function

3.6.3.1. Determination of the function
As I pointed out in 3.6.2., this function, together with the preaching function, constitute the actual activities of the P in the fifth P-saying. It is clearly indicated that the speech-function is dependent on Jesus. Thus the listening to and sensitivity for the words of Jesus play a decisive role. That the P's activity was here construed in terms of a mediator is very likely.

There is a difference in usage between λέγειν and λαλεῖν in the GJ which can be noticed also in this context by the shift in v.12f. The latter often expresses the vocal and speech-function itself, whereas the former one gives expression to the contents of what has been said.[102] The choice of the verb λαλεῖν to express the P's speaking what he hears may stress the speech activity itself and thus indicate that the P is a mouthpiece of the absent Jesus. This fact will be of some importance later on in the investigation (6.4.3.4.).

Further information concerning the P's future speaking is not found in the text. His speech is described as resulting from a constant readiness to and sensitivity for (ὅσα ἀκούσει) the continuing teaching of Jesus. Jesus, too, does not speak on his own but mediates through his speech what

---

[102] Further examples of differences in usage in the GJ: 1:37f. 3:11. 4:26. 7:12f. 7:26. 8:12. 8:30f. 12:29. 16:29. 19:10.

he has been taught by the Father (8:28). Considering the P's direct relationship with Jesus, this teaching speech may be characterized as revelation.[103] The contexts in which λαλεῖν is used connote some sort of revelation to most of its occurrences in the GJ.[104] The P will, thus, through his speaking what he hears, mediate revelation. This description of the speech-function, comes very close to the notion of prophecy, a fact strengthened by the parallelism which reflects an even clearer prophetic function: ἀναγγέλλειν τὰ ἐρχόμενα (See 3.6.4.1.).

3.6.3.2. Comparative material

The function of the P is, as I just stated, similar to the function of the prophet who also communicates revelation from God. God speaks to the prophet, the prophet listens and speaks accordingly. Such was the function of Moses.[105] Such was also the function of the prophet like Moses according to Deut.18:18: δώσω τὸ ῥῆμά μου ἐν τῷ στόματι αὐτοῦ, καὶ λαλήσει αὐτοῖς καθότι ἂν ἐντείλωμαι αὐτῷ. According to Num.24:13 Bileam regarded his activity in a similar way.[106] David regarded his life's work to be to communicate spiritual, inspired speech from God.[107] Such is also how one regarded the activity of the prophets in different parts of the Early Church.[108]

A similar kind of speech, here characterized as teaching and revelation of the Spirit, can be detected in other passages of early christian literature. Elsewhere (Excursus 3.8.), I have treated the closest parallels, namely, those sayings in the synoptics which deal with the disciples' trial before a court of law. There the Spirit speaks through the disciples. In the synoptic sayings, the disciples will speak what they receive,[109] which corresponds very well with the P's λαλεῖν ὅσα ἀκούσει. The difference is that in the synoptics the disciples receive and speak, whereas in the GJ it is the Spirit that receives and speaks. The speech function in the synoptics

---

[103] Cf Kothgasser, 1972, 36.

[104] See Porsch, 1974, 211, and de La Potterie, 1972, 182.

[105] Through the whole Leviticus until Num.36 there is a continuous shift: God spoke (λαλεῖν) to Moses, and he spoke, (λαλεῖν) in his turn, to the people.

[106] ὅσα ἐὰν εἴπῃ ὁ θεός, ταῦτα ἐρῶ.

[107] 2 Sam(LXX:2 Kgs).23:2: πνεῦμα κίου ἐλάλησεν ἐν ἐμοί, καὶ ὁ λόγος αὐτοῦ ἐπί γλώσσης μου. Cf Acts 2:31.

[108] Acts 3:21. Notice in the context (3:24) the parallel function expressed by καταγγέλλειν which comes very close to the parallel function in John 16:13, expressed by ἀναγγέλλειν. Hebr.1:1. James 5:10. 2 Peter 1:21.

[109] Explicitly expressed in Mk.13:11: ὃ ἐὰν δοθῇ ὑμῖν...τοῦτο λαλεῖτε.

is found in a forensic context but has, at the same time, a teaching and revealing function. There is, thus, also in the synoptic sayings a kind of doubleness residing in the composition where, as I have shown several times earlier, within a forensic context the didactic function receives the stress.

It is a similar kind of speech to the P's that the disciples deliver in different contexts in Acts. They will be inspired by the Spirit and speak what it makes them speak, even in tongues (2:4). Their experiences, what they have seen and *heard* (ἠκούσαμεν), urge them to speak (4:20). Apollo, burning in the Spirit, speaks what he has received through teaching (18:25). In different ways the disciples, just like the P, function as mediators when they speak. Thus, the inspired speech (with prophetic overtones) is not just a johannine phenomenon but is apparent also in other early christian traditions.[110]

3.6.3.3. Concluding remarks

One could ask if there might be any special reason for using λαλεῖν ὅσα ἀκούσει instead of the equally general λέγειν in connection with ὅσα ἀκούσει. There are some indications that λαλεῖν is preferred when emphasizing the P's speech function as prophetic teaching and revelation. The combination with ὅσα ἀκούσει strengthens precisely this aspect. The use of λαλεῖν is, however, due rather to literary conventions than to a deliberate choice.

As I mentioned in 3.6.3.2. λαλεῖν is, on important occasions, used in the LXX to express inspired prophetic speech. Those occurrences can not have been unimportant to the author of the GJ.[111] It is also notable that the three writings in the NT most concerned with inspired preaching and other inspired activity (the GJ, Acts, and 1 Cor.) differ substantially from the rest of the NT in the use of λέγειν-λαλεῖν. These three writings contain the half of all the occurrences of λαλεῖν in the NT.[112] This statistical data is worth taking into account when one observes that in these writings λαλεῖν is usually found in a context of preaching, teaching, or revelatory speech, often inspired and with prophetic overtones.

The conclusion concerning the speech function is that it belongs to the

---

[110] It is notable that the Pastorals, in this case, offer considerably less material for comparison than in the previous cases. The only passage of any interest is Tit.2:15. There, in a way reminiscent of the functions of the P, λαλεῖν is joined to the words παρακαλεῖν and ἐλέγχειν. λαλεῖν is not, however, determined in any special way.

[111] Cf Michaels, 1975, 236.

[112] The figures are based on Morgenthaler, 1958.

didactic frame of the P's functions, as I have argued. The P will speak audibly and mediate Jesus' teaching and revelation similarly as the OT prophets communicated God's revelation. The difference between the prophets and the P is that the former are inspired by the Spirit, whereas the latter is the Spirit itself.

3.6.4. The preaching function

The preaching in v.13 represents the P's second activity according to this saying. Although repeated in vv.14 and 15, it is on account of the object τὰ ἐρχόμενα in v.13 that it gets a more precise and, at the same time, a more debated meaning.[113]

The verb expressing this function, ἀναγγέλλειν, has a rather general meaning: to report, proclaim.[114] As a verb which is parallel to λαλεῖν it is, therefore, well suited.[115] It occurs in neutral as well as in religious contexts, to which the two other occurrences in the GJ testify (4:25 and 5:15). I have, in the fifth saying, choosen to translate ἀναγγέλλειν with 'preach', a word appropriate to such a religious, didactic context.[116]

---

[113] The much debated issue is what τὰ ἐρχόμενα refers to: 1) Future events, situations and problems in general? 2) The trial and death of Jesus? 3) A motive in the genre fare-well-discourses? 4) The Apocalypse of John and its contents?

Alt.1), which is the least complicated, is frequently opposed since it might ascribe a revelatory power to the P, a fact with which some scholars for dogmatic and other reasons can't agree. Joüon, 1938, 24f, attaches, for example, great importance to the prefix ἀνα- and says that it corresponds to 're' in latin. It would mean to 'annoncer une chose comme une redite' and to render ἀναγγέλλειν in the GJ 'une valeur unique, redire'. Joüon's argumentation is, however, unjustifiably forced. For further argumentation concerning alt.1) see Thüsing, 1960, 153; de La Potterie, 1965, 95; and Kothgasser, 1972, 42ff.

Alt.2). See Isaacs, 1983, 398: τὰ ἐρχόμενα 'seems to be a reference to the passion, as an eschatological event in which the final judgement of the world will have already taken place'. Isaacs' argument is untenable. Even if the GJ does not refer to 'a distant future', it does refer to a time after the glorification and removal of Jesus.

Alt.3). Wilckens, 1980, 193 note 19.

Alt.4). Sasse, 1925, 274.

[114] Liddell-Scott, 1968, 100. Liddell-Scott translates all the verbs in this wordgroup with 'proclaim'. Concerning the similarity between them see Schniewind, 1964, 56.

[115] Cf John 16:25 where λαλεῖν once again functions as a parrallel expression, now in relation to ἀπαγγέλλειν. Cf also LXX Is.41:22, a passage I shall have reason to turn back to.

[116] It is difficult for me to follow Arndt-Gingrich, 1957, 51, who do not count John 16:13f as 'didactic speaking' which, according to them, would lead to the translation 'preach', but renders it with 'proclaim', since it refers to "the proclamation of what is to come in the future through the Spirit". This form of proclamation is, indeed, didactic and justifies the translation 'preach'.

I pointed out that the speech function indicated a communication pattern of a prophetic nature. This becomes even clearer in the case of preaching. The author of the GJ has probably choosen to express himself with the verb ἀναγγέλλειν in order to make his reference to the prophetic function clearer,[117] as the object τὰ ἐρχόμενα indicates.

Young[118] has shown that several similarities exist between Isaiah and the GJ, including the use of the verb ἀναγγέλλειν. In Isaiah it often carries the meaning 'reveal' due to the intimate connection with God as its subject. Is.41:23 and 44:7 are of special interest since the verb takes the object τὰ ἐρχόμενα (the prefix ἐπ- does not matter in this case). As far as I know, this construction is found only in these cases in Isaiah and the GJ. In both occurrences the ability of preaching the things to come legitimates the claim to a prophecy of divine origin and authority. In Is.41:23 it is expressed: ὅτι θεοί ἐστε. He who is able to preach the things to come is a real and trustworthy mediator of the revelation from God.[119] This is the most important function of a prophet.

The prophetic aspect of mediation or communication is also found in John 16:14-15 where ἐκ τοῦ ἐμοῦ λήμψεται resp. λαμβάνει specify both the contents and the origin of the preaching.[120] One might, therefore, say that τὰ ἐρχόμενα and ἐκ τοῦ ἐμοῦ λ. function as parallel attributes to ἀναγγέλλειν, and, thus, supplement one another.

Establishing certain prophetic features in the P's preaching-function does not mean, however, that one can specify a form for it. There is nothing said about such forms in the text. It is not so much a question of form but of the quality and authority in the entire activity of the P. This prophetic authority may be expressed more or less strongly. In connection

---

[117] Concerning the prophetic background of the use of ἀναγγέλλειν in the GJ see van Unnik, 1979, who works with the saying in 4:25. His arguments are to a large extent relevant also to 16:13.

[118] Young, 1955, 224-226.

[119] Cf Deut.18:18-22.

[120] I have difficulties understanding Thüsing, 1960, 153 note 41, and 158, when he says that the saying ἐκ τοῦ ἐμοῦ only says something about the origin of the P-preaching and must not be understood partitively (that the P receives and preaches a part of what Jesus has). The two alternatives do not exclude each other. There is nothing in the text hinting at such an opposition. Neither can the saying in 10:32, ἐκ τοῦ πατρός, be brought forward as an argument in favour of Thüsing's thesis. The definite article in the expression ἐκ τοῦ ἐμοῦ does not function in the same way as it does in 10:32. In the latter case it belongs to a noun; in 16:14-15 it substantivizes a pronoun and specifies thereby what belongs to the pronoun, i.e., Jesus.

with most of the other functions I have also pointed to prophetic features. The preaching function in 16:14f is, however, more clearly prophetic in character.

3.6.5. The guiding in all truth

3.6.5.1. Determination of the function

Guiding in all truth is, as I have stated before (3.6.2.), the result of the P's speaking what he hears and preaching the things to come. This guiding has all truth as a goal.[121] Truth[122] denotes in this case, just as in the rest of the GJ, divine revelation, but here revelation in its entirty. As the result of speech and preaching, it is difficult to give 'guiding' a special meaning. In general it means that the P will supply the disciples with complete knowledge about Jesus and from him. The GJ as a whole does not contribute to a further understanding of the guiding function since there is no direct correspondance to it. To say that the function (to guide in all truth) is generally didactic is not, however, too daring a statement.

3.6.5.2. Comparative material

The conclusion, that the guiding in all truth is generally didactic, can be strengthened by referring to extra-johannine texts.[123] Two passages in the LXX[124] shed light on this function in John 16:13: Ps.25(24):5 and Ps.143(142):10. These two texts are usually mentioned by commentators[125] as the main background to 16:12-15, at times with some objections.[126] The former text has a wording similar to John 16:13: ὁδηγεῖν

[121] The text-critical question, whether one shall read ἐν or εἰς, plays a minor role when one judges this function of the P.If one has to make a choice, however, I prefer to read ἐν. Cf Brown, 1966-70, II, 703: "along the way of all truth", and his discussion about the matter on p. 707.
[122] It is in this context that the expression 'the Spirit of truth' occurs for the third time. Cf 3.2.2.
[123] Concerning the NT cf Acts 8:31. This passage concerns the understanding of the Scriptures. Through the inspiration of the Spirit Philip functions as a guide to the Scriptures and, subsequently, as a preacher of Christ (v.35).
[124] In the LXX it is usually God who is the one who guides. The background of this guidance is seen to be the exodus from Egypt and the wandering through the desert (for example Num.24:8 and Neh.9:12, 19). The experience and expectation of the guidance of God is treated also in other contexts, especially in the Psalter (for example Ps.23(22):3. 73(72):24). In several cases the desire for God's guidance is formed into a prayer (for example Ps.27(26):11. 139(138):24.).
[125] E.g. Barrett, 1978, 489. Lindars, 1972, 505.
[126] For example Michaelis, 1967, 100.

ἐπὶ τὴν ἀλήθειάν σου. ὁδηγεῖν is here parallel to διδάσκειν. This parallel structure is also to be found in 143(142):10, but in this text nothing is said about truth. Instead, the Spirit is mentioned as the subject of the guiding.

It is not only, however, the Spirit who guides in the LXX, but also hypostatized wisdom. Sap.9:9-18 indicates that the connection which exists between the GJ and the wisdom tradition may effect certain notions of the Spirit in the GJ. Wisdom guides a man's deeds (v.11), knows what is just according to God's commandments (v.9),[127] and in v.17 wisdom is placed on an equal footing with the Holy Spirit. Without wisdom and the Holy Spirit man would lack knowledge about God. It does not seem unreasonable to compare the relation between them to the relationship between Jesus and the P. Both are sent by God to give knowledge about him.

3.6.6. The glorifying function

It is, as I have pointed out (3.6.2.), a distinctive feature of the glorifying not to be a separate activity but the result of two other activities, namely, a taking from Jesus and a communication to the disciples. The consequence of this mediation, carried out by the P, is the glorification of Jesus. It seems, thus, correct to say that the glorifying indirectly belongs to the pattern of didactic functions (which I have found in the P-sayings) as a consequence[128] of other such functions.[129]

One could ask, what does the glorification of Jesus by the P result in?[130]

---

[127] Cf also Sap.10:10.

[128] Glorification as a result of some other process is mentioned elsewhere in the GJ. A similar approach is to be found in 11:4, where Lazarus' disease causes the glorification of Jesus; in 14:13, where the promise to answer prayers aims at glorifying the Father through the Son; and in 21:19, where the death of Peter will lead to the glorification of God. This is the only case where a subject other than the Father, the Son, or the Spirit is to be found.

[129] There is in the GJ a peculiar tension between the activity ofthe Spirit as a consequence of the glorification of Jesus (7:39) and the glorification of Jesus as a consequence of the activity of the Spirit (16:14). This shows how relatively unconcerned the author of the GJ is about logical and temporal inconsistencies in the exposition. 12:28 may give a clue to the question how the GJ's author can juxtapose temporal inconsistencies.

[130] The term δοξάζειν itself is, according to Schlier, 1964, 268 note 14, "ein unübersetzbarer Begriff". According to him it is only possible to render the contents of the word in a paraphrase. It is a word which "das Ansehen Jesu machtvoll austrahlen lässt".

Through the mediation of the P it will become clearer who Jesus really is, what origin he has, and what power he possesses. His unity with the Father, the divine character of his mission and revelation will become evident.[131] This unity, and the authority emanating from it, is strengthened by the statement in v.15a. Everything that the Father has belongs to the Son. The P will take from that which belongs to the Son and proclaim it which, then, leads to glorification.

This glorifying of Jesus is not, however, an end in itself. The ideas seem to move in a circle. It is ἐκ τοῦ ἐμοῦ the P preaches to the disciples, and it is in the preaching Jesus is glorified, i.e., the unity with the Father becomes apparent. This unity consists in ὅσα ἔχει ὁ πατὴρ ἐμά ἐστιν. This ἐμά, however, is the source from which the P (see the preceding verse) appropriates the material for his preaching, an interpretation confirmed by v.15b. The intention of this circular argument may have been to authorize the GJ's tradition (see further 4.4.3.) among other christian traditions and the advocates of jewish belief.

3.6.7. Conclusion

The fifth P-saying expresses, on the whole, four functions: two general and two more specific ones. Let me just say a few words about the former ones.

The guiding in all truth has an introductory role and is of didactic character. The fifth P-saying is , indeed, the most didactic one of all. The field of activities (v.13) of the guiding is said to be 'all truth', i.e., the divine revelation which ultimately is concerned with the Word that became flesh, with Jesus' life, death, resurrection, and with the consequences of these events.

Glorifying, on the other hand, may be said to be the function which covers all the others and is their ultimate goal. As, according to the GJ, Jesus' work ended in his glorification and that glorification also meant divine life-giving to the world, so the work of the P means a glorifying of Jesus whose life-giving work and revelation are thus continued.

It seems, therefore, reasonable to regard the fifth P-saying as a summary and conclusion of the P group of sayings.

---

[131] Cf Haenchen, 1980,494: "...die wahre Herrlichkeit Jesu an den Tag bringt...eröffnete den Weg zum Vater".

3.7. Concluding summary

This chapter investigated whether the three dimensions proposed in ch.2 could endure an analysis of the individual P-sayings, and, above all, the functions ascribed to the P by them. I claim that I have answered the question in the affirmative. All three dimensions are to be found in the P-sayings, although not every dimension is found in each saying or with equal clarity. The dimension of the farewell situation is least visable. This might be due to the fact that it indicates a *situation* rather than a function. The forensic dimension is more noticeable. It never, however, dominates the description of any of the P's functions. It forms the background against which the descriptions of the other functions are pictured. It is important that the background remains background, so that it does not play the central role in the determination of the P's functions. That role should rather be assumed by the didactic dimension. This dimension is included in all the sayings, in some cases very clearly.[132] In other cases one observes it only upon closer examination.[133]

Thus, the teaching and preaching functions dominate according to the P-sayings themselves. In different ways, in different contexts, and partly to different receivers, the P will teach while reminding of all that Jesus said, witnessing about Jesus, reproving and judging the world, guiding in all truth, and preaching the things to come. All these activities coalesce in the glorification of the Son by indicating his identity with the Father.

To teach on behalf of Jesus legitimates, of course, the P's authority within the congregation. His teaching can not be questioned, as cannot the Father's or the Son's. It is obvious, however, that this revelatory authority must, in some way, be related to human teaching authorities in the johannine community. He who represents and embodies the P can, of course, claim to represent and embody the true tradition from God. The interaction between the teaching authorities and the question of authority itself are the subject of the next chapter's investigation.

3.8. Excursus

The P-saying in 15:26 comes closest to persecution-sayings and promises about the Spirit found in the synoptics. (Mk.13:9-13. Mt.10:17-22. 24:9-14. Lk.21:12-19. 12:11-12.).[134] Nevertheless, the johannine text has been for-

---

[132] 14:26 and 16:12-15.
[133] 14:16f. 15:26f. 16:7-11.
[134] See Brown, 1966-70, II, 695. His tableau on p.694 is instructive.

med in its own way. The question is, what kinds of conclusions can one draw from the resemblance? Brown[135] posits that the persecution context in John 15:18-16:4a, owing to its correspondence to the synoptics, has not only rendered the P in 15:26 an unmistakable forensic character, but also has contributed to the overall picture of the P and its functions in the farewell-discourse. διδάσκειν in John 14:2, among other things, would correspond to the function ascribed to the Spirit in Lk 12:12, although the context otherwise does not indicate such a correspondence. That the basic functions in the GJ resp. the synoptics, according to Brown, would be different (in John to accuse the world, in the synoptics to defend the disciples in front of other authorities) does not bother him. This must be all credited to the "new orientation in the johannine development". It deals, in both cases, with a "forensic setting".

Brown's argument is, of course, to some extent correct. He seems, however, to view the situation from too narrow a perspective. The synoptic tradition 'falls down' in the farewell-discourse, especially in one passage (15:26 and its context), and sheds light forewards and backwards over the rest of the P-sayings. The tradition-historical explanation is presented at the expense of the textual. διδάσκειν in 14:26 is not primarily used here with regard to the tradition, but because of the associations and thoughts belonging to the verb itself in its immediate context as well as in the GJ as a whole, as I have tried to show in 3.3.3.

Gryglewicz[136] says that the author of the GJ has taken over the three verbs διδόναι, διδάσκειν, and λαλεῖν from the tradition. At the same time he is of the opinion that it is difficult to draw the line between what comes from the tradition and what is the author's own contribution. Gryglewicz's conclusion is sound: "Uns scheint aber, dass wir dem Verfasser des 4. Evangeliums die von ihm bevorzeugten Worte doch mit einer gewissen Wahrscheinlichkeit zuschreiben können, obwohl alle griechischen Worte der Aussagen über den Heiligen Geist der Tradition entstammen können".

Bultmann[137] is of quite another opinion: "Mit Mk 13:1...hat v 26 aber nichts zu tun".[138]

I wish to draw the same conclusion concerning "the forensic setting" of the P-sayings. As I have tried to show in 2.2., the P-sayings are found

---

[135] Brown, 1966-70, II, 699f.

[136] Gryglewicz, 1979, 48f.

[137] Bultmann, 1950, 426, note 5.

[138] Cf also Sasse, 1925, 272, who says that the function of μαρτυρεῖν in John 15:26 is quite different from that of the corresponding synoptic pericopes. The synoptics deal with a "Verteidigungsrede", John 15:26 with "ein Kerygma...im evangelistischen Sinne".

in the GJ where the forensic dimension is dominant. If one draws out the consequences of Brown's argument, the forensic dimension is due to the fact that "the forensic setting" from the synoptic sayings about the Spirit have shed their light not only upon the P-sayings in the farewell-discourse but also on the character of the GJ as a whole. I don't think, however, that Brown would be willing to draw this conclusion. I would like to approach things from the opposite end. The forensic dimension of the GJ has led to the fact that the author may have taken the forensic shaping of the Spirit from the synoptic apocalypse.

I add some further notes regarding Brown's exposition. If the influencefrom the synoptic tradition has been as decisive as Brown thinks, there is reason to ask why the synoptic verbs $\lambda\alpha\lambda\varepsilon\tilde{\iota}\nu$ and $\delta\iota\delta\acute{\alpha}\sigma\varkappa\varepsilon\iota\nu$ have been changed to $\mu\alpha\varrho\tau\upsilon\varrho\varepsilon\tilde{\iota}\nu$ in 15:26. If they were good enough for the forensic shaping in the synoptics, they should have functioned well enough in the GJ. The fact that $\delta\iota\delta\acute{\alpha}\sigma\varkappa\varepsilon\iota\nu$ is instead used in 14:26, a passage that does not have the same forensic close-context, could hardly be used as a counter-argument. The author of the GJ seems to attend more to the composition of his own work than the shape of other traditions.

One important conclusion could be drawn from a comparison between the GJ and the synoptic tradition. The exchange of $\delta\iota\delta\acute{\alpha}\sigma\varkappa\varepsilon\iota\nu$-$\lambda\alpha\lambda\varepsilon\tilde{\iota}\nu$ for $\mu\alpha\varrho\tau\upsilon\varrho\varepsilon\tilde{\iota}\nu$ might have been made in order to make this verb fit into the johannine terminology in general and its forensic terminology in particular.

This conclusion can be compared with the statement of Porsch:[139] "Die Bedeutung des Zeugnisses im Joh.ev. überhaupt und besonders in diesem, von Prozessmotiv bestimmten Abschnitt würde die Umwandlung des syn $\delta\iota\delta\acute{\alpha}\sigma\varkappa\varepsilon\iota\nu$ bzw. $\lambda\alpha\lambda\varepsilon\tilde{\iota}\nu$ in ein (Joh.) $\mu\alpha\varrho\tau\upsilon\varrho\varepsilon\tilde{\iota}\nu$ und damit auch die Wahl des Titels $\pi\alpha\varrho\acute{\alpha}\varkappa\lambda\eta\tau\sigma\varsigma$ durchaus erklären und rechtfertigen". Porsch is right concerning the verb but draws somewhat far-reaching conclusions concerning the title. More components are necessary to explain the title, as I have tried to show in ch.2.

The exchange from $\delta\iota\delta\acute{\alpha}\sigma\varkappa\varepsilon\iota\nu$-$\lambda\alpha\lambda\varepsilon\tilde{\iota}\nu$ to $\mu\alpha\varrho\tau\upsilon\varrho\varepsilon\tilde{\iota}\nu$ has not been made, however, to render the function a more forensic meaning. Instead, it is a reasonable conclusion that $\delta\iota\delta\acute{\alpha}\sigma\varkappa\varepsilon\iota\nu$ indicates that $\mu\alpha\varrho\tau\upsilon\varrho\varepsilon\tilde{\iota}\nu$ in 15:26, with regard to its contents, leans in the didactic direction. In that case this verb would link up with two of the dimensions I have described in ch.2: the forensic (from the perspective of composition) and the didactic (from the perspective of the contents).

---

[139] Porsch, 1974, 321.

4. The didactic triad

4.1. Introductory.

The receivers of the GJ are referred to three personal authorities after the resurrection and glorification of Jesus. The first, self-evidently sovereign one, is the glorified Jesus. The other two are the P and the Beloved Disciple (hereafter referred to as the BD).[1] On the one hand, these three authorities are autonomous entities, each one having been delegated his own task. On the other hand, their functions are so interdependent that the post-Easter situation, according to the GJ; would have been impossible if any one authority were missing. In their relations to one another they reflect something of the complexity characteristic of the Early Church which, while striving to maintain the traditions concerning the earthly work of Jesus, at the same time saw the fulfillment of that work in his death and resurrection, reflected upon it within a tradition of working with the Scriptures, and adapted it to meet the problems of the delay of the parousia and the expiring group of eyewitnesses. This complexity could be 'converted' into the didactic terms revelation, interpretation, teaching and mediation of tradition. It is within this didactic process (directly related to the origin of the GJ as a writing) that the three authorities are to be placed.

It has been pointed out by several scholars[2] that it is possible to relate the three authorities with one another and that these resultant relation-

---

[1] It is correct to name these three as the authorities of the post-Easter situation. If one, on the other hand, treats the presentation of the life of Jesus before his death and resurrection, one must add John the Baptist to the list. His authority is, however, restricted to the role of forerunner, which is played out when Jesus occurs on the stage. Cf Windisch, 1927, 128. where he states that the GJ depends on the continuity of three witnesses sent by God: John the Baptist, Jesus, and the P. This statement is misleading, partly because it does not take into account the time element for the validity of the authority, and partly because it overlooks the importance of the BD. Culpepper, 1983, 48, presents another alternative: "...its (the GJ's) authority is established on the witness of the Beloved Disciple (an eyewitness), the reliability of the narrator, and the words of Jesus about the Paraclete". I think, however, that he makes too much of the distinction between the BD and the narrator in this respect, and too little of the glorified Jesus.
[2] See recently, e.g., Stuhlmacher, 1983, 13.

ships are of importance for the legitimacy of the johannine tradition. This is the case primarily concerning Jesus and the P, secondarily concerning the P and the BD, and thirdly concerning Jesus and the BD. In this chapter I intend to assort the relevant material from the GJ concerning these relationships, claiming no originality in doing so. In addition, however, I intend to show that these three authorities constitute a cooperative unity around which moves the whole question of authority in the GJ moves. One could draw the relations and the unity graphically in a very simple way:

Jesus

The P   The BD

4.2. Jesus-the P

4.2.1. Identity and subordination

It appears from the interpretation of ἄλλος παράκλητος in 3.2.2. that the P is conceived as somehow parallel to Jesus.[3] The P-sayings assign the same things to the P as are said about Jesus in the entire GJ.[4] Nevertheless, what is said about Jesus goes beyond what is said about the P. The parallelism between Jesus and the P concerns their identity in the matters of origin and function. Within this identity, however, is also a scheme of subordination. The P represents the third stage in the chain of subordination: the Father - the Son - the P. Thus, many of the functions of the P correspond to characteristics found in the relationship between the Father and the Son. Although there is a direct connection between the Father and the P in that the Father is the one who gives (14:16), and sends (14:26) the P and in that the P comes (15:26) from the Father, it should be stressed that what the P is and does is carried out through "die Vermittlung des Sohnes".[5] The Son asks the Father to send the P

[3] Cf Bultmann, 1950, 437; Brown, 1967, 127 note 1. He expresses this thought very clearly: "The career of the Paraclete is parallelled in every detail by the earthly ministry of Jesus".

[4] Bornkamm, 1949, 12, and Brown, 1967, 126. One can also find these parallel sayings assorted and in certain cases systematized in tabular form in Bultmann, 1950, 437; Kothgasser, 1971, 571; Haacker, 1972, 218f; Painter, 1975, 66; and especially in Porsch, 1974, 237-239. Concerning the similarities of the prophetic features see Isaacs, 1983, 399-402.

[5] Porsch, 1974, 239.

(14:16). The Father sends the P in the name of the Son (14:26). A more active mediation is described in 15:26 and 16:7. In both instances the Son is the one who sends, in the first instance with the elucidation 'from the Father', in the second one without such yet, as v.5 indicates, it is on account of the Son's close relationship with the Father that he here sends the P.

It is precisely this aspect of mediation which gives the P a subordinated position in relation to the Son. Also, it should be pointed out, the main concern of the GJ's presentation has to do with the relation between the P and the Son.

4.2.2. The thought of succession

In 2.3. I mentioned the starting point concerning the parallel between Jesus and the P. The P-sayings belong to the farewell-discourse genre based on the model of similar farewell-discourses in the OT and apocryphal literature. The relation between persons in these discourses can be characterized as a "tandem relationship",[6] in which the dying man ordains a successor to take his place after his death. This pattern is to be found, e.g., in the relation between Moses and Joshua or between Elijah and Elisha. The successor is pictured in a similar way as was his predecessor. He continues the task of the predecessor but, in addition, interprets the predecessor's message. The interesting point of comparison in this context is the fact that someone succeeds another, takes over his functions, yet there is no presupposition of an exact affinity in the description of the two persons. To say, e.g., that Jesus is pictured like Elijah is an incorrect statement.[7] The role of the Spirit in this act of succession is also evident in the above mentioned examples. Joshua was filled with the Spirit of knowledge ($\pi\nu\epsilon\tilde{\upsilon}\mu\alpha$ $\sigma\upsilon\nu\acute{\epsilon}\sigma\epsilon\omega\varsigma$) in the LXX (Deut.34:9) as a consequence of the laying on of hands by Moses. Elisha asked for and received the Spirit of Elijah in double measure (2 Kgs (LXX:4 Kgs). 2:9, 15.). It is also appropriate here to take into account the promise and the prediction in Deut.18:15 concerning 'a prophet like Moses'. John 1:21 is probably an allusion to this passage. The saying in Deut.18:15 not only indi-

---

[6] Brown, 1967, 120; Isaacs, 1983, 402. Cf Bornkamm, 1949. The latter worked most thoroughly with this theme but from the point of view of the notion forerunner-fulfiller.
[7] For a treatment of the Jesus-Elijah issue see Martyn, 1978, 12-28. He shows that the GJ gives a "divided picture" in this regard. On the one hand the GJ polemizes against a resemblance between them; on the other hand there are several "Elijah-like traits" in the GJ's picture of Jesus.

cates that the thought of succession appears at an early date in the biblical tradition, but also that prophetic overtones are found in it. Against such a background one can expect prophetic features appearing in the presentation of the P, as I demonstrated in ch.3, especially 3.6.4.[8]

The similarity between these OT prototypes of tandem relationship and the relationship between Jesus and the P is thus found in the thought of succession. The difference does not consist in the fact that the task and the message of the predecessor survives in the activity of the successor, but, in the case of the P, that the predecessor as a person and as the object of faith is made living. The most important task of the P is to make Jesus present in the congregation.[9] The pneumatology of the GJ in general and the P-sayings in particular, are characterized by a "christologische Konzentration",[10] which has the effect of both establishing the importance of the P and showing his dependent and subordinate role. The fact that the Spirit, pictured as the P, is elaborated in a special way in the GJ compared with the synoptics is, among other things, due to two historical conditions considered problematic in this gospel: a) The dying out of the eyewitnesses of the earthly life of Jesus, and b) The delay of the parousia.[11] As it becomes more difficult to overcome the distance to the historical Jesus and more painful to await the parousia, the role of the P to make Jesus present in his absence becomes increasingly important. There is reason to ask if the coming of the Spirit has been regarded as the parousia itself. Jesus returns simply as Spirit.[12] The contexts of the P-sayings in 14:16 and 16:13-15 could indicate such. In both cases the P-saying is immediately followed by sayings concerning the parousia of the glorified Jesus. This formal parallelism also seems, as U.Wilckens shows,[13] to tie together the two comings of Jesus (in the earthly Jesus and the glorified Christ) in the P. It is therefore justified to say like Schnackenburg,[14] that the P's task, within the frame of the johannine 'program', is to make the Christ of the faith 'transparant' in the earthly Jesus.

[8] Cf Michaels, 1975, 246, and Meeks, 1967, 304f, note 3, where the prophetic feature as well as other similarities between Jesus and Moses are emphasized.
[9] de La Potterie, 1977, 201: "de rendre Jésus lui-meme présent dans la communauté".
[10] Porsch, 1974, 405.
[11] Brown, 1967, 128-131.
[12] Woll, 1981, 88. For him, however, it is rather a solution of a problem of authority - against charismatic inflation - than of the problem of the parousia.
[13] Wilckens, 1980, 194f.
[14] Schnackenburg, 1977, 289.

4.2.3. Detailed parallels

The parallelism between Jesus and the P contains several aspects. Regarding their origin, both are given and sent by the Father. Concerning their reception, both are rejected by the world while they are received by the disciples. Above all, however, there is a parallelism in their functions. It is precisely concerning their *functions* that there is a continuity between them.[15] I have earlier argued that the P is what he does. In this sense the most important continuity between Jesus and the P consists in what they actually do. Both serve the Word and carry forth revelation.

One common aspect of their activity is the tension between independence on the one hand and dependence on the other. In this context it is worth noting the kinds of restrictions placed upon their independence, as illustrated by the following tableau:

Jesus	*The P:*
8:28 ἀπ'ἐμαυτοῦ ποιῶ οὐδέν	16:13 οὐ λαλήσει ἀφ'ἑαυτοῦ
12:49 ἐγὼ ἐξ ἐμαυτοῦ οὐκ ἐλάλησα	
(cf. 14:10, 24)	
8:26 ἃ ἤκουσα παρ'αὐτοῦ ταῦτα λαλῶ	16:13 ὅσα ἀκούσει λαλήσει
8:28 καθὼς ἐδίδαξέν με ὁ πατὴρ	16:14 ἐκ τοῦ ἐμοῦ λήμψεται
ταῦτα λαλῶ (cf. 12:50)	

As independent speakers both are dependent upon a 'superior'. Both listen to this superior, receiving from him what they must say and do. Both are described as mediators of a message. This position of mediation presupposes closeness to the superior. Jesus and the Father are one (10:30) as is made clear in 1:18, where Jesus is said to have his place εἰς τὸν κόλπον τοῦ πατρός. In this passage, closeness-mediation is indicated through the usage of the verb ἐξηγεῖσθαι. As to the P, the listening and speaking in 16:13 in a similar way indicates a relationship of closeness-mediation.

Concerning specific functions, the task of mediation is presented in similar ways. I follow the order of the P-sayings.

a. Both agents are said to be with and in the disciples. Jesus: 3:22; 13:33; 14:20, 25; 15:4, 5; 17:23, 26. The P: 14:16f.

b. The teaching function is the most obvious parallel. The teaching of the P (14:26) corresponds to the teaching of Jesus in several passages: 6:59; 7:14ff; 8:20; 18:19.

---

[15] Müller, 1974, 48.

c. It is more difficult to discover a parallel in the reminding function found in 14:26. Jesus' reminding of his own words according to 15:20 indicates, however, such a similarity in function.[16]

d. Witnessing is a function carried out by both. The difference here is that the P, according to 15:26, witnesses about someone else, while Jesus, at least according to 8:13f, witnesses about himself.

e. The e-function has a formal correspondence in 3:20. The function can be better demonstrated in some other passages, however, if one defines (as I have done in 3.5.2.) this function as preaching judgement. The whole revelation in Jesus can, under certain circumstances, be seen as a result of this function, i.e., when this revelation is rejected in unbelief (3:19).

f. The 'guiding in all truth' according to 16:13 has no formal parallel concerning Jesus, but such is intimated in 14:6 and 10:3.

g. The parallel concerning the 'speaking what he hears' is treated above.

h. The prophetic preaching in 16:13 has its parallel in 4:25.

i. Finally, 17:1 and 4 show that the glorification in 16:14 is also a part of Jesus' function.

4.2.4. Summary

The comparison between Jesus and the P has shown that both, while acting independently, also represent an absent superior from a subordinated position. The representations are so in accord with the life of the superior that through these representations he is made alive and present. Prototypes of this relationship can be found both in the OT and in the apocryphal tradition. This mode of representation is worked out in the functions ascribed to Jesus and the P. The common feature of these functions is the mediation of knowledge of various kinds: revelation, prophecy, tradition, and reflection. It is, thus, appropriate to characterize both Jesus and the P as didactic mediators.

---

[16] Haacker, 1972, 219. The ticklish question here is if this being reminded of a word of Jesus - even though it is put in the mouth of Jesus - is not (at least partly) a result of the post-Easter process of reflection. It would, in that case, strengthen the similarity between Jesus and the P concerning this function.

4.3. Jesus-the BD

4.3.1. Introduction of the BD

The BD is, just as is the case concerning the P, a figure without direct parallels in the synoptics. He is as enigmatic as is the P. The question of the possible historical identity of the BD has especially excited the curiosity of scholars. Is someone in the circle around Jesus hiding behind this figure? Or is he a person without anchoring in history, a literary creation who is meant to represent a tradition or group of some kind in an ideal way, e.g., heathen christianity[17] or a wandering group of prophets?[18] Is the BD simply intended to give a picture of the ideal disciple?[19] Research concerning the first altenative (the identification of the BD within the circle around Jesus) has always been speculative and leads into blind alleys.[20] For my investigation, therefore, the task of establishing the historical identity of the BD has held little value. The other approach (the BD as a literary creation), however, has proved to be more interesting and, as I see it, can shed light upon a methodological question concerning the GJ which I have dealt with earlier.[21] When one has to make a choice between different interpretations, one should try to avoid either/or reasoning. The intention of various expositions in the GJ often seems to be to include various aspects of a certain notion in one saying.[22] This is the case also concerning the BD. It is not reasonable to search for a particular

---

[17] Bultmann, 1950, 369; Pamment, 1983, 367.

[18] Kragerud, 1959, 87-92. Cf page 116 where the BD is described as identical with the johannine circle. Cf also Schlier, 1964, 269, who instead of a group of prophets sees charismatics in the congregation symbolized by the BD. It is, however, doubtful that Schlier means that the BD is a purly symbolic figure.

[19] One of the latest variants of this opinion is found in Wilckens, 1980, 201: "Der namenlose Jünger ist also seiner Funktion nach nichts anderes als der im vorösterlichen Kreis der Zwölf bereits anwesende Jünger der nachösterlichen Zeit. Von daher erklärt sich seine Namenlosikeit. Er ist sozusagen das proleptisch verklärte Spiegelbild der anwesenden Jünger". Cf Lindars, 1972, 34, who relates this ideal discipleship to the failure of Peter. Another variant of this view is found in Watty, 1979, 212. According to him, the anonymity of the BD may indicate some kind of pastoral care. New generations of disciples must not be repulsed by the feeling that they do not belong to the inner circle of famous names around the earthly Jesus. The BD thus becomes the unknown ideal disciple with whom they can identify themselves. This explanation, however, seems strained.

[20] See the argumentation in Minear, 1977, 105.

[21] See 1.1. and 1.3.

[22] E.g. the words $\pi\nu\epsilon\tilde{v}\mu\alpha$, $\check{\alpha}\nu\omega\vartheta\epsilon\nu$, $\dot{\alpha}\nu\alpha\beta\alpha\acute{\iota}\nu\epsilon\iota\nu$, $\dot{v}\psi o\tilde{v}\nu$. See Cullmann, 1948. Richard, 1985.

historical person behind the enigmatic designation when one takes into consideration the silence of the synoptics concerning the BD and the contours of the individual BD-pericopes themselves. On the other hand, to regard this figure only as a symbolic abstraction is also problematic. The two main arguments of Lorenzen[23] are here convincing: a) The BD is always mentioned in connection with other concrete persons such as Peter,[24] Mary, and Jesus. b) At several important points in the passion story this disciple is said to be an eyewitness and the guarantor of the reality of the death and resurrection of Jesus.

One can draw the conclusion that there should be a both-and concerning the historical/symbolic interpretation of the BD. That is, he represents a historical personality yet displays, in the GJ, ideal and symbolic features.[25] The same can be said about several other figures in the GJ: Andrew, Philip, Nathanael, Thomas, Jesus' mother. That the BD is not mentioned by name is remarkable, since the author of the GJ is otherwise very careful to identify the persons in his gospel.[26] This pseudonymity can have several explanations. Firstly, considering his central position in the community at the time of the origin of the GJ (21:24), the BD would have been so well known to the readers/listeners that the pseudonym had a self-evident historical origin to which we no longer have access. Furthermore, it was unthinkable in the synagogal tradition of scriptural interpretation (see further ch.5) that a teacher/preacher (the BD can be seen as such in his role as originator of this gospel tradition) would quote himself by name.[27] In addition, a pseudonym gives rise to other associations than does the use of a name and, in this context, it could be argued that such a convention could have served the purpose of strengthening the position and authority of this particular disciple. The Moses-Benjamin typology,

[23] Lorenzen, 1971, 77ff.

[24] Cullmann, 1976, 75, states correctly that, if the BD is only an ideal figure, Peter, who is the regular counterfigure of him, must also be of that character.

[25] Lorenzen, 1971, 80; Roloff, 1968-69, 141; Thyen, 1977, 293, expresses the matter drastically: The BD is "keinesweges ein blosser Homunculus aus der literarischen Retorte seines Erzeugers". Instead, as a "literarische Figur" he must "auf der Ebene des johanneischen Christentums" have had "eine tatsächliche Entsprechung". Thyen calls it "ein historischer Pendent" to the BD. Cf also Hawkin, 1977, 141: "an historical figure with paradigmatic significance". Brown, 1979, 31. Or, as concisely expressed by Gunther, 1981, 134: "idealized historical personality". Culpepper, 1983, 47.

[26] Watty, 1979, 210 exposes this doubleness well. He calls it "the passion for precision and detail and the prevalence of anonymity". Watty's own explanations of the anonymity are not convincing, however.

[27] Maybaum, 1901, 19.

an example of such a usage of pseudonymity, is treated by Minear.[28] Benjamin, the most beloved of Josef's 12 sons is, in Moses farewell-discourse in Deut.33:12, designated as $\mathring{\eta}\gamma\alpha\pi\eta\mu\acute{\epsilon}\nu\sigma\varsigma$ $\mathring{\upsilon}\pi\grave{o}$ $\varkappa\upsilon\varrho\acute{\iota}\sigma\upsilon$. Jub.43:11 also indicates that this tradition concerning the beloved Benjamin was kept alive. A version of Test.Benj.11:1 further supports this particular tradition, mentioning Benjamin as the executor of the good things that emanates from God's mouth.[29] The second part of Deut.33:12 which concerns the protection of 'the Lord all days' also exhibits certain similarities to the responsibility Jesus assumes concerning the BD in John 21:22. No matter how one judges the validity of this last correspondence, it should indicate the range of possible associations concerning the pseudonymity of the BD. The enigma of the BD is, in this respect, not more remarkable than is the logos language in chapter 1. That the logos language refers to Jesus is as obvious as are its allusions to the wisdom tradition.[30] Pseudonymity can imply plurisignificance.

4.3.2. The relevant passages

If one assumes that a certain doubleness is inherent to the figure of the BD (historical person with symbolic and ideal features) the question regarding his historical identity is not as interesting as is discovering what the final redactor behind the GJ wished to say by employing this figure as he did. Before going into this question I should mention which passages of the GJ I shall take into account.

Four texts are certain in that they explicitly deal with 'the disciple whom Jesus loved': 13:23-26; 19:25-27; 20:2-10; 21:1-24. Three are disputed since an anonymous disciple is mentioned but without direct reference to the BD: 1:35-40; 18:15ff and 19:34ff. I take the last two into consideration, but disregard the first. 1:35-40 is excluded because the first explicit presentation of the BD takes place in 13:23-26. The anonymous disciple in 1:35-40 is also of less actual or theological interest.[31] I include 18:15ff

---

[28] Minear, 1977, 110-114.

[29] This version is preferred by Charles but not by Charlesworth.

[30] I have difficulty with the argument of Roloff, 1968-69, 143-151, that the anonymity is best explained by a comparison to the teacher of righteousness in Qumran. No doubt there are certain similarities, but to draw the conclusion that there has been a direct influence is problematic. If there is any influence, it is rather indirect than direct, as I have argued in 3.2.2. Similarities can be due to the fact that one drew from the same sources, e.g., the OT and apocryphal traditions.

[31] So Lorenzen, 1971, 45f. Cf, however, Thyen, 1977, 274. His conclusion that "jene rätselhafte Gestalt des Lieblingsjüngers vorbereitet wird" in this passage seems somewhat far-fetched. Brown, 1979, 33, is on the same line as Thyen. The BD is the unnamed disciple in 1:35-40 but he "achieved his *identity* in a christological context" (13:23-26).

in the text material about the BD partly bacause of its similarity with
20:2-10[32] and partly because several motives here are strikingly similar
to the rest of the accepted sayings.[33] I also accept 19:35f since these verses
are very much like 21:24.

4.3.3. The actual parallels

One can demonstrate the parallels between Jesus and the BD in the same
way as I described the relationship between Jesus and the P. The purpose
of the figure of the BD is "ihn so klar wie möglich als 'Christusparallele'
darustellen".[34] This can not be demonstrated with the same detail as was
the case concerning the P. Rather, here the parallelism consists in basic
circumstances and motifs.

It is important to note that the relationship between Jesus and the BD
is similar to the relation between Jesus and the Father. Although several
of the texts confirm this fact, this is most obvious in 13:23. The BD recli-
nes at the meal ἐν τῷ κόλπῳ τοῦ Ἰησοῦ. It is generally accepted that
this expression refers to in 1:18 where the Son is in the κόλπος of the
Father.[35] These statements are particularly important since they, in both
cases, serve to introduce the respective figures. In these statements a special closeness between the persons is established. In 1:18 this closeness renders the Son such a knowledge of the Father that he is able to explain
and interpret the Father to the world. 13:23-26 seems to ascribe a similar
knowledge to the BD. What is said directly about the Son in 1:18 is illustrated in the 'ideal' scene with the BD in 13:23-26.[36] It is very difficult
to imagine the pericope as being an actual event in detail.[37] This close-

---

[32] Cf Neirynck, 1975, 139ff; Becker, 1981, 435.

[33] Lorenzen, 1971, 50.

[34] Kragerud, 1959, 74. The parallel motif itself is described on pp. 131ff.

[35] Lorenzen, 1971, 83f, says correctly that the saying in 13:23 has a concrete meaning,
while 1:18 is to be understood metaphorically. In addition, he says that the relation between Jesus and a man can never be identical with the relation between the Father and
Jesus. The former can only resemble the latter, being a copy of it.

[36] See Schnackenburg, 1970, 101.

[37] Why would, in that case, Peter have to ask Jesus via the BD? Such a procedure has
no correspondence in the synoptics (Mt.26:22. Mk.14:19.), where every disciple asks Jesus
directly. In Luke (22:23) they talk to one other without asking Jesus. One has, of course,
tried to explain this peculiarity. For a survey of the problem see Haenchen, 1980, 461.
Brown, 1966-70, II, 574, presents - as he says himself - an unsatisfying and not very probable proposal of a "technical" kind. The placement around the table would create such
a distance that a mediation would be necessary. But how is one to imagine the room and
the meal, if the distance between 13 persons causes a communication problem? Schulz,
1972, 175, and Bultmann,1950, 367, mention the fear of the disciples as a cause. This

ness, a kind of intimacy, is expressed in the formula ὃν ἠγάπα ὁ Ἰησοῦς, which is used here for the first time.

The exposition in 19:25-27 strengthens this aspect of closeness. The BD takes over Jesus' place as son and, by doing so, embodies the earthly sonship of Jesus in his absence including the tasks and authority emanating from it.[38] It is a farewell-situation like the one I presented in 2.3.1. Like Joshua and Elisha "schlüpft er (the BD) in die Rolle des Testamentvollstreckers Jesu, indem dieser ihm seiner letzten Willen bekundet".[39] The fact that Jesus is glorified and leaves the world is not always presented in the GJ as an advantage. Difficulties must have arisen within the johannine community because the incarnate Jesus was no longer among them. The designation of the BD as 'beloved son' may have been one answer to that dilemma. It is possible to maintain such an interpretation no matter how one interprets the role of Mary in this pericope.[40]

The scene at the cross illustrates another parallel between Jesus and the BD, that of subordination. Jesus neither sent nor authorized himself butacted on God's initiative, which is also the case concerning the BD. Jesus gives the BD his place in the community and thereby marks the BD's dependence on him. The scenes in 13:23-26 and 21:20-22 confirm this fact. One might, however, raise the objection that the motif of subordination applies to all the disciples (e.g.13:16) and that the BD in this respect displays only a general condition of discipleship. It is, nevertheless, such a consistent feature of the exposition of the BD that it deserves special notice. The subordination and lack of independence does not prevent the BD from being active and independent. It is the same tension as can be seen concerning Jesus: one acts independently but on behalf of and in obedience to a superior. Brought to a head one might express the paradoxical in the relationship so: the more subordinated, the more authoritative.

explanation seems even less satisfying. The proposal of Kuhn, 1969, 69, about an influence from the Qumran congregation concerning a certain speech order at the meals is more interesting. In analogy to such a custom the BD would have a higher rank and rightly speak before Peter. This explanation focuses, in any case, on the relation between the BD and Peter and the BD's position within the circle of the disciples. This observation seems more important than the historical explanation one gives.

[38] It is, of course, possible to say like Dauer, 1968, 82: "...dadurch, dass der Jünger Sohn der Mutter Jesu wird, wird er gleichzeitig auch Jesu Bruder - noch bevor Jesus seine anderen Jünger als Brüder grüssen lässt. So hat der Jünger auch hier der Vorrang vor allen anderen Jüngern". But to maintain the thesis, as Gunther, 1981, 129, that the BD is his german brother is misleading. Gunther's argumentation is, in several respects, good but does not much support his thesis.

[39] Langbrandtner, 1977, 33.

[40] Cf Thyen, 1977, 285.

We have touched upon a third parallel motif - both Jesus and the BD appear as mediators. Concerning Jesus see 4.2.3. In the case of the BD one can trace the motif in most of the relevant texts. One of the more important purposes of 13:23-25 seems to be to show the BD's role as mediator.[41] It is the most reasonable explanation of the exposition. Access to Jesus is mediated by the BD. A similar kind of mediation is requested from the BD in 18:15f. Because of his connection ($\gamma\nu\omega\sigma\tau\delta s$) with the high priest and his servants, the BD is able to bring about Peter's access to the courtyard of the high priest. Peter is dependent on this mediation.[42]

This mediation has prophetic overtones in 21:7.[43] The BD is the only one who is capable of recognizing and revealing Jesus on the shore. It is due to this discovery that Peter can act as he does.

In different ways the BD is thus presented as a mediator between Jesus and the disciples. The last aspect of this motif to be discussed is the witnessing about Jesus and the events around him in order to awaken faith (18:35, 21:24).[44] The BD is so close to Jesus and the decisive events of his life that he is the trustworthy witness of all that concerns Jesus. He is also capable of identifying the risen Lord, which indicates that he has made use of and done justice to the interpretative key in the GJ, the resurrection. He holds, then, an unique position as an interpreter of the

---

[41] Cf for the opposite opinion Schnackenburg, 1970, 101: "...nicht die Rolle eines Mittlers...sondern wird als der Vertraute Jesu vorgestellt." I can not accept his statement for two reasons: partly because the role as mediator seems so convincingly clear, and partly because I can not see any contradiction between the two parts of Schnackenburg's statement. On the contrary, it is precisely by being "der Vertraute Jesu" that the BD is capable of playing "die Rolle eines Mittlers". Hawkin, 1977, 143, is on the same line as Schnackenburg. He denies the BD's role as mediator "between Peter and the disciples". Hawkin draws the conclusion: "This is simply not true to the text." Of course not! The role of mediator concerns rather the communication between Jesus and Peter. The purpose is to show the BD's special access to the person of Jesus. Hawkin's second argument, that "nothing is mediated to Peter" is also misleading. The role as a mediator implies a two-way communication, i.e., also from Peter to Jesus. It is true that the development of the scene is remarkable but this does not change the BD's function as a mediator. I can not agree with Hawkin's conclusion: "Certainly in this pericope nothing of significance is said about the relation of Peter to the Beloved Disciple". But if so, why does Peter have such a distinctive role in the pericope? And what kind of inconsistency does Hawkin wish to attribute to the final redactor of the GJ when he, two pages further on (145), writes about 20:2-10: "The relation of the Beloved Disciple to Peter is the key to the interpretation here".

[42] I will return to the motif of competition in the relation between Peter and the BD in 4.4.3.

[43] Minear, 1977, 115.

[44] Cf Roloff, 1968-69, 138.

Jesus tradition and its meaning. Thus, the BD could be seen as an exegete and interpreter whose task is to awaken faith. The BD is not a revealer himself but mediates the revelation for the revealer. Seen as a mediator, both the resemblance to and the difference from Jesus' person and task is apparent.

4.4. The P-the BD

4.4.1. Introductory

Most of the relevant comparative material between the P and the BD has already been presented. Before reviewing it I wish to mention a further similarity which goes beyond what was presented earlier. At the beginning of the chapter I stated that these two figures, together with Jesus, are the post-Easter authorities in the johannine community. What the P and the BD have in common, however, and that which distinguishes them from the glorified Jesus is that they carry out their activity on earth among men. Their activity is to be experienced by men and have an effect on them. Jesus remains, of course, the dominant authority but has, in turn, authorized the P and the BD to represent and carry this authority into effect. Later I shall show that they, rather than being in competition, are mutually dependent upon one another.

4.4.2. The parallels

The most important similarity between the P and the BD is found in their closeness to Jesus. Both are appointed to their functions either by Jesus or on his request. The relation to Jesus is, in both cases, direct. They have exclusive access to Jesus which gives them a correct and deepened knowledge about him and makes them capable of giving $\mu\alpha\rho\tau\upsilon\rho\acute{\iota}\alpha$ about Jesus. This testimony concerns actual events during the earthly life of Jesus as well as their meaning (19:35 and 14:26). It also includes the capability of discerning the nature of future events and situations for the disciples (16:13 and 21:2-7), indicating the presence of prophetic features as well.[45]

---

[45] 13:23-25 also points to similar prophetic features concerning the BD. Jesus acts and speaks like a prophet in this context. Jesus is revealing the traitor and the BD 'assists' him. Cf Bultmann, 1950, 367.

Such witnessing suggests another common feature. Both the P and the BD function as mediators. Owing to their closeness to Jesus they stand, in a special way, between him and the disciples and the world. In this context the BD holds an exclusive position in relation to the other disciples, especially in relation to Peter. One is justified in speaking of a motif of competition between the BD and Peter, through which the BD receives a certain superiority or, at least, has his authority and position reinforced. I shall soon return to this. It goes too far, however, to say that the BD, through his closeness to Jesus and because of his function as a mediator, comes into "eine eigentümliche Konkurrenz zum Parakleten".[46] Instead, the P's and the BD's parallel relationships to Jesus here serve the purpose of linking them together in a front (more or less sharply pictured) against others, especially Peter.

Let me, however, before proceeding with the theme of competition between the BD and Peter, mention the third similarity between the P and the BD. Both manifest the peculiar tension between independence and subordination. They transmit only what they are given through seeing (19:35), hearing (16:13), receiving (16:14), and recognizing (21:7). Thus, both remain trustworthy and reliable.

4.4.3. The purpose

What purpose does the parallelism between the P and the BD serve? In order to answer this question one must first discern the purpose of the BD-sayings. The main theme of these sayings concerns the relation to Peter, their purpose being to point out the BD's superiority.[47] This is not acomplished by playing down Peter's role but by elevating the BD's.[48]

---

[46] Thyen, 1971, 354. So also Langbrandtner, 1977, 115. At the same time Langbrandtner admits, however, that the BD could be seen as "eine zeitlich begrenzte Verkörperung des Parakleten". It seems a bit contradictory that he in another place (p.58 note 1) says: "Dass sich hinter dem Parakleten eine irdische Person verbirgt ist abwegig". In many other respects I share Langbrandtners view of the BD (pp. 28ff), especially regarding the parallelism between the Father and Jesus and between Jesus and the BD which is seen in terms of mediation, and also regarding the BD's function as a guarantor of the tradition and the competition with Peter.

[47] Cf Becker, 1981, 437: "Konstitutiv für die Deutung von L (the BD) ist ferner die Verhältnisbestimmung zu Petrus".

[48] Cf Hawkin, 1977, 146: "It is not so much that the importance of Peter is played down; rather the attempt is to elevate the importance of the Beloved Disciple." Cf also Thyen, 1977, 290: "...mit Hilfe der fraglosen Autorität des ersteren (Peter) diejenige des letzteren

In 13:23-25 Peter is, as usual, described as the spokesman of the disciples but, nevertheless, he is dependent on the mediation of the BD. Peter can reach Jesus only indirectly. In 18:15f Peter depends upon the BD's contacts to gain entry to the scene where the last act of Jesus' drama occurs. In 20:2-4 the BD runs faster than Peter to the grave. There is no reasonable cause for such a note from the redactor other than the wish to establish the BD's superiority also concerning the testimony about the resurrection. It is true that Peter enters the grave before the BD, but it is said of the BD that he 'saw and believed' (20:8).[49] The same superiority is ascribed to the BD at the meeting with the resurrected Jesus in 21:2-8. Peter's reaction is mediated. The BD tells him what he sees and only then does Peter act. Jesus' remarks concerning the BD in 21:20-22 serve the same purpose, especially since Peter is snubbed by Jesus. Peter's concern for the BD is superfluous since the BD, through his direct relation to Jesus, is given special and direct care.[50]

Thus there is an obvious attempt to describe the relationship between Peter and the BD as one characterized by competition. This does not only apply to them as individuals but also concerns what they represent: two different traditions and two different ways of transmitting knowledge about the revelation in Christ.[51] Lorenzen[52] has observed that the BD occurs in pericopes which display aspects similar to certain pericopes of the synoptic tradition. These passages are, in the synoptics, about Peter, whereas in the GJ they concern the BD. In the GJ the BD remains the main actor.[53] When the BD is described as a trustworthy mediator of the tradition about Jesus, this judgement concerns the tradition found in the GJ. It seems clear that the confrontation with Peter at the same time re-

(the BD) und damit ja seines Evangeliums selbst zu etablieren und befestigen". There is a slight difference between Thyen's and my way of regarding the issue. Thyen draws such an harmonious picture that there is no room for tension or competition in it. I think, however, that the motif of competition is important. It is, however, mainly reflected through positive arguments. It is therefore not correct to play down Peter's role in the GJ by stating that " 'Peter' stands for a negative strain in the gospel". Watty, 1979, 211.

[49] Cf also the difference between ϑεωρεῖ and εἶδεν in v.6 resp.8.

[50] Similar conclusions concerning these passages are found in Brown, 1979, 82f, and Maynard, 1984, 535-542. Brown calls it "the consistent and deliberate contrast" between Peter and the BD.

[51] A brief and good exposition of the two "traditions" (the BD's and the "Petrine" one) is to be found in Gunther, 1981, 135-140.

[52] Lorenzen, 1971, 107. Cf Moreton, 1980, 216.

[53] Lorenzen, 1971, 88.

veals a confrontation between two traditions.[54] It is evident that the tradition found in the GJ is the BD's, but to define Peter's tradition exactly is problematic. It could be the synoptic one in a broad sense,[55] or even other traditions or gospels. Whatever it was, Peter has been seen as the representative and guarantor of this tradition. For my further investigation the question is not decisive. The important thing to notice here is that the GJ, through the figure of BD, intends to legitimate the tradition to which this gospel gives voice. The BD's function is, thus, to elevate the GJ to 'canonical rank'.[56] One could ask if there is not a correlation between the GJ's christology and the BD. If the BD and/or the circle around him provided the highly developed christology of the GJ, the BD, among other things thereby contributed to the strengthening of his own authority. Thus, the the BD's parallel relationship to Jesus has as one result the fact that the higher the christology was pushed in the GJ the higher would be the 'rank' attached to the BD. And, of course, the greater the authority of the BD the more he is able to develop and establish his own tradition.

From this perspective it is easier to answer the question concerning the purpose of the parallel relation between the P and the BD. The BD not

[54] Brown, 1979, 83, is on the same line but does not speak of traditions but of "the Johannine community symbolically counterposing itself over against the kinds of churches that venerate Peter and the Twelwe". Cf Cullmann, 1976, 94, who speaks about two groups of disciples, one "more important by virtue of its number and the continuity of its common life, ... represented by Peter". The other, represented by the BD, would be "smaller and rest on a more inward relationship".

[55] Later traditions in the Early Church, e.g.Irenaeus, the muratorian fragment and Clement of Alexandria, give the GJ a special position in relation to the synoptic gospels. This might be an indication of an identification of Peter with the synoptic tradition. Cf Merkel, 1978, XIIIf, Cullmann, 1945, 34, and Cullmann, 1976, 72f. A good survey of the whole question about the relation between the GJ and the synoptics is found in Blinzler, 1965, 16-71.

[56] Dauer, 1968, 92f; Thyen, 1977, 292; Kragerud, 1959, 46ff, is of quite another opinion. As "Traditionsgewährsmann könnte er schlechterdings nicht ungeschickter dargestellt werden". His argument is not convincing. It reads as follows: If the BD were "Traditionsgewährsmann", why is he nonexistent in ch.1-12? Should he not have witnessed those words and deeds of Jesus as well? Why does he not receive secret revelations as is usual in apocryphal gospel traditions?

The first argument is a crude argumentum e silentio. If it were applicable one could maintain analogically that the P, who is also nonexistant in ch.1-12, had nothing to do with the origin of these chapters. More important, however: when Kragerud argues in favour of the unity of the GJ, including ch.21, (pp.15-199), he implies that the BD's witnessing according to 21:24 also embraces the events and traditions of which an account is given in ch.1-12. 21:25 indicates that the reference is to the whole GJ.

only receives his authority from Jesus but also is closely related to the P. Considering the role of the Spirit in connection with the formation of the OT tradition and the expectations regarding the Spirit at the arrival of the messianic time, it is logical to expect that the one who is able to demonstrate some contact with this Spirit will be taken seriously and believed. If so, one could ask why Jesus, in the the GJ, did not furnish the BD with the Spirit by an ordination through which the necessary functions as transmittor and interpretor of the Jesus tradition would be embodied. Such would no doubt have been easier, at least from a more recent point of view, than building on complex parallelisms. I shall intimate at least one important answer to this question: such a total identification presupposes a claim to exclusivity that the texts do not express. The legitimation of the BD did not mean the elimination of other traditions. The claim is that the BD and his tradition should be regarded equal to other traditions.[57] No claim is made that the activity of the P is restricted to the BD. When, however, the BD is described as the main authority behind the GJ, the BD illustrates the P in an ideal way.[58] One can also say that the BD represents the P and embodies him.[59] Thus the BD becomes the first fulfillment of Jesus promise of the P.[60] Both figures thus shed light upon each other in a fruitful way: The P renders the BD *legitimation;* the BD renders the P *concretion.*

[57] Cf Cullmann, 1945, 27ff. The GJ, just as any of the synoptics, does not intend to "verdrängen", "ersetzen" or "ergänzen" the other gospels but to "...ein sich selbst genügendes, das Christusgeschehen nach seinem wesentlichen Offenbarungsgehalt erschöpfend darstellendes Evangelium bieten". The GJ has no "polemische Absicht" against the other gospels.

[58] Brown, 1967, 130. It is unsatisfactory to disregard the direct relation between the BD and the P because of literary critical considerations. So Becker, 1981, 439: "Doch nirgends wird L mit dem P ausdrücklich in Beziehung gebracht, noch eine Ausgleich zwischen beiden Gestalten versucht. Dies hängt sicherlich auch mit der Mehrschichtigkeit des Joh zusammen".

[59] Kragerud, 1959, 82. Hill, 1979, 151, does not share this view: "It is far too sweeping to suggest that the author of John - the Beloved Disciple - is in some way an 'incarnation' of the Paraclete". Hill's hesitation depends on the fact that he does not see in the BD the prophetic features which he finds basic to Jesus and the P. I have tried to show that the case is the opposite. The BD has prophetic features and appears in prophetic contexts. The prophetic features are, however, not such that they alone constitute the basis for a parallel relationship. There are, as I have shown, other important features which support the parallelism, so that one is indeed justified in speaking of an incarnation or embodiment.

[60] Roloff, 1968-69, 149. Culpepper, 1975, 268: "the BD fulfilled for the Johannine community the role of the Paraclete".

4.5. Concluding summary

The preceding exposition has shown that there exist parallelisms between Jesus, the P, and the BD. Jesus, in his unique task, is sent by the Father to represent and present him. When this mission has come to an end Jesus appoints the P and the BD to replace and represent him. Jesus thus makes himself dependent upon both of them. Without them the mission of Jesus would be ineffective. The P and the BD, on the other hand, are also dependent on Jesus. All they say and do emanates from him. This is the condition under which they act as mediators. The P and the BD are also mutually dependent on one another. Through the BD the P will communicate with the disciples. Through the P the BD receives the power and authority which is required to make the disciples listen and obey. Further, one should inquire into the historical development within the johannine community concerning the relation between the P and the BD.[61] If (and there is much in favour of such an interpretation) ch.21, especially vv.20-24, indicates that the death of the BD caused problems in the johannine community (bearing in mind the expectation of the parousia and the function of the eyewitnesses), and if the final fixation of the GJ consequently was entrusted to the community, the role of the P will point beyond the BD himself to his 'successor' or fulfiller. The P will, then, serve to guarantee that as the BD had been an inspired transmitor and teacher but so also will those who complete his work with the same authority and power.[62]

The P is thus intimately connected to a context dealing with revelation, teaching, and the transmission of tradition. If one accepts the relations within the didactic triad as I have described them, it will be seen that, in the case of the P, the stress, from a functional point of view, is laid on the didactic dimension. It becomes difficult to emphasize other dimensions, e.g., the forensic one. Those dimensions are, of course, (as I have shown in ch.2) parts of the literary exposition of the GJ, but are not as

---

[61] Cf concerning the following Thyen, 1977, 293.

[62] A similar argument is found in Culpepper, 1975, 269. Further developed in Culpepper, 1983, 43ff, where he mentions the narrator, the P, and the BD as "the three figures which have interpretative roles in the gospel". The narrator, it seems, is the 'successor' of the BD. See also Brown, 1979, 101. The P was "the moving Spirit behind the interpretation of the tradition as passed on by the Beloved Disciple. After the death of the Beloved Disciple, the community understood that the work of the Paraclete continued in the disciples of the Beloved Disciple."

central as is the didactic dimension. The P's primary task (just as are Jesus' and the BD's) is to mediate the revelation, especially the revelation in Christ with its consequences for the disciples and the world. Thus the P, as the teaching authority in the community takes, for the first time, concrete form in the BD. The question is now whether one can say anything more about the traditions of this teaching and the context in which such traditions evolved. That is the task of the next chapter to investigate.

5. The type of didactics

5.1. Introductory

So far in my investigation I have tried to show that a) the dominant activity of the P (in the literary redaction of the GJ) lies within the didactic field (ch 2.), b) this didactic activity is variously realized in actual functions ascribed to the P (ch 3.), and c) what was subsequently termed the 'didactic' function belongs to the three authorities of the post-Easter situation: Jesus, the BD, and the P (ch 4.). The actual teaching activities of the P have been described in previous chapters. The next step is to ask, against what kind of background was such a description of the P's activity possible? If one can answer this question by describing the manner in which similar kinds of teaching occurred in other historical contexts, one should be able to arrive at a better understanding of the didactic function of the P in the GJ.

5.2. The connection to the service

The central areas of the P's activity, as the previous material has indicated, are teaching, preaching, and mediation of tradition within the community. The locus for such activities in the Early Church was, no doubt, the liturgy.[1] In the service the Scriptures were read and interpreted. In the service the risen and living Lord came to his people. In the service the Spirit and its gifts were made living in a special way. Traditions in the NT other than those represented in the GJ show clearly that this was the case. It has also been pointed out by several scholars[2] that the GJ in many respects reflects the influence of liturgical conventions. Impor-

---

[1] Wilckens, 1980, 199.
[2] For example Corell, 1950, 52-62; Barrett, 1950, 5f; Cullmann, 1962, 38-112; Aune, 1972, 72f.

tant here is the 'liturgical' patterning of parts of or the entire GJ.[3] The prologue's hymnic character (ch.1), the johannine exposition of the 'sacraments' (3:3-8. 6:5-58. 21:4-13), Jesus' intercession (ch.17), reveal a connection to a service characterized by vivacious activity. The GJ resembles a play, a liturgical drama[4] which gives life to what has happened and continues to happen in the revelation of Jesus. It is precisely in this dramatized service that the tension of the johannine eschatology is released: what has happened and and will happen happens now.[5] In the middle of that tension the P is acting.

Neither, however, for the early christian service in general[6] nor, more specifically, for the community of the GJ was the liturgy creationed out of a vacuum. It is reasonable to assume that the synagogue was the initial locus of the johannine community.[7] In that after the separation from the synagogue this service remained the model for the christian service,[8] there is no reason to doubt that the early christian service was established

[3] Le Déaut, 1971b, 522. A more intricate hypothesis is found in Raney, 1933, e.g., p.12. He proposes that the prologue, the discourses, and the High Priestly Prayer (ch.17) are written as prose hymns to be sung by chorus-singers either as a prelude or as a postlude to the readings in the common service. The most specialized investigation in this regard, however, is the one by Guilding, 1960. She thinks the whole GJ to be built around a three year cycle of Old Testament lectionary readings. She also attempts to prove the existence of such a lectionary at this time. See Miller, 1971, 34, and the reviews mentioned there; Morris, 1964, 41-52; McNamara, 1972, 46f; Morris, 1983, 130f. Cf also the statement in Blinzler, 1965, 76: "Es ist bisher noch niemandem gelungen, eine konsequente Logik in die liturgischen Rahmenwerk des Joh nachzuweisen". Nevertheless, it seems evident that Guilding has emphasized an important aspect of the background of the GJ. That her conclusions are sometimes doubtful does not remove this fact. One such unfortunate conclusion concerns the P. She interprets the P against the background of the new year feast and sees him primarily as an advocate or intercessor and, secondarily, as a comforter. Her argumentation is not convincing. A 'case study' similar to Guilding's can also be found in Reim, 1983(a), 101.For a fuller treatment of the difficulties concerning the lectionary hypothesis, including the one presented by Goulder, 1974, see Morris, 1983, 134-149.
[4] The dramatical character of the GJ is described by Martyn, 1979, not, however, in the context of the service.
[5] See Bühner, 1982. He explains "die Verschränkung der Zeitebenen" (p.224) as a result of "die kultische Denkstruktur" (p.226) basic to the GJ. There is "eine Grundschicht kultischen Denkens" in the GJ which is "christologisch getragen und pneumatisch zugespitzt" (p.227).
[6] The expression 'the early Christian service in general' does not imply that I regard this service uniform in all respects and in all places.
[7] ἀποσυναγώγους in 16:2 is an indication of that.
[8] Rowley, 1967, 242; Dugmore, 1964, 1-8.

upon elements of the synagogue's service as is existed in Jesus' time.[9] Indeed, the prototype of the 'liturgical drama' can be found in the service of the synagogue.[10]

Thus, in establishing the background of the P one must start from the hypothesis that the teaching which occurred in the synagogue's service is of special importance. With regard to Jesus' activity in this respect, one should remember that the syngogue in the GJ is often described as being the stage of Jesus' teaching and preaching activity. As the synagogue provides the frame within which this activity naturally took place,[11] it therefore becomes necessary to describe the character of the teaching tradition of the synagogue in order to understand the didactic function of the P in the GJ.

Before beginning this description one remark should be made. Judaism at Jesus' time had two didactic fora: the synagogue with its service, and the school with its teaching discourses. It is, thus, appropriate to differentiate between the functions and character of the synagogue and that of the school, a differentiation which seems, at least partly, to coincide with the distinction between halakah and haggadah, where the haggadah is the result of the activity of the synagogue and the halakah is the result of the school activity. It is, however, impossible to draw a sharp dividing line between these two fora due to the simple fact that they were situated under the same roof.[12] Sometimes the teachers were invited to preach and often the expositions of the synagogue were followed by school discourses. The crossover went in the other direction also. There were people from the synagogue, e.g. the hazzan, among the school staff. Nevertheless the two fora should be treated separately in order to emphasize the individuality of their characters.[13] Their relationship has been characterized by

---

[9] One should be cautious to attempt to determine the various components of the synagogue service in NT times. The generalization of McNamara, 1972, 37, seems, however, balanced: "The constant parts of the synagogue service were prayer, the reading of lessons from Scripture, followed where possible by a homily". Cf Dugmore, 1964, 11: "...instruction and prayer. This division of the service has existed from the earliest times".
[10] Georgi, 1964, 131ff and his references to Krauss, 1922, 135 and 170f.
[11] Hruby, 1971, 59.
[12] Zunz, 1892, 352. Cf Bloch, 1957, 1267; Rowley, 1967, 228ff; Patte, 1975, 31 and 55; York, 1979, 83-86.
[13] One could ask if it is not possible to explain, at least partly, the difference between the synoptics and the GJ on the basis of the different characters of these fora. One could, concerning Gerhardsson, 1961, ask if his difficulty to include the GJ in his thesis is not due to the relation between the two fora: the synagoue and the school. In this context I just wish to note that Borgen, 1965, 3, says that "John's environment seems to have

A.T.Hanson as: "...a different atmosphere but the same tradition".[14] In my investigation I shall concentrate on the synagogue and its didactics.

5.3. Teaching in the synagogue

Teaching in the service consisted of three parts: reading from the Scriptures, a translation to the vernacular language (the Targum), and, in some cases, exposition-preaching. It is impossible to prove that the scriptural readings followed set lectionary cycles.[15] It is, however, probable that the Scriptures were read according to the lectio continua order.[16] The reading was divided into two parts: the seder-reading from the Torah and the haftarah-reading from the prophets. The latter was related to the former on the basis of similaries in content or certain words.[17] As the Torah enjoyed an absolute position in relation to the rest of the OT (including the prophets), the seder-reading was construed to be of more importance than the haftarah-reading in the synagogue service. This fact is reflected in the targum translation. The reader was allowed to read only one verse of the seder passage before the translator, the methurgeman, translated. In the case of the haftarah-passages, however, one was allowed to read three verses before the translation occurred. Since the translator was not allowed to use any written text, the Torah passages were translated verse by verse in order to insure that the ground text was adhered to closely. Even though the translator often mediated a traditional translation, the practice itself reflected the absolute position of seder-passages, as mentioned above.[18]

The targum translation provided the intermediate step between the reading from the Scriptures and its exposition. In that the reading was not an end in itself but was aimed at making the Scriptures understood while actualizing them,[19] a translation had long been necessary. It is not

been a 'school' of a church after the break with the synagoue" as distinguished from Philo's which is said to have been the synagoue. I have difficulties in seeing the justification for making such a distinction, especially concerning "John's environment".

[14] Hanson, 1983, 22.

[15] A short survey of the research in this matter is found in Perrot, 1973, 24-36.

[16] 'Lectio continua' would indicate a certain order but not in a technical sense, i.e., as in a set cycle. However, cf the argument regarding the lectio continua used in such a technical sense during NT times in Perrot, 1973, 141-152.

[17] Bowker, 1969, 72.

[18] McNamara, 1966, 65.

[19] Le Déaut, 1971(b), 510: "...de *faire comprendre* le texte à un auditoire concret".

possible to determine exactly how long the practice had been in use, but according to jewish tradition it had been a custom since Ezra's time.[20] They were, as I said above, oral translations which did not arise *ad hoc* but were the result of a tradition of translation. This tradition was later codified in the different written Targums. The dating of the written Targums is an old matter of dispute, which I need not here review.[21] Although one should be weary of assigning the written Targums too early a date, it is evident that they contain traditions which are much older than the documents themselves. It is reasonable to assume, following Le Déaut, that many of the traditions in the written Targums go back to and are representative of the Judaism of the first century C.E. and, consequently, that they are contemporeous with NT Christianity.[22] And more importantly: the hermeneutical principles reflected in the Targums are much older than the written Targums themselves as can be seen from the LXX,[23] especially in the book of Jubilees, and from Ps.Philo. One can, therefore, compare these principles (as far as they are possible to systematize)[24] with those found in the NT. It is my belief that the interpretation of the NT and especially the GJ gain much from such a comparison.[25]

The transition from the translation to the exposition, the homily, was not a difficult one in that the Targums themselves displayed a paraphrasing and interpreting tendency and, also, because both the translation and

---

[20] Le Déaut, 1965, 37f.

[21] For a further discussion see Zunz, 1892, 65f; Le Déaut, 1965, 37f; Bowker, 1969, 14; York, 1974. A short and instructive survey of the whole targum issue is found in Lentzen-Deis, 1970, 195-200.

[22] See also Schäfer, 1970, 305 note 5; Miller, 1971, 34; Reim, 1983 (b), 13.

[23] Concerning the LXX as an interpretative translation see Hanson, 1983, 10-14.

[24] Their "popular" (Le Déaut, 1963, 59; Hanson, 1983, 23.) and "atomistic" (Patte, 1975, 75) character makes it difficult to systematize them.

[25] The basic importance of the Targums for the interpretation of the NT is pointed out by, among others, McNamara, 1966, 260, and Le Déaut, 1974, 244. McNamara gives, in this respect, the Targums preference over the rabbinic, apocalyptic, and Qumran writings, because the Targums were the best known by the most jews. The importance of the Targums for the johannine literature has long been observed in handbooks (McNamara, 1972, 142-159), monographs (e.g. Borgen, 1965), and articles (recently Reim, 1983(b). Concerning the trend of the research see Miller, 1971, 30f. There is reason, however, to take the warning of Chilton, 1980, 177, seriously: "The probability that elements in the Targums are early is no reason to assume that the Targums in their present form underlie the New Testament". Also p.178: "...Targums should be combed for early material (even if expressed in the language of a later age) which might illuminate the N.T., but I fear the optimistic assumption that the Targums predate the N.T. may lead us seriously astray".

104

homily, from the beginning, were often performed by the same person.[26] Not until later, demonstrably in the first century C.E.,[27] was the exposition differentiated from the reading and translation, the homily thus becoming a teaching task entrusted to the scribes. Consequently, in NT times it must have been difficult to draw sharp borderlines between reading and translation on the one hand and exposition on the other. The scene from the synagogue in Lk.4 indicates that such a blurring of borders occurred.[28] Jesus acts both as the reader ($\dot{\alpha}\nu\acute{\epsilon}\sigma\tau\eta$ $\dot{\alpha}\nu\alpha\gamma\nu\tilde{\omega}\nu\alpha\iota$ v.16) and as an interpreter of the particular scriptural passage ($\dot{\epsilon}\varkappa\acute{\alpha}\vartheta\iota\sigma\epsilon\nu$... $\mathring{\eta}\varrho\xi\alpha\tauο$ $\lambda\acute{\epsilon}\gamma\epsilon\iota\nu$ v.20f). The relationship which existed between the Targum and the homily has been examined by R. Bloch,[29] who concluded that because they reflect similar hermeneutical attitudes and are so closely interwoven, the Palestinian Targum (PT), in particular, should be considered as exposition, midrash. No matter how one evaluates the details of Bloch's conclusion, one is convinced by her argument that the essential features of the translation and exposition should be approached in terms of the hermeneutical attitude which is reflected in them, an attitude which should not be restricted to a certain literary genre, midrash.[30] Midrash is something more than the writings called Midrash. One should rather speak in terms of a midrashic attitude which is comparable to the

---

[26] Moore, 1927ff., I, 304. Cf McNamara, 1972, 70f.

[27] Moore, 1927ff., .I, 305.

[28] Here the translation is missing. The most probable reason for its absence can be attributed to the process of redaction. As Luke lets Jesus read from the LXX there is no need for a translation. The historical background has not been of importance to Luke in this case.

[29] Bloch, 1957, 1263-1280. Bloch's research is summarized in Vermes, 1961, 7 note 2.

[30] The thesis which considers midrash to be a literary genre has lately been maintained by Wright, 1967. He has not, however, been well received. See among others Le Déaut, 1971(a); Miller, 1971, 43f; Patte, 1975, 117. Patte also tries, pp.315-324, to establish a "normalization" of the terminology concerning midrash. He distinguishes between a "convictional level" and a "symbolic level". To the former belong "hermeneutical axioms", to the latter "literary genres". Patte's argumentation is clear and provides a certain structure. The danger of drawing too tightly the border lines concerning the terminology becomes evident in Hruby, 1971, 90: "In rein literarischer Hinsicht steht Midrash im Gegensatz zur Halacha, zur normativen Gesetzesdeduktion...". Patte's disposition may provide some elucidation here.

NT hermeneutical attitude in general and, in my case, to that of the GJ.[31] It is necessary, therefore, to determine the characteristics of this hermeneutical attitude.

5.4. The character of the synagogue teaching

An important feature common to all teaching in the synagogue is that it is exposition of the Scriptures, exegesis. Its main purpose is to make the text intelligible to the audience which is present. The first stage in this process is the targum translation. This translation may be more interesting from the hermeneutical point of view than the actual expositions, the homilies, since one does not expect to find as explicit a hermeneutical attitude in the targum as one has reason to do in homilies themselves. All translations are, indeed, interpretations, but the intentions and consequences of most translations are not always as conscious as are those found in the targums.

The hermeneutical attitude of the targum can be defined in the words of Le Déaut:[32] "Traduire, c'est bien comprendre et transposer". In the targum translation, passages from Scripture are explained and adapted at the same time. Such translations do not only transpose from one language to another but also adapt the text to the situation of the audience. Consequently there is a tension between loyalty to the passage being translated and respect to the community and situation in which the translation is made. This tension can also be seen as a paradox.[33] That is, the intention of the midrash exegesis is on the one hand to explain a text which, as a completed text, posseses supreme authority. Yet, on the other hand this exegesis functions to keep the same text open, protecting it from

---

[31] See Le Déaut, 1971(a), 278: "What is profitable for the exegete is not to relate the text (of Paul) to a midrash which is analogous in the strict sense, but to recognize in the two the same hermeneutical methods". Cf also Le Déaut, 1974, 289: "The Targum appears especially useful by reason of the exegetical methods it employs in its approach to Scripture. The phenomenon of 'targumism' can illustrate similar cases in the NT, on the level of oral tradition as well as of the redaction and subsequent transmission of the texts". Targumism shall, according to Le Déaut, 1971(b), 508, be seen "comme attitude des Anciens face au texte sacré".
[32] Le Déaut, 1971(b), 522.
[33] Seeligmann, 1953, 181.

petrification in order to allow it to speak to every new situation.[34] A similar tension exists between the two 'loci' of the revelation, i.e., the Scriptures and the worshipping community.[35] These two loci give rise to a hermeneutical circle. The targumic translation of the Scriptures is made for a worshipping community whose life is structured by the Scriptures as understood by its interpretative tradition. The worshipping community could thus regard itself as the 'embodiment' of the Scriptures, the Scriptures 'incarnated'. The Scriptures gave the community its identity. Consequently, the tension between the Scriptures and the community was a fruitful one in which no hermeneutical 'gap' developed.

Another factor which contributed to the shape of the relationship between the community and the Scriptures had to do with the nature of the biblical writings themselves.[36] One can maintain, like Bloch, the view that the later literature in the OT canon actualizes the contents of older books.[37] It is also possible, going one step further as Seeligmann does, to regard the midrashic attitude as characteristic of biblical writings and to speak about "die weitgehende Beweglichkeit von Erzählungen und literarischen Motiven in der Bibel". The biblical stories become more or less occasional stages in a predominately oral development of tradition. Thus, the formation of the canon does not entail the drawing of sharp borderlines. This is relevant concerning the midrashic attitude and its method of interpretation. If it is relevant concerning midrash as a literary genre is a question of greater dispute. Wright[38] is of the opinion that after the canon was closed there was still present the need to actualize, adapt, and interpret both the writings themselves and other early traditions. He finds it impossible, however, to agree with Bloch, Vermes, and others that ear-

[34] It is interesting here to point to certain similarities with the apocalyptic literature. Both actualize God's old promises and show that they are fulfilled. There is a common openness in the interpretation of the Scriptures. The difference between a midrashic and the apocalyptic interpretation is in the temporal mode employed. The Midrash is interested in the Scriptures' meaning for today, the apocalyptic in its meaning for the future. Cf Bloch, 1957, 1276. This is, however, partly a chimera. Apocalyptic exposition often lets the ancients (e.g.Enoch) speak about and to the future which, however, is the same as the reader's present.

[35] For the following see Patte, 1975, 80f.

[36] Stressed especially in Seeligmann, 1953, 151ff; Bloch, 1957, 1271ff; Aune, 1972, 71f; Weingreen, 1976, IX; Hanson, 1983, 7-10, with several good examples. Cf already Zunz, 1892, 38 and 180.

[37] Cf Patte, 1975, 119.

[38] Wright, 1967, 132-135.

lier revised versions and redactions of the OT be parts of this genre. The question is, however, if Wright is not attempting to define a literary genre without taking seriously enough into consideration the vagueness of the borderlines among literary genres in Judaism. The authors were perhaps more conscious that they were writing within a certain tradition than in a particular literary genre. Many authors 'performed midrash' without intending to 'write a midrash'. Le Déaut, says of Wright's method that it cuts down a wood in order to make a box of matches.[39]

The midrashic hermeneutical attitude can also be approached through the notions 'confinement' and 'freedom'. An explicit teaching about the Scriptures would asume that one was strictly confined to them, whereas an implicit teaching (expressed in the Targums and Midrashes) could involve a dynamic creativity quite different from the static quality of explicit teaching.[40] Whether or not it was possible to maintain the harmony between the two types of teaching is difficult to say. Such seems doubtful, however, if the words of Juda ben Ilai[41] are representative: "He who translates a verse with strict literalness is a falsifier, and he who makes additions to it is a blasphemer". In many cases blasphemy seems to have dominated over falsification. The 'motive of adaptation'[42] (to change the meaning of the word of Scripture to suit the thought and behaviour of later times) has been strongly stressed. That it has been possible is due, in part, to what Neusner calls "creative philology" and "creative historiography".[43] Creative philology discerned a meaning in every apparently meaningless detail. Alternative vocalizations offered further possibilities for such treatment.[44] 'Context' was also approached differently than in modern exegesis. One could make use of the immediate context if one wished, or simply leave it aside if such better suited ones purposes. The basic rule was that the entire scriptural corpus could provide the proper context. Within this context one could operate quite freely,[45] using such

---

[39] Le Déaut, 1971(a), 269f and 273.

[40] Concerning the words "explicit" and "implicit" see Patte, 1975, 23-27.

[41] Tos.Meg.4:41. Kidd.49a. The translation is taken from Moore, 1927ff., I, 304. See also Bacher, 1906, 57.

[42] Seeligmann, 1953, 172.

[43] Neusner, 1960, 50.

[44] Patte, 1975, 56. Concerning the concentration on the actual word of Scripture cf Miller, 1971, 38.

[45] Miller, 1971, 66. See also Hanson, 1983, 25, who emphazises more the importance of the immediate context.

'categories of interpretation' as play upon words, associative meanings, double meanings, and similarity in sound.[46]

This manipulation of context functioned somewhat similarly in creative historiography. The rabbinic principle, "There is no before or after in the Scriptures",[47] resulted in a 'telescopic attitude' regarding the relationship between the Scriptures and history.[48] Any special information in a text (time, place, persons) could be seen to represent the whole of Scripture and could, therefore, be related to or compared with quite different contexts in the Scriptures.[49] Here, it seems, the seed of an 'ahistorical view of history' is to be found. That is, in spite of the OT's emphasis on historical events, God's mighty deeds, it is not the historical events in themselves that are decisive but the truths and values which can be read out from them and actualized in different times and situations. As Neusner[50] puts it: "Midrash thus exchanges the stability of language and the continuity of history for stability of values and the eternity of truth". From one point of view this can be seen to be a kind of typological interpretation[51] or, from another point of view, one can discern here the beginnings of allegorical interpretation.[52] Both cases reflect a common conviction: the Scriptures say more than they seem to say at first glance and it is, therefore, the task of and the gift to the community, in times of need, to discern the hidden meanings.[53] Consequently, the evolution

[46] Seeligmann, 1953, 157ff. See also Klein, 1982, who through many examples shows two aspects of targumic interpretation which borrow from other contexts in order to arrange and make the translation instructive. He names these features associative and complementary translation.

[47] Sifre to Num.9:1. See also Daube, 1953, 32.

[48] Patte, 1975, 67. On p.70f he illustrates with a good example, observed by Le Déaut, from Neofiti I concerning Ex.12:42, which describes the four nights of world history. They are identified with each other by being related to the same day, the 15th of Nisan. The identification ends up in interaction, so that one night can be understood in terms of another, etc.

[49] When France, 1983, 102f, speaks about the actualization of the biblical story in the Targums he draws quite another conclusion: "...the motive for this expansion is not some other biblical text which produces a 'midrashic' combination of biblical themes, but rather the desire to interpret the biblical story in the light of the contemporary theological climate". I doubt that this conclusion is correct.

[50] Neusner,1960, 50.

[51] Le Déaut, 1965, 25.

[52] Philo's hermeneutical work with the OT-texts moves in this direction. See Hanson, 1983, 18ff.

[53] Cf Le Déaut, 1971(b), 519. The Scriptures have never been seen as a 'mummy' but as the living word of God, directed to today with a permanent meaning to "la communauté liturgique".

of tradition in the synagogue was not systematic. It does not strive after the formulation of correct teaching but rather intends to maintain an open attitude to the Scriptures. This attitude results in a multiplicity of theological conceptions which do not necessarily fit well together.[54] This indicates a certain interpretative flexibility which is possible in that, not wishing to to exempt oneself from the Scriptures and God's will in them, one reaches deeper into the Scriptures in order to be able to perform God's will in every time.[55] From this comes the name Midrash,[56] and the term midrashic hermeneutics.[57]

5.5. Midrashic hermeneutics and the GJ

The most obvious connection between midrashic hermeneutics and the GJ is found in John 5:39: $\grave{\varepsilon}\varrho\alpha\upsilon\nu\tilde{\alpha}\tau\varepsilon$ $\tau\grave{\alpha}\varsigma$ $\gamma\varrho\alpha\varphi\acute{\alpha}\varsigma$. It is likely that $\grave{\varepsilon}\varrho\alpha\upsilon\nu\tilde{\alpha}\nu$ in this passage serves as the equivalent of *dārash* even if, in the LXX, $\zeta\eta\tau\varepsilon\tilde{\iota}\nu$ usually stands for *dārash*, while $\grave{\varepsilon}\varrho\alpha\upsilon\nu\tilde{\alpha}\nu$ never does.[58] If one allows that John 5:39 refers to a midrashic use of the Scriptures, two important observations follow: a) There is no polemic against such a use of the Scriptures in the GJ's exposition, rather, Jesus accepts the practice since its purpose is to win eternal life. The inclusion of Jesus in the text is not performed by an adversative connection of the clauses but through $\varkappa\alpha\acute{\iota}$. The midrashic attitude to the Scriptures is, thus, a precondition for making the adjustment to Jesus which the text has in view. b) The Scriptures' witness about Jesus is stressed in such a way that Jesus is assigned the same dignity as the Scriptures. The Scriptures give eternal life (v.39). So does Jesus (v.40). The words of Moses are authoritative but actually speak about Jesus (v.46). Interpreting the Scriptures (the words of Moses) using the wrong key gives neither eternal life nor belief in Jesus (v.47). As Jesus is the real content of the Scriptures, the object of search should be Jesus

---

[54] Patte, 1975, 75; Le Déaut, 1971(a), 270.

[55] The effect is that the step from explanation to exhortation, parenesis, is not a large one. They are two necessary sides of the same thing. Cf Le Déaut, 1971(b), 520.

[56] The word itself, Midrash, occurrs only in two passages in the OT: 2 Chr.13:22 and 24:27. The verb *dārash,* however, occurs often and means 'search' in a religious sense. See Bloch, 1957, 1263. Cf also Zeitlin, 1953, 21ff.

[57] A practical and instructive example of how a saying from the OT can be interpreted in different 'midrashic contexts' is to be found in Chilton, 1983. The range and the multiplicity of the different interpretations are striking.

[58] See among others Bultmann, 1950, 201 note 4; Brown, 1966-70, I, 225; Cothenet, 1977, 94f.

himself.[59] Thus a proper Midrash should have the Word, manifested in the historical Jesus, as its object. The hermeneutical work now concerns the words and deeds of Jesus. The resurrection and ascension (in the johannine sense) of Jesus can be said to give dignity to these words and deeds in a way that corresponds to the canonization of the OT. The Jesus tradition was understood by the johannine community as analogous to the Scriptures and was, therefore, subjected to the same midrashic activity.[60] Thus, this Jesus tradition could be approached as creatively as were the Scriptures, both in the synagogal tradition of interpretation and, de facto, in the GJ.[61] Elsewhere (3.3.4.2.) I have pointed to the saying in 2:22 as evidence of the johannine community's shaping of tradition from the point of view of the resurrection. It can also be noted here that the Scriptures and the words of Jesus were seen to be of equal authority. This equality results also in a 'reciproque process'.[62] The Scriptures witness about Jesus, while Jesus reveals the secrets of the Scriptures.

[59] Le Déaut, 1971(a), 275f; Porsch, 1974, 224: "Jesus tritt damit an die Stelle des Bundes-gesetzes". In the process of canonization the NT collection of writings becomes this object. The gospels correspond to the five books of Moses in the OT. Both groups of scriptures, the Pentateuch and the Gospels, at the same time derive from and describe their media-tors of revelation. The latter is, however, superior. See Cullmann, 1945, 26.

[60] Miller, 1971, 63f. That such a way of acting found concrete manifestation in the service of the Early Church is seen from Acts 17:2f. Cf Hruby, 1971, 64. Quite another conclusion seems to be drawn by France, 1983, 121, although his argument is rather unclear. It is worth noting that when France speaks about the christian gospels he refers only to the synoptics. He has nothing to say about the GJ in general and its relation to jewish histo-riography in particular. Therefore his study, which deals with the "historical character of the gospels" and their relation to "various documents or literary tendencies in the je-wish world of the first Christian centuries"(p.99), is of little value to me.

[61] Aune, 1972, 69. See also note 3, where Aune refers to Freed, 1965, 129. Freed shows that the GJ, in its technique of citation, is not primarily interested in the quotation itself. The quotation rather serves and is adapted to the contextual, compositional, literary, and theological purposes of the author. See also the sayings by Freed, p.129f: "His methods presuppose and reveal a thorough training in the Jewish scriptures and tradition and a thorough knowledge of their content. ...the evidence...is strong...in several cases for the use of the traditions of the Targums". I do not, however, find his conclusion convincing that the GJ derives from a christian school which felt obliged to defend and strengthen the synoptic tradition by adducing OT texts. The relationship between the GJ and the synoptic tradition is not so harmonious, as I showed in my investigation of the relation between the BD and Peter (4.4.3.). For a survey concerning the GJ's use of the OT see also Hanson, 1980, 157-176, and 1983, 113-132.

[62] Miller, 1971, 44.

I pointed out in 5.3. that midrashic hermeneutical principles are found in books and traditions which are older than those reflected in written Targums and Midrashes. The wisdom literature in particular provides some of the best examples of midrashic interpretation in the Scriptures.[63] It has been pointed out that the wisdom tradition played an important role in the theological thinking behind the GJ, most obviously that of the prologue.[64] These two facts strengthen the validity of comparing the GJ with midrashic hermeneutics.

The basic similarity between Midrash and the GJ is that both types of interpretation are *homiletical* rather than *historical*.[65] In both cases interest is directed towards actualizing what was said, written, or happened at some earlier point in the present with its particular possibilities and needs.[66] This kind of interpretation approaches what I earlier (5.4.) called an ahistorical view of history.

5.6. Concrete similarities

The realization that an ahistorical view of history or 'telescopic attitude' is reflected in the GJ can shed light upon its eschatology. The 'realized eschatology' found in the GJ can in many respects be explained by the fact that the GJ was given final shape after the expectations of the parousia had cooled and its delay had become a problem in the johannine community.[67] If one approaches the realized eschatology of the GJ from the perspective of the midrashic exposition of the Scriptures, it becomes clear that it represents more than a solution arising out of severe embarrasment. The timeless quality of realized eschatology which, from the point of view of history is troublesome, serves the purpose of illuminating cons-

[63] Bloch,1957, 1273f; Vermes, 1961, 8. Wisd.9-11 is a useful example of such a Midrash. Cf Wright, 1967, 109.

[64] So, e.g., Brown, 1966-70, I, CXXII: "...the fourth evangelist saw in Jesus the culmination of a tradition that runs through the Wisdom Literaure in the OT". Concerning the prologue's relation to wisdom literature see p.523: "Thus, in the OT presentation of Wisdom, there are good parallels for almost every detail of the Prologue's description of the Word".

[65] Bacon, 1933, 156f. Cf Johnston, 1970, 152: "The Fourth Gospel is a dramatical evangelical and pastoral treatise rather than a history". A case study of the discourse in John 6 as a homily has been presented by Borgen, 1965.

[66] Bloch, 1954, 33. Cf Bonnard, 1980, 10f: "Ainsi, le quartième évangile serait au service d'une anamnèse de type actualiste: Jesu raconterait dans l'Histoire ce qui se passe aujourd'hui dans l'Eglise".

[67] Brown, 1967, 128f.

112

tantly valid truths and values which can be read out from individual persons and events. It is therefore justified to speak about a "two-level drama" in the GJ[68] in which past and present are constantly being interwoven. A constant actualization and adaptation is thus made possible. This telescopic attitude could also explain the sometimes troublesome fact that the GJ (in spite of its realized eschatology) presupposes the parousia, resurrection, and judgement. The way in which esachatology is presented in the GJ does not remove the parousia but rather serves to actualize and adapt the revelation.in Christ to the present. I therefore prefer the notion of an *actualizing* rather than a *realized* eschatology.

This timeles quality must be, of course, effected through the composition of the GJ. The above mentioned freedom in handling contexts, as found in the midrashic exposition of the Scriptures, is one such compositional techique appropriated for this purpose in the GJ. Much of the textual material occurs in different contexts in the GJ than in the other gospels, and the order of pericopes is, as well, often other than that found in the synoptics. It is not necessary to establish the literary priorities for these observations to have validity. The clearing of the temple in ch.2 is usually mentioned as one of the best examples of a pericope which enjoys another context in the GJ than in the synoptics. For my study the P-saying in 15:26 is another example.[69] Contexts could also be arranged in order to make the reader see a traditional bit from another angle and thus give it another meaning, or at least make the message more explicit. The feeding miracle and its interpretations in ch.6 offer an example of such recontextualization.

In the same way as there is no before or after in the Scriptures, there is, in the revelation in Christ, no before or after in the light of the resurrection in the GJ. As the goal of the presentation is to achieve an actualization of this revelation, one is free to arrange the textual material accordingly. The many literary critical attempts to reconstruct the material in order to make a better fit would thus seem to be of no avail.[70] Unnatural joints and breaks did not actually matter to anyone used to the synagogal

[68] Concerning the possibility of adapting this expression to time see Martyn, 1979, 136f. Cf also Martyn's statement on p.148: "It is precisely the Paraclete who creates the two-level drama".
[69] Concerning a tradition historical treatment of this saying see Excursus 3.8.
[70] Cf Cullmann, 1976, 4: "Instead of building one idea upon another, the early Christian would rather consider the same truth from different perspectives, with the result that some sections appear to be either intolerable repetitions or irreconcilable contradictions which would not give this impression to a redactor or even to an original author".

tradition of scriptural exposition.[71] These viewpoints do not exclude the possibility of practising literary criticism on the GJ. They support, however, the thesis advanced in the introductory chapter, that the GJ in its present shape constituted a meaningful entity both to the final redactor and to the readers/listeners of the GJ. Even the problematic ch.21 may have been seen as a natural addition to the entire gospel, even if it was not a part of the johannine tradition from the beginning. The existence here of the BD indicates an attempt to graft this chapter organically on to the previous material.[72]

The multidimensional model I developed in ch.2 regarding the GJ's composition also becomes more understandable against the background of the synagogal interpretation of the Scriptures. A free and lively association was a part of this tradition of interpretation. If one could give an interpretation which clarified different aspects of the material and, in addition, was able to present the material in a way which exploited its associative range, much was gained in the actualization of the interpretation. This seems to hold true for general questions of composition, the more immediate contexts, and even individual words.[73]

[71] A concrete example on how the Targum tradition can shed light upon a problematic passage in the GJ is found in Schwarz, 1982.

[72] The whole question whether ch.21 was originally an integral part of the GJ or is a later additon has recently been critically reviewed by Minear, 1983. He questions strongly the common opinion that ch.21 is an appendix and maintains instead that there are factors which speak strongly in favour of its original integrity. Minear's argument is in many respects convincing, especially his starting point in the communication situation, p.98: "As exegets we are under obligation to recover as fully as possible that original line of communication between the narrator and those first readers". To me it seems especially important here to bring forward the service background. The following statement of Minear, p.97, illustrates the problem in a nutshell and sheds light, with regard to the GJ, upon the distinction made earlier between Midrash as a literary genre and the midrashic attitude: "Our reaction will depend to some degree upon our image of the Evangelist. If we view him primarily as a literary figure, obliged as an author to meet certain literary standards of a consistent continous style, then we will take the apparent aporias here and elsewhere in the gospel very serious indeed. If, on the other hand, we view him primarily as a prophetic figure, more concentrated with dilemmas faced by his churches and concerned to mediate to the traditional materials relevant to those dilemmas, those aporias in literary style and structure will seem both less surprising and less serious". See also Hartman, 1984, 29.

[73] The statement of Bloch, 1954, 31, moves on the same line: "Le symbolisme du Quatrième Évangile, l'intéret qu'il porte à la signification des noms, son penchant pour les jeux des mots, etc, seraint aussi à rapprocher de certaines tendances midrashiques".

That the use of the enigmatic term παράκλητος also could be the result of such association seems probable. The notion of 'creative philology'
may also be applicable to the P, even if this title does not immediately
express the same kind of ambiguity as is the case concerning e.g. ἄνωθεν
in John 3:3,7.[74] In ch.2 I dealt with the ambiguity of the verb
παρακαλεῖν and the noun παράκλησις and the possibility that these two
words are a background of and starting point for the use of παράκλητος
in the GJ. I also pointed out their connection with synagogal exposition
and teaching as can be seen from Acts 13:15 (cf 2.4.3.). Thus, the P can
be understood as the one who performs the activities of the verb and the
noun when viewed against the background of the synagogue's exposition
and teaching.

The list of examples of such creative philology could be enlarged. I
shall mention here but one more, the BD. On the one hand it is evident
who he is and what he is doing. On the other hand the BD is an enigmatic
figure and we cannot (as was the case with the P) with any certainty determine that to which the term refers. I have earlier (4.3.1.) mentioned some
possible reasons for this anonymity. In addition, there is also the factor
of ambiguity and associative plasticity which allows the description of the
BD (as well as of the P) to point beyond what is immediately evident,
making possible renewed actualizations of him as an inspired transmitor
and teacher in the same way as I have mentioned that the entire gospel
seems to function (4.5.). It is worth noting that this enigmatic ambiguity
concerns precisely the two figures who, together with Jesus,[75] make up
the didactic triad described in the previous chapter.

Finally, I should like to deal with the similar treatment of the comple-
ment confinement-freedom in relation to the objects of the interpretation,
the Scriptures and Jesus. It is characteristic of midrashic exegesis to take
as its starting-point a particular passage in the Scriptures. This confinement is both inescapable and fruitful. The same exegesis is, however, free
to use every acknowledged method in order to actualize and adapt this
material. This attitude can be seen in the GJ in general and in the P-sayings in particular. A similar kind of confinement of the P to Jesus is made
clear in 16:13f: "...not speak on his own, but will speak what he hears;
...from me he will receive". Here again the midrashic attitude is reflected.

---

[74] See Cullmann, 1948, 364f.
[75] According to Cullmann, 1976, 17, a similar ambiguity can be seen concerning the presentation of Jesus in the GJ: "The simultaneity, the identity of the incarnate Jesus and
the exalted Christ, is often expressed in the Gospl of John by use of ambigous expressions."

The revelation in Jesus has more to say than it appears at first glance. It is a deep source from which one might draw, and it is valid to attempt to do so.[76] At the same time the actualizing freedom of the P is mentioned. This is indicated in the saying regarding the reminding activity in 14:26. I earlier (3.3.2.) discussed what this saying suggests in the matter of how tradition was shaped in the circle behind the GJ. This interpretative and adaptive reminding corresponds to the creative actualization found in the midrashic interpretation of the Scriptures, of which I gave an account in 5.4. It is the same actualization which is intended in the guiding in all the truth (16:12f). The P's witnessing about Jesus in 15:26 shows that Jesus and the P have replaced the Scriptures both as the object for searching and reflection (Jesus) and as the witness of this new object (the P). Their relationship is similar to that between Jesus and the Scriptures. The difference is that the new witness, the P, enters after Jesus whereas the earlier witness, the Scriptures, preceded him. The apparent difference between the Scriptures and the P (that the Scriptures are both object and witness whereas the P is only witness) is explained by the fact that the Scriptures can function as an object only so far as it functions as a witness (5:39). That the process of actualization was also expected in new and unknown situations can be seen from the saying $\tau \grave{\alpha} \; \grave{\epsilon} \varrho \chi \acute{o} \mu \epsilon \nu \alpha \; \grave{\alpha} \nu \alpha \gamma \gamma \epsilon \lambda \tilde{\epsilon} \iota$ (16:13).

The degree to which this freedom in actualization might be allowed to progress is not mentioned in the GJ. The only way of measuring such a freedom is to compare the results of the johannine tradition[77] with other early christian traditions, especially the synoptic.[78] The difference between these traditions is well known. At the same time it is evident that the gospel traditions have co-existed in the same canon for more than 1500 years, which indicates the range of midrashic interpretation of the

---

[76] There is reason to beleive that this statement (16:13) is directed to those who were of the opinion that the johannine tradition had taken too much freedom with the Jesus material.

[77] This can partly be seen from the GJ itself. Reim, 1983(b), 4, has pointed out that one can trace (from the GJ's way of applying the targumic messianic understanding and interpretations) a critical selectivity when these interpretations are adapted to Jesus. The GJ agrees with some of them. It distances itself from others by assigning them to the speculations of the people.

[78] The concrete cases in the GJ where it is possible to trace the influence of the interpretations of the Targums are not made up of material from the extra-johannine tradition but rather constitute is a johannine "Spezificum". Reim, 1983(b), 13.

Scriptures tolerated in the christian context.[79] The common tie to the object of revelation has been so strong that the considerable variations in exposition have even been treated positively. This gives a picture of 'die Wirkungsgeschichte' of the christian midrash.

5.7. The midrashic hermeneutics and New Testament prophecy

I earlier in this chapter observed that the further the process of canonization of the OT advanced, the more apparent was the need of and possibility for a midrashic exposition of the Scriptures. Canonization produced a defined object for worship and reflection. The thought (within important parts of Judaism) that the prophetic voice, carried by the Spirit of God, had ceased speaking in Israel after the prophetic activity of Malachi,[80] contributed to the notion that the OT was an object for worship and reflection. The prophets were thought of having commented upon and interpreted the Torah. When they ceased speaking these tasks were taken over by tradents who, besides the Torah, now also had the prophetic tradition as a further object for exposition. The great difference between the prophets and these tradents consisted in the possession of the Spirit. The former possessed it, the latter did not.[81] In classical Judaism the Spirit was so strongly connected with prophecy that it could be defined as 'the Spirit of prophecy'.[82] It is also possible to posit the inverse, that the expectation of the Spirit in messianic times implied an expectation of the return of prophecy.[83] It is, consequently, within the Judaic apocalyptic circles

---

[79] Cf from a somewhat different point of view Brown, 1979, 163, who states that "the church's hermeneutical decision to place it in the same canon as Mark, Matthew, and Luke" means that "the Great Church...has chosen to live with tension".

[80] Tos.Sot.13:2. Sanh.11a. Yoma 9b. Sotah 48b. (Further textual evidence is found in Aune, 1983, 374 note 1.) See further, e.g., Zeitlin, 1953, 26; Schäfer, 1972, 94f; Hill, 1979, 33; Aune, 1983, 103-106, pleads energically in favour of revising the view that Judaism thought prophecy had ceased after Malachi. As far as I can see, however, the view of the cessation of prophecy was held by the main stream of Judaism.

[81] Patte, 1975, 118f; Seeligmann, 1953, 176f.

[82] Schäfer, 1972, 21-26. Hill, 1979, 33.

[83] Schäfer, 1972, 106-115. Cf Hill, 1979, 35f. He distinguishes between "the expectation of a new era of prophecy" and "the expectation of an eschatological prophet". The former expectation constitutes, according to Hill, "a peripheral element in the hopes of Judaism". The latter is "more significant, perhaps". Such a distinction seems laboured. Prophecy and prophets have always belonged together.

which regarded "the eschaton as imminent" that the thinking concerning the Spirit and prophecy is most vivid.[84] Thus, when the Early Church proclaimed itself to be the bearer of the Spirit, it also regarded itself as the bearer of a renewed prophecy which in turn influenced its view on revelation, authoritative teaching, and the mediation of tradition.[85] The use of the Joel prophecy in Acts 2:17-22 clearly illustrates how the outpouring of the Spirit and prophecy were held together in this way. It is not difficult to show that this was a common notion of early christianity. Luke, Paul, and the Apocalypse indicate this especially clearly. It is not so easy, however, to get a satisfying answer to the question concerning the actual nature of early christian prophecy.[86] Hill[87] has recently examined the question and attempted a general definition which serves as a "reference-point" in his work on early christian prophecy: "A prophet is a christian who functions within the church, occasionally or regularly, as a divinely called and divinely inspired speaker who receives intelligible and authoritative revelations and messages which he is impelled to deliver publicly, in oral or written form, to Christian individuals and/or the Christian community". This definition seems to cover the ground rather well. One should notice, however, that it stresses the aspect of direct revelation in prophetic activity at the expense of inspired work with already existing traditions.[88] Hill repairs the mistake a little bit later,[89] but it is not, unfortunately, included in the definition. Making this adjustement, it seems valid to speak of "prophetic insight" as well as "prophetic foresight".[90] This does not mean that the direct revelation of new material corresponds to 'foresight', whereas the work with already existing tradi-

---

[84] Aune, 1983, 104.

[85] One could also express it through the words of Hanson, 1983, 183: "...early Christianity represented a 'back to the prophets' movement".

[86] Dautzenberg, 1975, 24. A renewed survey of the whole question is found in Aune, 1983. It is a hugh collection of material but the conclusions are not always convincing.

[87] Hill, 1979, 8f. For a critical discussion of Hill's definition see Aune, 1983, 10.

[88] See also Aune, 1983, 339f. He makes a questionable distinction between prophecy and divination where "prophecy is direct revelation while divination is indirect revelation".

[89] Hill, 1979, 14: "the prophet's consciousness of being called to deliver a message directly given by God does not imply a total abandonment of tradition: the prophet drew upon, modified and added to the religious traditions of Israel, sometimes rejecting them, sometimes affirming them".

[90] Hill, 1979, 61. Isaacs, 1983, 398, says that the OT prophet "was forthteller rather than foreteller". It seems to be a rather strained definition, even if the intention is laudable: to stress the fact that the prophet's revelations were more often conveyed in the form of sermons and proclamations than in that of visions.

tions is to be thought of as 'insight'. The two entities interface with each other. All prophecy is, actually, 'insight' into the nature of past, the present, and the future which gives a deeper understanding and knowledge of both the not-yet-revealed and the already-proclaimed. Concerning the past it is therefore justified to talk about "la prophétie rétrospective".[91] In this context it is appropriate to bring together what is called "charismatic exegesis" and prophecy. As far as I can see, Aune's[92] dislike of this association is unjustified. His criterion of prophecy (that it is "direct revelation") should not make it impossible to regard the authoritative interpretation of existing scriptures and traditions as "direct revelation" as well, especially as it is dependent on the inspiration of the Spirit.[93] If one accepts that the inspired interpretation of the Scriptures has something to do with prophecy, one is led to discern prophetic activity in rather 'usual' preaching situations. They need not deal exclusively with prophetic insight, nor need the terms prophet/prophetic/prophecy occur in the context in order to trace prophetic activity. Rather, one should have a "functional approach" when studying early christian prophecy and its occurrence in the texts.[94] I have in mind here the sermon by Paul in Antioch in Acts 13,[95] and Stephen's speech in Acts 7.

[91] Cothenet, 1977, 93.
[92] Aune, 1983, 339-346.
[93] Aune, 1983, 340, states that the interpretation of the Scriptures is "inspired".
[94] Hill, 1979, 4. Cf Isaacs, 1983, 392. Hill and Isaacs trace this functional characteristic of prophet and prophecy in different areas. Hill deals with these notions in early christianity; Isaacs with its OT correspondances. Cf also in this context the double description of functions in Hawthorne, 1975, 108, which presupposes that "the prophet participated in two events: 1) in an extraordinary one...a revelation given by the Spirit... 2) in an ordinary event such as preaching the gospel in language intended to scrutinize, judge, lay bare the secret thoughts of unbelievers and bring about their conversion".
[95] I have difficulty in sharing the dislike of Aune, 1983, 345, in regarding this text as a prophetic homily. The hesitation of Hill, 1977, 125ff, to designate this sermon as prophetic is less pronounced. He opposes the view that the prophecy is dependent upon the way in which the Scriptures are interpreted. He wants, instead, to identify the prophetic feature as "the exhortation to repentance and obedience". Hill's distinction (p.127 note 66) between "inspired teachers" and "prophets", where the activity of the former would be "the interpretation of the Old Testament" and "the exposition of the Scripture", while the latter would not, seems somewhat artificial. I have difficulty seeing why the sermon in Acts 13 can not also be seen as prophetic in regard to the interpretation of the OT. A broader view of prophetic teaching and interpretation is found in Hawthorne, 1975, 107. Hill has, however, a statement that strengthens my argument for a "functional aproach": "...if we look at the content of the speech, rather than at its formal structure, we may discern the utterance of a prophetic spirit...".

Making this connection between inspired interpretation and prophecy has certain consequences for my investigation. I have earlier (2.4.) shown that παρακαλεῖν-παράκλησις often appears in contexts with prophetic overtones. Considering the fact that the paraclesis had its place within the regular teaching/preaching of the christian community, it is natural that prophecy also belonged to this context. I do not claim that all paraclesis was prophecy.[96] This was made clear in 2.4. Prophecy was, however, one important part of the paraclesis.[97] It is difficult to draw distinct borderlines here. The prophetic feature seems to include both "intelligible propheteia" and "didache".[98] This 'borderline crossing' aspect of prophecy is in accord with my conclusions of chapter 2. Against this background one can ask to what extent it is possible to trace the explicitly prophetic features of the P. I earlier alluded to such features while describing the P's functions (ch.3). The conclusions of that chapter reinforce the 'functional approach' mentioned above. That the P in many respects is represented as a prophet is reflected in the functions ascribed to him.[99]

The most important prophetic features of the P are found in the dependance on and similarity to Jesus. I have already stressed this fact in 4.2. Michaels[100] finds this correspondence so striking that he says that it would be as natural to replace ἄλλος προφήτης with ἄλλος παράκλητος in John 14:14. This proposal seems, however, to restrict the functions of the P to too narrow a field to do justice to the multidimensional model I described in ch.2. Michael's proposal has, on the other hand, the advantage of making the reference to Jesus more obvious. Irrespective of the validity of Michaels' suggestion in this particular instance, his general point is supported by the johannine texts. In the GJ Jesus is pictured as a prophet like Moses[101] or, perhaps better said, against the background

[96] I think Müller, 1975, 26, goes too far in saying that the paraclesis is the "übergeordnete Funktionsangabe" of prophecy. It is interesting, however, that Müller, p.41., because of this "Funktionsangabe" calls the christian prophets "Parakleten".

[97] Cf Ellis, 1970, 58: "paraklesis is one way in which Christian prophets exercise their ministry and, in this context, is a form of prophecy". Indeed, Ellis' statement concerns the question "in Luke's thought", but the saying is valid in a broader sense. A more detailed discussion on the question is found in Cothenet, 1977, 79-84.

[98] Hill, 1979, 128. Cf Hawthorne, 1975, 105: "proclaimer of divine revelations as well as one who was a preacher of the Good News in the more traditional sense". Concerning the differences between prophecy and teaching see Cothenet,1977, 102.

[99] Cf Cothenet, 1972, col 1320; Boring, 1978, 113f; Hill, 1979, 150.

[100] Michaels, 1975, 248. Cf the point of view of Boring, 1978, 119: "παράκλητος... an appropriate surrogate for προφήτης."

[101] Hill, 1979, 54.

120

of expectations of a prophet greater than Moses.[102] These expectations, raised by Deut.18:15, are always in the background. Jesus' task is to mediate knowledge from and about God, knowledge which is 'normally' not available yet which is nevertheless necessary, both for a correct understanding of God and for proper obedience to him.It is the task of the prophet to mediate revelation in the form of both new and adapted knowledge. When the P suceeds Jesus, this prophetic mediation is continued. The only time the verb $\pi\varrho o\varphi\eta\tau\varepsilon\acute{v}\varepsilon\iota\nu$ is used in the GJ (11:51), it refers to the high priest Caiaphas. It is interesting to note that the prophetic function he performs is defined as $\mathring{\alpha}\varphi'$ $\dot{\varepsilon}\alpha\upsilon\tauo\tilde{\upsilon}$ $o\mathring{\upsilon}\varkappa$ $\varepsilon\tilde{\iota}\pi\varepsilon\nu$. This is indicative of the same kind of independence I discussed in 4.2.3. in regard to Jesus and the P. Caiaphas performs the two previously mentioned prophetic functions of 'insight' (interprets the meaning of Jesus' life and death) and 'foresight' (foretells the future).[103] These same prophetic features are also valid concerning Jesus and the P.

There are several other similarities between early christian prophecy and the functions of the P. I shall not make a detailed list here,[104] but wish to mention one more aspect concerning the P as the one who interprets and actualizes the Scriptures. The P broadly performs the Spirit's functions regarding mediation of knowledge. This type of mediation has its closest correspondence in jewish notions regarding the functions of the OT prophets. I mentioned earlier that their main task was to interpret and actualize the Torah. Possessing the Spirit they also had access to knowledge through direct inspiration. They embodied God's Spirit and were therefore capable of acting as authoritative mediators through interpretation and actualization. A new phase begins with the revelation in Jesus: Jesus is the fulfillment of the Scriptures and replaces them both as the source of revelation and as the object of interpretation and actualization. The Spirit of the new prophecy is located in the figure of the P. He is the one who guarantees that the interpretation of the revelation in Jesus is indeed possible, just as was the case concerning the prophet's interpretation of Torah in the OT. The realization of this function, however, is effected by the BD in the GJ. I mentioned earlier that he exhibits pro-

[102] Meeks, 1967, 319; Isaacs, 1983, 402ff. Cf Bornkamm, 1949, 19f.
[103] Boring, 1978, 120 note 1.
[104] See the detailed exposition in Boring, 1978, 113-120. Concerning the similarities to the OT prophets see Isaacs, 1983, 393-399.

phetic features.[105] The prophetic prototype is found in in the OT prophets but the actual continuity in interpretation and actualization is preserved in the methods of the synagogal use of the Scriptures. The synagogue provided the johannine community with examples of scriptural exposition. The community differed from the synagogue in that its object of interpretation was Jesus and because its prophetic spiritual equipment, the P, was to stay with them forever.[106]

Against such a background it seems unwise to distinguish too sharply between synagogal and early christian preaching.[107] That one can go wrong here is especially true concerning the GJ. Müller, for example, sees the synagogal preaching primarily as exposition of biblical texts, whereas he thinks this activity is absent from prophetic preaching. The difficulty of such a distinction becomes clear in a quotation from Mül-

[105] I have difficulty in following Schnackenburg, 1977, 302f, who is of the opinion that the teachers and preachers of the johannine community did not regard themselves as prophets but as inspired (by the Spirit) tradents and interpreters of the revelation in Christ, with the BD as their primary authority. Schnackenburg goes so far to say that the johannine community "von 'Propheten' in ihren Reihen nichts wusste und nicht wissen wollte". Prophecy was not "die Weise, in der sie das Wirken des Geistes erfuhr". It seems unwise, in the light of the OT and the expectations of the Spirit-prophecy in messianic times, to distinguish between prophets and inspired tradents and interpreters. It is, at bottom, the same thing.On the other hand, the P and the BD are not pictured exclusively as prophets but have other characteristics. But as I have stressed earlier the borderlines between prophecy and preaching are vague and difficult to draw. One has to concur with the statement of Boring, 1978, 114: "In a functional understanding of christian prophecy it is better not to distinguish between the inspired teacher or exhorter and the prophet". Cf also the cautious attitude of Isaacs, 1983, 394: "It is doubtful whether a rigid distinction can be made, either in Judaism or Christianity, between prophecy, preaching and teaching".

[106] The thought of the P's remaining with the disciples (14:16) has its correspondence in the notion of the Spirit as resting on the prophets in the rabbinical writings, the Targums, and the Midrashes. See Schäfer, 1972, 159f. That the disciples' possession of the Spirit is stressed in the GJ is partly due to the fact that Jesus in this gospel is pictured as Shekinah (1:14). In the person of Jesus God again is present in the midst of his people. This Shekinah is the condition for the presence of the Spirit. God's Shekinah was in a special way connected with the temple. Jesus as the new temple (2:20f) represents this Shekinah and makes the presence of the Spirit possible. In this context one is reminded of the previous mentioned prophecy of Caiaphas in 11:51. By virtue of his position as high priest he was able to prophecize, since the temple is the place of the Spirit. Schäfer, 1972, 135-143.

[107] Müller, 1975, 238: "Die Synagogenpredigt wie die entsprechende christliche Predigt ist ja ein erbaulicher Lehrvortrag. Nicht so die prophetische Predigt: sie ist andrängende Ansage neuer Wirklichkeit".

ler:[108] "Erstere (i.e. the prophetic preaching) ist selbst das Wort des Kyrios bzw. geschieht durch ihn, tritt also mit unerhörter Autorität auf, während letztere (i.e. 'die in Analogie zur Synagogenpredigt stehende christliche Homilie') Auslegung des göttlichen Wortes ist". As I have shown earlier, the task of the P is: a. to *mediate* authoritatively the Word of Jesus (since he does not speak on his own but what he hears and receives from Jesus) and, b. to *interprete* Jesus' earthly revelation by deepening and actualizing it. Müller's argument becomes even more confusing when he parallels prophetic preaching with "Nahesachatologie", and the situation after this Naheschatologie had cooled with "die Homilie analog synagogaler Übung". He modifies his position later, but only in one direction: "Schon zur Zeit des Paulus gab es neben der Gestalt prophetischer Predigt die andere, die ihren Ursprung in der Synagogenpredigt hatte". He says, however, nothing about the inverse, e.g., prophetic utterances in the homily. His understanding of prophecy is, thus, one-sided. Prophecy, according to him, has nothing to do with the exposition of texts or the mediation of tradition but is only concerned with an immediately revealed message. The P-sayings show that it is not possible to maintain such a standpoint in regard to the GJ. Both forms stand side by side in the GJ, if they are not indeed interwoven into each other. The P is able to interpret because of his immediate contact with the Lord himself. And inversely, his interpretation expresses prophetic features. This description also fits the eschatological view of the GJ earlier defined as actualizing eschatology.

5.8. Prophecy and the Jesus-tradition

If one is willing to relate early christian prophecy to the process by which the new source of revelation, the earthly Jesus, was interpreted, one lands up in the discussion about how creative such a prophetic activity was in regard to the Jesus tradition.[109] It is, of course, valid to discuss the degree

---

[108] Müller, 1975, 239.

[109] The starting point for this discussion is in many respects the thesis developed by Bultmann, 1972, e.g., 127f and 163. A critical survey on the issue is found in Aune, 1983, 233-245. His conclusion concerning the problem is negative: "While the theory is not an apriori impossibility, the critical methodology for detecting and demonstrating the prophetic origin of such putative sayings of Jesus has not yet been developed" (p.245). I think, however, that Aune goes too far when he states: "In spite of the theological attractiveness of the theory, however, the historical evidence in support of the theory lies largely in the creative imagination of the scholars" (p.245).

to which such prophetic activity was interpretative. The fact that such a process occurred in the Early Church must, however, be regarded as unquestionable.[110] It is remarkable that many scholars, in spite of being aware of the fact that the gospel tradition has developed in different ways and in different situations, are unwilling to ascribe this process to prophetic activity.[111] One can understand this standpoint concerning the synoptic tradition with its 'tighter' character. But when one comes to the GJ, it is difficult to understand this unwillingness to link the transformation of the traditions about Jesus together with prophetic activity. Hill, as one example of such a standpoint, deserves to be quoted: "...the discourses in the fourth gospel: these may indeed be homilies composed around sayings of Jesus himself and presented in the form of a speech by Jesus himself, but there is no certain evidence that they emanated from a Christian prophet or prophetic circle".[112] There is reason to ask, however, how it was otherwise possible to legitimate such a thorough transformation. The apostolic witness must, as I see it, display an authority of equal merit: the inspired prophetic voice. The model of this prophetic activity is found in the synagogal tradition of scriptural exposition with its particular purposes, methods, and limits. It is a similar complementary relation to the one I pictured between the BD and the P. The P renders the BD legitimation; the BD the P concretion (see 4.4.3.). From this perspective one can understand that the results of such transformations were regarded to be neither secondary nor of less value than the 'genuine' words of Jesus. *Authenticity* does not, at least not in the GJ, depend upon the degree of

---

[110] Cf Dunn, 1977-78, 179. Dunn's critique of Bultmann's thesis is marked by this double attitude: Bultmann is right in his thesis that early christian prophecy had a creative role concerning the Jesus-tradition, but the degree of such a creative influence is exaggerated. Dunn's statement (p.182) is symptomatic: "The creative role of prophecy was balanced to a considerable extent by the conserving role of teaching..."

[111] One example of such an unwillingness is Aune, 1983, 233-245. His conclusion (p.245) is significant: "The point of issue is not whether early Christianity exercised a creative role in the formation, reformation, and transmission of the sayings of Jesus; they certainly did. The point of issue is the identity of those who were largely responsible for the creative additions and modifications in the traditions". The question of *identity* is important, of course, but the question of *authority*, which is even more important, is not discussed.

[112] Hill, 1974, 270. He seems, however, to have modified his view a little in his book on prophecy. Instead of saying that prophetic utterances have entered and become a part of the Jesus-tradition, he claims that these prophetic utterances have taken up autentic logia and used them in different situations. Hill, 1979, 168. This standpoint is, however, more a consession to the thought of prophetic influence on the Jesus-tradition than an acknowledgement of the basic role of inspired prophecy in the interpretative work with the Jesus-tradition, especially in the GJ.

historicity of the Jesus-tradition but upon the *authority* by which it is delivered.[113] Prophecy, inspired by the Spirit, renders it the dignity of the Word of God.

It is, therefore, anacronistic to attempt to determine whether the P's 'reminding of all what Jesus said' and 'guiding in all truth' implies a deepening of already existing revelation or the addition of new.[114] Rather, they are interdependent processes which makes it impossible either to separate them from one other or to set up an opposition between them. The activity of the P "brings new revelations which complete the revelation brought by the pre-Easter Jesus, but it is precisely this revelation which is brought to completion".[115]

5.9. Summary

The intention of this chapter has been to show a world of thought and a context of interpretation as a background for the P's activity as mediator of knowledge. The result is that he can be seen as a preacher with prophetic features who interprets and actualizes the Scriptures within a concrete field of activity: the service. It is important to stress that this description does not cover the entire significance nor all functions of the P. The description given in this chapter must, however, be regarded as central.[116] It has also the advantage of proposing one further aspect for the understanding of the background of the figure of the P. That is the topic of the next chapter.

[113] Hill, 1979, 179; Hawthorne, 1975, 117. Hawthorne's survey of the question (pp.110-118) is instructive, and his conclusions are balanced and sound.

[114] So e.g. Kothgasser, 1972, 32f.

[115] Boring, 1978, 118.

[116] In Windisch, 1927, 127, there is a concluding description of the P which renders the P such a marked prophetic role that it comes close to total identification: "Kurz gesagt, mit dem Parakleten in Johannes ist eigentlich die Figur eines zeugenden, Rat erteilenden, lehrenden und die Zukunft enthüllenden Propheten zusammengeschmolzen".

6. The realization of the P's functions

6.1. Power or person

How is one to describe the P function in concrete terms? Is he a power, invisible and impalpable, or a person, visible and palpable? This question has a twofold origin in the text of the GJ itself. First, in the P-sayings as in the rest of the GJ there is no uniform way of describing how the P will be realized. Secondly, the P is, as is well known, connected with the Spirit.[1] The latter factor, in particular, has contributed to the idea of the P as a divine but abstract power. The description of the Spirit, apart from the the P-sayings, also contributes to such an idea. The Spirit is the power which renews, giving life and strength (ch. 3:5f; 6:63; 20:22). True worship is done in the Spirit (4:23).[2] The manifestations of Jesus' life are described with the aid of the Spirit, both in regard to his physical (19:30) as well as his internal life (11:33; 13:21).

To call the Spirit the P renders it, however, a more personal character. Already the word παράκλητος, with its personal references in secular contexts, carries such a connotation. The pronoun ἐκεῖνος in the masculine (14:26; 15:26; 16:8, 13f) is not only a necessary consequence of its masculine headword but also assigns the P a personal character as the successor of the earthly Jesus.[3] This is especially evident in 16:13, since it would have been more natural grammatically to use a neutral pronoun with the headword τὸ πνεῦμα. In addition to this personification, dependent upon the identification of the Spirit with the P, there are also features and functions which attribute personal characteristics to the notion of the P itself. It is not improbable that such an increasing emphasis on the personal character of the P is due to historical developments within, at least, that part of the Early Church to which the GJ belongs. R.E.Brown[4] has

---

[1] I remind the reader (See 1.2.)of the fact that I work with the text in its present form. Concerning the literary critical question about what might be primary and secondary in the connection the Spirit-the P, see Windisch, 1927, 130f. It is worth noting that the pouring out of the Spirit on the first Whitsunday in the Early Church often was seen as the fulfilment of the P-promise. See Casurella, 1983, 39 and 140.

[2] Observe that God here is defined as Spirit, thus not describing *who* he is but *what* he is.

[3] See Barrett, 1978, 482; Brown, 1966-70, II, 639 and 650.

[4] Brown, 1967, 124.

pointed out that the notion of the Spirit developed in the early Church from that of a divine, prophetic power to a more personal understanding. The reason for the increased stress on the personal aspects of the Spirit should, as I see it, be sought in the increasing embarrassment the community experienced with the continued delay of the parousia and the dying out of the apostles/eyewitnesses.[5] The longer Jesus is absent and the further the distance becomes between Jesus' life and that of the community's, the more important it is to stress the Spirit as Jesus' 'alter ego' and thereby give the Spirit a concrete and personal character. The personification of the Spirit in the figure of the P reflects the fact that it is "christology rather than pneumatology which dominates John."[6] The P is, in my opinion, a special variant of the idea of the Spirit, a variant supported by both the GJ's well developed christology as well as the embarrassment caused by the delay of the parousia. The functional parallel with Jesus, as I have mentioned earlier (4.2.2.), points in the same direction. The P is meant to be "Christus praesens".[7]

6.2. Realization - how and through whom?

Even if it is correct to say that the P, in the GJ, is thought of in personal terms, the question regarding his actual realization remains unanswered. The author of the GJ is anxious to stress that revelation, in the time between the glorification of Jesus and the parousia, does not display the same visible characteristics as was the case during Jesus' earthly life. It is evident that the understanding of revelation after Jesus' death became problematic for the johannine community (e.g. 16:16-18). The point of the Thomas pericope (20:29) is to prepare the disciples for this time. The 'blessed state' is to believe in spite of the fact that visible conformation of revelation is no longer possible. The P does not transmit concrete visual impressions about or from Jesus. Instead, he transmits orally what he hears. Further, he is not going to perform concrete signs or miracles as did some of the OT prophets and Jesus.[8] There is, thus, no connection in the GJ between signs and miracles, and inspired missionary preaching as, e.g., in Acts. At the same time, it seems to be an ambition of the GJ to

---

[5] Cf Brown, 1967, 128-132.
[6] Isaacs, 1983, 402.
[7] Cf Ricca, 1966, 169.
[8] Cf Isaacs, 1983, 399.

let the P be represented by concrete figures and their work, just as the P himself represents the absent Jesus in accordance with the third P-saying in 15:26f. As the P will witness about Jesus so also will the disciples (v.27). This does not mean that yet another intermediate step is introduced between Jesus and the community, but rather that the P works directly through concrete persons, often in very specific situations. I shall return to this soon.

One can not, however, simply say that each witnessing disciple represents the P, at least not to the same degree. This is due to the fact that the GJ is not consistent in its description of disciples and discipleship. Consequently, there is reason to ask to whom the P-sayings are actually directed in the GJ's text. No explicit addresse is mentioned, but the $ὑμῖν$, $ὑμᾶς$ which are used in the sayings indicate a reference to disciples in general. There is no clear indication that these pronouns especially refer to the group of 12. Not even the farewell-discourse as a whole is explicitly addressed to the twelve. Chapter 13 hints at associations to corresponding pericopes in the synoptics where the 12-group is mentioned. The only mentioning of a group in ch. 13, however, is $οἱ ἴδιοι$ (13:1), quite likely a reference to the true people of God compared with $οἱ ἴδιοι$ in 1:11 or with $τὰ ἴδια πρόβατα$ in 13:3f.[9] It seems to be a smaller group but no clear delimitation is made. The only certain thing is that the BD, Peter, and the traitor Judas are included in this group from the beginning. Judas leaves the company later. Three more disciples are mentioned: Thomas (14:5), Philip (14:8), and Judas nr 2 (14:22). No matter how one wishes to define this group one is justified in letting its description be as vague as it is in the GJ, which seems to serve the purpose of making possible an identification between the disciples addressed by Jesus in the text and the readers of the GJ. On the other hand, one can see that the GJ regards the 12 as a special group. All who wandered with Jesus are called disciples, but after the crisis reflected at the end of ch. 6, the twelve are presented as that group which remained faithful. This group is also, in a special way, selected by Jesus (6:70; cf 13:18).

Outside of the farewell-discourse one finds different persons doing those things which have been characterized as functions of the P. This is especially true concerning witnessing: the disciples in ch. 1, the samarian woman in ch. 4, the man born blind in ch. 9, Lazarus in ch. 11, and the women in ch. 20. Last but not least, there is also the figure who stands in a special way behind the GJ: the BD (Cf 4.4.2. and 4.4.3.). If

---

[9] See Barrett, 1978, 438.

one allows that the BD is the head of the group through which the functions of the P are realized, the result of the BD's work - the GJ - must also be included as the result of the P's activity. The GJ is a codification of a practical transmission and actualiation of the revelation in Jesus. Thus, the P-sayings do not function as a promise that was to become effective at the point of the GJ's final compilation. Rather, they reflect a process of interpretation within which they themselves already had been functioning and been proven effective, a process which, at a certain time, due to needs and problems of the johannine community, was codified in writing. This writing was held to be legitimate on account of the BD's special relationship to Jesus and the P. As I have said earlier (4.5.), this codification has the character of being a binding norm for the community but points, at the same time, beyond itself to the continous work and realizations of the P.

What has been said so far indicates that the question regarding the P's realization is not possible to answer in a simple manner. The GJ has not, as would be the case later in church history,[10] a single prophetic figure in mind as the one true realization of the P. On the other hand, the P-sayings do not seem to incite a 'democratization' of the P in the sense that every christian in every moment realizes the P.[11] The P is, rather, realized when the functions ascribed to him are performed by individual disciples.[12] This means that his realization, through the individual disciple, can take place more or less often and to a greater or lesser extent. As individual disciples performed these functions more often and to a greater extent, they appeared as more important realizations and embo-

---

[10] See Harnack, 1927, 426. About half a century after the origin of the GJ proposals were made that the P had been embodied in Paul. Montanus also claimed that he embodied the P in his preaching. It is worth noting that these two persons, who had been connected primarily with teaching and preaching (concerning Montanus also with prophetic claims), were associated with the P. This indicates that such an understanding of the P was possible and as natural as associations in other directions, e.g., the forensic. The P's *functions* were more decisive in this regard than its associations with the secular meaning of the title.

[11] 1 John 2:20 might possibly be seen as a step in that direction.

[12] Here I come close to the thesis of Johnston, 1970, e.g., 119, that the P is embodied in certain leaders in the community: the exegete, the teacher, the prophet, the comforter, and the witness. I think, however, that he puts too much stress on their roles as leaders. It is not because they are leaders that the P is embodied through them in certain functions. On the contrary, they become leaders since the P uses them in certain functions. The weakest point in Johnston's argument in this case, as throughout the book is, however, that the concept of the P is not presented as a person but as a power. Concerning a detailed criticism of this question see Malatesta, 1973, 540-543.

diments of the P. It is here that the embryo of the authority hierarchy, which is possible to discern in the GJ, is to be found.[13] In that hierarchy the BD assumes the highest position. But since the realization of the P is primarily connected with *function* and only secondarily with personalization, the BD is not presented as an exclusive realization but can (at the same time as his profound authority is marked) point beyond himself towards the P's further activity, when the time of the BD is over.[14]

One can say, then, that just as the P's overall function is to make the glorified Christ present within the community until he returns, a realization of the P also takes place every time someone performs a function which results in the presence of this same Christ, actualizing him in words. The difficulty with such a loose functional definition is that the problem of distinguishing between right and wrong actualizations of Christ remains unsolved a problem of which 1 John 4:1-3 is an indication.[15] The GJ itself reflects upon this problem only in so far that the exposition intends to show that the GJ itself is a legitimate interpretation and actualization of Christ from the perspective of his earthly life as well as of his glorified being.[16] The personal and concrete exposition of the P did not, thus, result in his identification with specific holders of certain tasks but to the tasks themselves, whether performed by individual persons or an entire congregation.

6.3. A concrete figure serving as model

6.3.1. Introductory

Thus, if the P is described as a person, there is reason to ask whether the GJ's author might have had some concrete figure in mind which provided the background upon which he drew the picture of the P. It is hard to imagine that the presentation of the P was merely an aggregate of

[13] See 4.4.2. and 4.4.3.
[14] Cf 4.5.
[15] Brown, 1982, 503, speaks about the need of "a criterion...for putting their Spirit to the test".
[16] See 4.4.3.

thoughts and ideas gathered from different sources.[17] No matter how such thoughts and ideas are said to fit together, they alone are too abstract to cover all aspects of the presentation of the P in the GJ. By this I do not deny that ideas were a part of the picture as well. These ideas ought in some sense, however, to be based in concrete reality.[18]

Indeed, attempts have been made to find concrete models for the exposition of the P. Bultmann's[19] proposal of the mandean Jawar figure, and Shafaat's[20] proposal of the qumranean Geber figure, are two such examples. The weakness of such proposals is either that the background figures are fetched from a time, a place, or a context too far distant from the particular situation of the GJ to have any reasonable probability of having influenced it,[21] or the model picks out one feature or function of the P and makes this the basis for the selection of a proper model (Shafaat). The latter is also charcteristic of the attempts to find the P's background in Jewish angelology.[22] One finds there features which shed light upon the figure of the P, but neither can this background alone explain the role and functions of the P. Apart from this weakness, however, one should acknowledge that the attempts to find a background to the P in angelology are more reasonable than were Bultmann's and Shafaat's proposals.

Of all the one-dimensional models offered, those which identify the P with personified Wisdom[23] are the best in that they both respect the func-

---

[17] Cf Boring, 1978, 117: "From wherever the word was derived, the occasion and model for its use was not an *idea* found in the Old Testament, Jewish, Hellenistic, Gnostic, or Mandean sources... ". See also Martyn, 1978, 3, who in the spirit of Bousset states that "johannine exegets cannot be satisfied indefinitely to move about in the realm of disembodied ideas". Instead, one should look for concrete contexts in which "to fix the locus occupied by John in the history of early Christianity".

[18] See e.g. Olsson, 1974, 267f. Olsson's interpretation of the P is in many respects very close to mine. His reference to *melīts* has the advantage of trying to find a solution of the hiatus problem, the forensic title - the didactic functions. The reference to *melīts* is, no doubt, a step in the right direction and is important for the interpretation of the P. It is, however, not concrete enough. Olsson's statement is revealing: "Thus the Hebrew-speaker had a *word* (my underlining) which covered both the 'kerygmatic' and forensic aspect..." (p.267). The reference shall, however, concern more than a word. It should also concern concrete phenomena which were experienced by the johannine community.

[19] Bultmann, 1950, 440.

[20] Shafaat, 1981.

[21] The critique of Bultmann's proposal has dealt with other problems in addition to its chronology but only this aspect of the critique is important for my argument. For a critical assessment of Bultmann see Michaelis, 1947. See also Schulz, 1957, 153.

[22] Mowinckel 1933; Betz, 1963.

[23] Riesenfeld, 1972.

tions of the P and can be applied to the GJ as a whole. Nevertheless, Wisdom alone, just as any other single background, does not offer a sufficiently complete or concrete model through which the actual background of the P can be explained.[24]

The basic criterion for a background figure for the P is, as I see it, that of being an empirical phenomenon with a probable nearness in time and space to the GJ's author and readers/listeners.[25] It also must be a phenomenon which, in as many respects as possible, corresponds to the functions of the P. It is neither possible nor desirable to demand a total correspondence in that such an identity would make other fields of association superfluous. I have earlier argued against such exclusiveness. The task is to try to find a model, corresponding to my argument in ch. 2, which covers the dominant dimensions.

6.3.2. Desirable characteristics

If my investigation up to this point has been correct, the desirable characteristics of a model (called X) for the P may be summarized as follows.

1. X shall stand in some kind of 'tandem relationship' to another figure 'Y' which displays similar tasks and functions (4.2.). X also ought to function as a replacement of Y in some way.

2. X shall have an independent authority but, at the same time, be subordinate to Y (4.2.).

3. This subordination implies X's dependence but also signifies a nearness to Y in terms of confidence as well as X's knowledge about Y's thoughts and will (4.2.).

4. Such nearness makes it possible for X to mediate Y's thoughts and words (4.2.).

5. It shall be possible to relate X to the service of both the early Christians and that of the synagogue (5.).

6. Since the GJ clearly displays a midrashic attitude in the exposition of the Scriptures and, at the same time, is the 'first work' of the P, X shall have some connection with theprocess in which the midrashic attitude finds expression. The functions of translation, actualization, and preaching shall be specially considered. It is worth stressing, once again, the freedom and, at the same time, the dependence of X in the interpretation (5.).

---

[24] A summary of the different proposals is found in Brown, 1966-70, II, 1137-1139.
[25] Cf Boring, 1978: "a concrete phenomenon present in the Johannine community".

7. X shall have prophetic features (3.).

8. The tasks, functions, and the mission of X's activity are of primary importance, the carrying out of a particular office is secondary (6.2.).

6.4. Proposal for a model

6.4.1. The Methurgeman

In the search for a figure which, in the best way, represents these characteristics, one ought first to consider the Methurgeman(M). He is the individual in the synagogue's service who translated the scriptural readings into a targum as well as, later on, mediated the synagogal preaching. The proposal to consider the M, in this context, seems reasonable. It is, therefore, astonishing that nobody, as far as I can see, has made this suggestion earlier. Only one scholar, Le Déaut, makes a hint in this direction.[26]

I shall now present material and arguments as to the probability of my proposal. Conclusion in this matter can only be tentative since the relevant material about the M is rather meagre and the jewish sources, from the NT perspective, are so late that it is difficult to achieve any certain results.[27] The contours which one can discern concerning the figure of the M are, however, clear enough so that a comparison with the P is possible.

If I can present material that makes a comparison possible, the methodological question arises whether it is correct to assume that the institution of the M had been established before the time of the GJ's compilation so that this institution could have inspired the GJ's author to describe

[26] Le Déaut, 1968, 392 in the text and in note 3; Le Déaut, 1971(a), 276. Le Déaut does not mention the M in his comparison, but *tannā* and *'amorā*? I deal with the latter title later in this chapter. It is symptomatic that it is Le Déaut who makes this association. He is the one who, more than other scholars, has realized the importance of the midrashic attitude of scriptural exposition and the method of targumizing for the interpretation of the NT. See e.g. 1971(a), 279 : "For the New Testament exegesis it is important to study the tendency to 'targumization' as a phenomenon of hermeneutics, together with its methods, psychological mecanisms and presuppositions". Cf Cothenet, 1977, 100, who in a somewhat different context says: "L'interprète quit doit traduire les discours en langues (1 Cor. 14:27) tient le rôle du meturgeman. Le prophète, chargé de la paraclèse, n'accomplit-il pas celui de l'homéliste à la synagogue?"

[27] A survey of the material is found in Billerbeck, 1922f., IV:1, 161-164 and 185-188. See also Zunz, 1892, 9 and 351; Bacher, 1899, 28 and 206; Elbogen, 1913, 187ff; Krauss, 1922, 134 and 176-181; Gächter, 1936(b), 171-184; Stauffer, 1963, 283-293.

the P's functions as he does. That is, do striking *similarities* justify the conclusion that the M was the actual historical *background* against which the P was drawn? Such would be difficult to prove. Yet, the information of the M, indeed late and meagre, can be interpreted *phenomenologically*. That is, the M can be seen to represent the synagogue's way of dealing with the Scriptures and its functions within the believing community. The established M-institution is a result of a process in which,long before the date of the written sources about it, the attitudes represented in the institution were an inherent part of that process. Such a phenomenological approach can also cope with the fact that, whereas the GJ presumably did not have its origin in Palestine but in Ephesus in Asia Minor,[28] or in Antioch in Syria,[29] the M-institution originated in Palestine.[30] It is, of course, true that there was no need for translations of the hebrew text into aramaic in the greek speaking diaspora, and thus the M-institution was superfluous there.[31] It is also true, however, that, for long time, there was a constant need for translations and interpretations both inside and outside Palestine, e.g., in Syria, especially in connection with the Christian mission in that the gospel was delivered in different languages.[32] Also, if the relationship between the GJ and the midrashic attitude has been correctly presented in chapter 5, the community behind the GJ might have been as well acquainted with the M-institution as it was with its results.

It seems valid, therefore, to interpret the similarities between the P's activity and the synagogue's way of dealing with the Scriptures by assuming that the latter provided the phenomenological background, especially as it concerns the M, to the figure of the P. If I can show actual resemblances between what is said about the P in the GJ with what we know about the M, I consider I have met the demand for a reasonable empirical nearness in time and space to the GJ made in 6.3.1.

[28] So Barrett, 1978, 131 (with some hesitation); Brown, 1966-70, I, CIIIf.

[29] Kümmel, 1972, 175: "somewhere in Syria...probably the best altenative". Becker, 1979, 50: "Mit Vorsicht...Syrien den Vorzug geben".

[30] Gächter, 1936, 174.

[31] Krauss, 1922, 177f. It would, of course, have been even more superfluous, as Krauss says (p.178), if the text was read in greek.

[32] See Krauss, 1922, 178, and the evidence he offers there. He says: "Meines Wissens ist der Umstand dass die Institution der Verdolmetschung des verlesenen Textes in einer bestimmten Form auch im Urchristentum bestand, noch nicht genügend beachtet worden.".

6.4.2. Presentation of the Methurgeman

Linguistically,[33] there are are three different terms for the M: $targ^emān$, $tūrg^eman$, and $m^ethurgēman$. Methurgeman, the latest term in the development has become dominant in usage. In a later stage the M was also called 'amorā'? The transition was gradual, 'amorā' being common by the middle of the 3rd century CE.[34] The functions attributed to these terms were, however, the same: to translate the readings from the Scriptures in the synagogal service and to mediate the exposition of the readings.

The M as an institution is, according to jewish tradition, said to have been established already during Ezra's time.[35] It is not possible, however, to prove that such was the case. In the beginning of the 2nd century CE[36] the translation of the reading of the Scriptures was probably a common practice in Palestine. If the translation of texts was then common it had presumably been in development for some time, exactly how long it is impossible to say.[37] There is an indication that such translation was in use during the time of the temple.[38] The same is true of the M's activity as a mediator between the preacher and the congregation in the service of the synagogue. The oldest proof in this respect concerns Gamaliel II, 90-110 CE, who was forced to be silent when his M was silenced.[39] It seems reasonable to assume that only if this kind of translation activity was widespread could the silencing of Gamaliel II's M have its desired effect. The custom was, thus, most likely commonly in use at least by the second half of the first century CE.[40]

[33] Concerning the etymology see Bacher, 1899, 206 note 2, and Gächter, 1936(b), 172 note 5.

[34] Gächter, 1936(b), 180.

[35] Billerbeck, 1922ff., IV:1, 161. It is worth noting that one, during the tannaitic time, was of the opinion that the maśkīl of the Psalter headings referred to an M who helped the poet recite the psalm in front of the congregation. See Gächter, 1936(b), 181.

[36] Gächter, 1936(b), 175.

[37] Gächter, 1936(b), 175; argues that common use presupposes a period of at least 50 years during which the use grew. "Es spricht alles dafür, dass die Sitte schon zur Zeit Jesu bestand".

[38] See Krauss, 1922, 179.

[39] Berakh.27b. See Gächter, 1936(b), 182, and Billerbeck, 1922ff., IV:1, 186.

[40] Gächter, 1936(b), 183, draws the conclusion: "Damit kommen wir in die Zeit der Apostel und Jesus selbst".

I doubt if the attempt of Billerbeck, 1922ff., I, 579, to anchor the M-institution in the NT itself (as an explanation of Mt.10.27) is correct. Only Gaechter, 1963, 343, seems to have followed Billerbeck here.

6.4.3. Detailed description

In what follows I intend to give as detailed a picture of the M as is possible. The description is based on an exposition of the characteristics listed in 6.3.2.

6.4.3.1. Tandem relationship

It is natural that the M, who functioned both as a simultaneous intepreter and as a mediator of a message (see 6.4.3.4.) did not work alone but had someone at his side who acted with him and was dependent upon him, i.e., the one who read the hebrew text and supplied the material for exposition. Seen in these terms, the M-institution might have existed in embryonic form in the synagogal service already in the days of the babylonian captivity, where some kind of translation in the service was presumably needed, as I have noted earlier (5.3. Cf 6.4.2.). The phenomenon of tandem relationship concerning the M is, however, reflected in another context. In Ex. 4:12-16 it is reported how Aaron was appointed as the spokesman for Moses in front of Pharaoh.[41] That the M-institution actually was seen in terms of this Moses-Aaron background is later indicated in TargNeofiti as well as in TargOnkelos on Ex. 4:16. Both render *l^epha̅* with M.[42] The conclusion that Aaron functioned as an interpreter and translator is drawn, in a non-aramaic speaking area, by Philo.[43] It is also of interest that in Ex. 4 Moses is described as holding such strong authority that he will appear as God (*le̅'lohim* 4:16) to Aaron. Aaron does not assume a divine position or authority but is placed in a relationship where the other is assigned almost divine dignity.

---

[41] The hebrew text uses *l^epha̅*. One encounters here, paranthetically, the instigation of the later custom where every rabbi of rank had his own M, as was the case concerning Gamaliel. The LXX translates στόμα. This passage is fully treated by Stauffer, 1963, 287.

[42] Another passage, in which a hebrew word is rendered by M in the Targums, is Gen. 42:23. Here it concerns the function of translation without any theological overtones. The hebrew text has *meli̅ts*, which has been thought to have some connection with the idea of the P. See Olsson, 1974, 267f. Cf, however, Betz, 1963, 139. It is worth noting that Olsson mentions Gen. 42:23 but not its Targum, where *m^ethurg^ema̅n* becomes the equivalent of *meli̅ts*. Olsson comes, actually, very close to a reference to the M saying that the P is "the true translator and interpreter" (p. 268, 270). Betz' argument against considering *melits* in this context is, on the other hand, unsatisfactory. His conclusion is due to his characterization of the P as a forensic figure. The P's "grundlegende forensische Dienst" makes, according to Betz, such a reference impossible.

[43] De Vita Mosis I:84. He paraphrases the passage: χρεία δ'εἰ γένοιτο ἑρμηνέως ὑποδιακονικὸν στόμα τὸν ἀδελφὸν ἕξεις.

Thus, the M stands in a 'tandem relationship' to another person in a way that is similar to the P's relationship to Jesus. The M does not, however, assume divine rank but is present in contexts where divine authority is infused into the activity.

6.4.3.2. Independent but in subordinated position

The M is, thus, no solo performer. He functions in a relationship with two other figures, the one who read the hebrew text and the one who was responsible for the exposition. In the former case it might be more correct to say that the M's task was defined by the recited text. The text itself is superior to and guides the M's work. In relation to this text the M had a double responsibility. On the one hand he was to render it faithfully in order to guarantee the sanctity of the Word of God, on the other hand he had to remain independent of the letter in order to realize the meaning of the text.[44] The M's task was to resolve the tension between a literal and a meaningful translation. This tension sheds light upon the fact previously (5.3) mentioned, that from the beginning the borderline between translation and exposition was unclear. The Targums witness to the fact that, in different situations different aspects of the text were stressed. Onkelos is a much more literal translation than Jonathan,[45] a difference which is also present in to the greek translations of the OT. Aquila's translation, for example, strives after a more literal rendering than does the LXX.[46]

Limitations upon the freedom allowed in translation were provided by passages like Deut. 4:2, in that the translator dealt with the Torah.[47] This limitation could be expressed by a formula[48] and had deep roots in jewish as as well in christian tradition.[49] On the other hand, freedom of interpretation could also be stressed. It even happened that rabbis demanded the M to diverge from the text.[50] Sometimes it was enjoined upon the M to

---

[44] Illustrative examples of this doubleness is found in Le Déaut, 1965, 17, 27f and 31f. The active role of the M in appropriating the text for instructive purposes is pointed out, with examples, by Klein, 1982.

[45] For a characteristic of the different Targums see Bacher, 1906, 58f; Kahle, 1959, 191-208; McNamara, 1972, 173-189.

[46] Kahle, 1959, 193f. Bowker, 1969, 25.

[47] LXX: οὖ προσθήσετε πρὸς τὸ ῥῆμα, ὃ ἐγώ ἐντέλλομαι ὑμῖν, καὶ οὐκ ἀφελεῖτε ἀπ'αὐτοῦ.

[48] οὖ προσθεῖναι...οὖ ἀφελεῖν.

[49] For documentation see Stauffer, 1963, 288ff.

[50] For the following see Leipoldt-Morenz, 1953, 76f.

embellish and correct.[51] At times the M was forbidden to translate certain texts which, because of their possible offensiveness, could easily be misunderstood.[52] One did not experience such kinds of translation or deletion as deceit, since the hebrew text itself was always recited. This reading, even if one did not understand it, guaranteed that the sanctity of God's Word was preserved.[53]

Freedom from the literal meaning of the text increased when the M also began to serve, to a larger extent, as a mediator of the exposition. This development presupposes that translation and exposition gradually became construed as separate activities. Exactly how and when the separation occurred is not clearly indicated by the material. After the reading of the text and the translation, anyone could be invited to speak or preach, even strangers. So is the case in Acts 13:15 although here the translation is missing. Later the class of possible preachers became more limited, consisting of professionals and, to some degree, ordained rabbis.[54] The degree of freedom in the preaching itself has, of course, varied from case to case, the range being from a literal translation of the preacher's word to the M's own improvisation, or even to M's acting for the preacher on certain occasions.[55] Here one can see a link with the notion of replacement, intimated in the first characteristic listed in 6.3.2.

The M's tasks were thus structured by the complements freedom - confinement and independance - subordination. A similar complementarity can, as I have tried to show, be seen in the P's relation to Jesus. The P will independently 'translate' and actualize the earthly Jesus' words and work in situations where Jesus is no longer present. The P is, however, subordinate to Jesus and teaches the disciples only what comes from him.

---

[51] Meg.25b. See also Klein, 1976, who, with several examples, shows an important technique of translation in the Targums from the Pentateuch, i.e., "converse translation". This technique includes, e.g., an insertion of a negative which does not occur in the hebrew text, changing the verb in clauses, and transforming a rhetorical question to a declaration.
[52] Meg.3.10. Meg.25a,b. Some of the relevant texts were: Gen.35:22. Ex.32:21-24. Num.6:22-27. 2 Sam.13. Some texts were not even allowed to be read in hebrew! (Especially Ez.1.) Cf the statement of Hermann, 1956, 48, referring to this fact: "Gottesdienstliche Übersetzung konnte also auch eine lehrkritische Tendenz enthalten". 1953, 76f.
[53] Bowker, 1969, 13.
[54] Elbogen, 1913, 197. Zunz, 1892, 351. Gächter, 1936(b), 181, points out that the increasing independance of the M is bound up with the improvement of the M's skills. In tannaitic time (-200 CE) ordained rabbis often acted as the M.
One could, of course, ask whether Paul in Acts 13:15 was invited to speak as a rabbi (he might still have been regarded as such) or as a layman.
[55] Keth.8 b. Yoma 20 b. Sota 40 a. Cf Zunz, 1892, 351.

6.4.3.3. The nearness

The M's ability to function in this tension between independence and subordination was due mainly to his nearness to a superior. This was especially the case when the M acted as a mediator of the exposition. The closeness of this working relationship was stylized when it became customary for the rabbis to have personal M:s. These M:s knew the thoughts and intentions of their teachers so well that, at the moment of exposition, the preacher could but intimate to the M what he wished to say presenting him with only the most important thoughts and passages from the Scriptures. Communication between the preacher and the M took place in a whispering tone.[56] The preacher was sitting, and the M had to bend to listen. The acquaintanceship was mutual, so that the preacher could confidently leave the actual exposition of the texts to the M.

A similar nearness has previously (4.2.) been pointed out in the relation between Jesus and the P. The P will not speak on his own, but speaks what he *hears* drawing upon knowledge which actually belongs to Jesus (16:13f). The P's origin, i.e., that he is sent by the Father and/or the Son, guarantees the claim of his particular nearness to Jesus.

6.4.3.4. Mediator

The preacher communicated in a whispering tone to the M material which provided the basis for the M's exposition. It was, then, the M's task to fill out, independently but from a subordinated position, the preacher's thoughts and, having created an entity out of them, announce this result to the congregation. He was the preacher's "ausführendes Organ".[57] The M functions, thus, as an active mediator between the preacher and the congregation. It is an ancient thought within Judaism that teaching was to be mediated.[58] The basic teaching, the revelation of the Torah, had been received from God and mediated to the people

---

[56] Sanh.7 b. Moed Q.21 a. Cf Zunz, 1892, 350f; Elbogen, 1913, 197f; Billerbeck, 1922ff., IV:1, 185ff.

[57] Wilckens, 1980, 192. One should note that Wilckens is not concerned with the M, but with the P. I have borrowed Wilcken's expression as a description of the M's function in order to illustrate my thesis that the description of the P, in this respect, fits the description of the M. I do not, however, agree with Wilckens' usage of the expression as a label of the P's entire activity. The P has, according to Wilckens, "überhaupt keine Selbständigkeit". The P, as well as the M, functions actively and in what could be called a 'sensitive' independence. Cf also the statement of Krauss, 1922, 177 note 3, that the M "den Sinn des den Vortrag eines Schriftgelehrten verdeutlichenden Erklärers hat".

[58] pMeg.4,74d. Cf Billerbeck, 1922ff., IV:1, 185f.

by Moses. Since the Torah had been received through mediation, it was also to be interpreted by a mediator. The M's activity could then sometimes be thought of in terms of Moses' activity and seen as a continuation of it.[59] An indication of how highly esteemed the M-function was is found in the fact that one could reverse this order and compare Moses with the reader of the text and God with the M.[60] The case mentioned earlier, when Gamaliel II was silenced because his M was silenced by the congregation, illustrates the M's power. The preacher, actually, was dependent upon his M.[61] Without the M the voice of the preacher could not be heard. Though it may not have been common to do so, the high esteem which the M occassionally held suggests that one should not deny a possible connection between the P and the M on the ground that they do not stand at the same level of respectability.[62]

There is reason to suppose that the M did not function as a mediator only in one direction, from the preacher to the congregation, but also in the opposite direction, from the congregation to the preacher.[63] The M mediated the questions put by the congregation to the preacher, and answered them on behalf of the preacher.

The similarity between the M and the P seems also, on this point, to be striking. One further note can be made. The figure of the BD can also, in part, be explained by making a comparison here.[64] One of the dominant features in the exposition of the BD is precisely his function as a mediator. This implies a mediation from Jesus to the disciples but also entails a mediation from the disciples to Jesus in 13:24f. The M functioned in a similar way.

---

[59] York, 1979, 76f.

[60] Berakh.45a.

[61] Cf, parenthetically, the basic role of the interpreter (διερμηνευτής) in connection with the glossolalia in the service according to Paul in 1 Cor. 14:28. If there is no interpreter present, the one who speaks in tongues should be silent.

[62] Concerning the later development in the Early Church cf the statement of Stauffer, 1963, 292 note 65: "Nicht nur die Amtsbezeichnung, auch die hierarchische Rangstellung des jüdischen Methurgeman ist in der Kirche dieselbe wie in der Synagoge". Cf also the statement of Schlatter, 1898, 52f, concerning the early christian M's position (in Jerusalem): "Wars auch nur ein untergeordneter Dienst, so war es doch eine thätige Mitwirkung bei der Ausrichtung des Apostelamts und eine Vertrauensstellung, die den Übersetzer leicht in enge Verbindung mit dem Lehrer brachte, den er begleitete, und die ihm mehr als der übrigen Gemeinde die genaue Kenntnis gab, was jener zu lehren pflegte".

[63] Taanith 4b. Cf Zunz, 1892, 351 and 368.

[64] Without mentioning the M, Minear, 1977, 118f, describes the BD's functions in the GJ in terms which are strikingly close to those of the M in this respect.

6.4.3.5. The service context

In chapter 5 I indicated that in several respects the P's functions parallel methods of scriptural exposition found in the service of the synagogue. Consequently, a model for the P ought to be sought in this context. If the result of the comparison is so far correct, the proposal of the M is self-evident. In the synagogue, it is the M who embodies the translating, interpreting, and actualizing work with the Scriptures. Concerning, then, the service context it seems sound to choose the M as a background figure to the P in that the M-institution presumably, in some way, was taken over by the early Church. Appropriating an argument from Eusebius (HE 39:16), Gächter[65] claims that such translation activity existed also in the johannine community and is reflected in the GJ itself. His analysis of the prologue[66] and the farewell-discourse[67] indicates that the author of the GJ has worked with an interpreter.

6.4.3.6. The midrashic attitude

It is clear that the M was closely related to the midrashic activity of the synagogue. The midrashic attitude was characterized by a desire to make the Scriptures understandable, to actualize their contents while adapting them to new situations. In this process of translation and exposition the M was one of the main actors.[68] This does not mean that the midrashic attitude has its origin in the M-institution. Such an attitude is rather due to the interaction between worship and everyday life. The attitude has, however, one very important representaive in the M. It is the M who personifies the attitude's confinement to the Scriptures as well as its freedom from them. Consequently, the M guides while serving as a model for the community's traditional way of relating the Scriptures to everyday life.

The P is related to the Jesus-tradition in a way which is similar to the midrashic attitude's relationship to the Scriptures.[69] The midrashic attitude to the Jesus-tradition in the GJ can be said to be derived from the P and to have been legitimated by him. There are obvious similarities between the M and the P on this point. Both shall guide and serve as

---

[65] Gächter, 1936(b), 186f. Cf Stauffer, 1963, 292; Cf also Schlatter, 1898, 52, who is of the opinion that the translationfunction existed already in the bilingual congregation in Jerusalem. The apostles had an M in order to be able to speak to both groups.

[66] Gächter, 1936(a), 104f and 111.

[67] Gächter, 1934, 205f.

[68] Cf the characterization by Le Déaut, 1971(b), 513: "...le traducteur devient exégete..."

[69] Cf Carrez, 1981, 332: "Le Paraclet est agent actualisateur du mémorial de Christ, rend actuelle sa parole..."

models. There is, however, also an important difference between them. The P, being the Spirit of God, represents a higher order of authority than the M.

Let me also make a side reflection here. The midrashic attitude, as it can be observed in the targumic translations, was primarily meant to be expressed orally. The targumic translation, for example, was not allowed to follow a written source so as to prevent the evolution of a written authority which was equal to the Torah. We know, nevertheless, that the oral tradition became very firm, and that it was codified in written texts later. The direct, spontaneous translation gradually became a chimera in that it also included traditional interpretations. Consequently, when the M began his work, half of it was already done. It was sufficient for him to clearly formulate the contents of the tradition. The tradition itself represented the life of the extended actual passage, and each version reflected one stage of a long process of working with the Scriptures.[70] A similar development can be discerned concerning the P's activity. His functions indicate that he, primarily, acted orally through human mediators. The BD probably had a leading position as the P's mouthpiece. The P himself seems to appropriate, according to the GJ, even a bit of this functon when the BD is going to die/has died. The P is thought of continuing this work (Cf 4.5.). None the less, as has been pointed out several times earlier, the P's activity is first codified in the GJ. The established assumption, that the GJ originated in stages, is a reasonable one. The johannine tradition grew, was modified and redacted before receiving its final form. Such a process implies an intermediary stage between oral and written form, which I have noted was true also in the case of the Targums. It was the lot of both the M-institution and the P to have their work codified in spite of the fact that such was not the intention (with certainty concerning the former; in all probability concerning the latter) from the beginning of their respective traditions.[71]

6.4.3.7. The prophetic feature

It is difficult to prove that the M displayed prophetic features. I have not been able to find any explicit evidence of such. This is not surprising if one takes into consideration the fact that prophecy was thought to have been removed from Israel in the time of Malachi. There are, on the other

---

[70] Le Déaut, 1971(b), 522.

[71] Concerning the P-sayings as promises which take their point of departure in the present shape of the GJ while, at the same time, reflect the process of tradition, see 6.2.

hand, no descriptions of the M which make a comparison between the M and the P impossible in this respect. Rather, the use of implicit arguments makes it possible to imagine the M as some kind of prophetic figure or at least as performing some prophetic functions, especially when speaking on God's behalf.

I have earlier (6.4.3.1.) mentioned that Aaron's duties as Moses' spokesman in Ex.4:12-16 are described in terms of M's activity in TargOnkelos and TargNeofiti. When this saying is taken up again in Ex.7:1, Moses assumes an almost divine authority while Aaron functions as his prophet. This pericope reflects the OT thought that prophets were *mediators* between God and men.[72] There is a shift of emphasis here in that Moses, usually regarded as a prophet and mediator,[73] becomes superior in divine authority to the prophet Aaron. One has, obviously, used the notions of prophet and mediator on different levels and in different contexts.[74] TargOnkelos renders *nāvi'* here with M. This indicates that it has not been impossible to regard the M as a bearer of certain prophetic features. The thought of mediation, in connection with the task of actualization, may have been the connecting link between the notion of prophecy and the M.[75]

There is not sufficient material to claim that the M was a prophetic figure, but it is also incorrect to maintain that he completely lacks prophetic features. The common denominator, mediation, indicates that there is no real obstacle, even in this respect, to the proposition that the M served as a model or background figure to the P.

[72] See Hermann, 1956, 46.

[73] This aspect is emphazised by Josephus. See Ant.Jud. 3:87. Cf Fascher,1927, 156ff; Schlatter, 1932, 57f.

[74] Philo illustrates the variety of prophetic mediators. The non-jew Bileam, De Vita Mosis, I, 277, and even the heathen god Hermes, De Leg. ad Gaium 99, could function as prophetic mediators. See also Hermann, 1956, 47.

[75] It is also possible to argue indirectly and compare the M with the early christian prophets in the service. They mediated an authoritative message from God to the congregation and translated, so to speak, God's will into intelligible words. The congregation understands itself 'simultaneously' addressed by the prophet and by God. Cf Minear, 1968, 5: "In any Christian gathering, the words of a prophet, whether oral or written, were sure to carry great weight, because they relayed a message from the God who was being worshipped... The listeners would realize that they were being addressed simultaneously by the prophet... by Christ, and by the Most High God..." This is a type of simultaneous mediation similar to the M's. The difference is that the originator of the message in the M's case is visibly and audibly present, while in the prophet's case he is said to be absent or invisibly present. Functionally, however, they seem to be similar to one another.

6.4.3.8. Function not office

Early on in the synagogal tradition, the M-function was not performed by appointed officials since anyone in the congregation could be invited to perform as the M (See 6.4.3.2.). Even individuals who were under age were capable of acting as the M.[76] This indicates that the M did not always carry out spontaneous translations, explanations, and expositions but, rather, transmited memorized traditions.[77] It was, then, originally more important to adhere to fixed traditions since the activities of translation and exposition were not differentiated.[78] Later the reading and translation, on the one hand, and the exposition, on the other, were separated. Thus there developed a need for qualified people to serve as M:s.[79] The level of ability which was later demanded is reflected in the fact that the designation 'amorā' later stood for the superior rabbi himself.[80] It is, of course, difficult to say how far this development had come in NT times. It is indisputable that there at this time existed officials who acted as M:s in individual cases (as was the case concerning the M of Gamaliel II). It is, however, impossible to prove that the M-institution had a fixed character during NT times. It is probable (especially when one considers the need for translation outside Palestine) that this institution had, at this time, a rather loose character and therefore that it was primarily the function which was of primary interest. It was of less interest who performed the function, since this role varied according to individual circumstances.

If this judgement is correct, it is in accordance with my conclusions concerning the P in 6.2. The P is realized through the individual disciples when they perform the functions ascribed to the P. This has little to do with any fixed structure of officials. At the same time, however, it is possible to discern a tendency towards a structure of authority based on the role of the P. Such a tendency is similar to the development I pointed out concerning the M-institution. The conclusions here seem to validate a phenomenological comparison of the P and the M.

---

[76] Meg.4.6. Cf however TosMeg 4:21. Cf Elbogen, 1913, 187f; Billerbeck, 1922ff., IV:1, 162ff.

[77] McNamara, 1966, 65; McNamara, 1972, 48-50. Cf Patte, 1975, 64, where the problem of the targumic translation as fixed tradition is discussed. The risk of inherent contradictions is obvious.

[78] Moore, 1927, 304; Cf Krauss, 1922, 179f, and Stauffer, 1963, 287. See also 5.3.

[79] See 6.4.3.2.

[80] Gächter, 1936(b), 181.

6.5. Summary

This chapter has argued, for the first time, that the M can provide a concrete background figure for the P, and that it enjoys a reasonable phenomenological and historical claim as such. At several points I have presented detailed information, but more decisive is that the argument in favour of the M-institution as a background for the P also sheds light upon essential features of the GJ as a whole, both regarding its composition and its contents. This also elucidates the primary realization of the P in the GJ: the BD. I have earlier (4.4.) shown similarities, as well as differences, between the P and the BD. Both the similarities and the differences may, in several respects, be explained against the background of the M. The P is Jesus' permanent M, whereas the BD functioned as an occasional one. The notion that the GJ was the first concrete result of the P's activity also fits in well against the pattern of the M-institution.

One might ask why the M played a significant role as a model for the GJ's author while it seems not to have been important to the rest of the NT. One cannot give any simple answer to this question. I think, however, that it is possible to say that the author of the GJ has *not* choosen this background figure in order to let it have a basic influence on the formation of the GJ. The M as a background figure is, rather, a natural consequence of the GJ's background in the synagogal tradition of interpreting the Scriptures. One can only speculate why such was the case, and there is no reason to do so here. I should like to stress also that the M was not of such importance that the GJ was built up around this figure. The M rather fit well into the general frame of the way divine revelation and tradition is reflected in the GJ as a whole. It is, as I should wish to call it, the *organic* relationship between the M's role in his context and the P's role in his, that makes the M an acceptable background figure for the P.

7. Epilogue

7.1. Retrospective review

This investigation has now come to an end. As I stressed in the introductory chapter I do not claim to have presented *the* solution to the riddle of the P. I hope, however, to have contributed to the elucidation of some of the methodological questions which surround the interpretation of the P and, above all, to a better understanding of the P's function according to the P-sayings and in the GJ as a whole.

One result has been the proposal of a multidimensional model which eliminates the frustration of searching for only one solution to the P's problem. Thus, it has been possible to do justice to the ambiguity of the idea of the P in the presentation of the GJ. The P is, in a broad sense, a forensic title which was familiar to the receivers of the GJ. As such it belongs to the important court-process motif found in the GJ. Further, the P is presented in a farewell situation which engendered associations to other farewell situations within the literary frame of reference of the receivers. Such associations stress the aspects of exhortation, comfort, and continuity. The 'successor', in the GJ, the P, guarantees the continuation of his predecessor's work by remaining with the disciples forever and, also, by the codification of the predecessor's words and works. Most important, the word παράκλητος is used to present the Spirit as the one who carries through christian paraclese. Paraclese is in this context understood as teaching-proclamation-preaching. This conclusion is made possible through reference to one field of usage of παρακαλεῖν-παράκλησις in the NT. The basic role of the P might then be defined as didactic.

This multidimensional model is found to be valid through the examination of the functions of the P according to the P-sayings. Thus, the original methodological point of departure holds true, i.e., the P is what he does.

It has also been shown that the P's basic didactic role corresponds to the interaction between Jesus, the P, and the BD in the GJ. All three function as mediators of revelation in different situations and with different authority yet they are mutually dependent upon one another.

I have also proposed a background against which the P's actual teaching activities can become better understood, i.e., the synagogue's way of interpreting and exposing the Scriptures. The synagogue's midrashic attitude has been investigated and its fundamental importance to the GJ's interpretation of the revelation in Jesus has been stressed.

Finally, as a consequence of the synagogal background, a proposal for a concrete background of the P has been made. The M and the M-institution have been approached phenomenologically as representing the synagogue's way of dealing with the Scriptures. It is not possible to prove the validity of this proposal, yet it remains highly reasonable. It sheds, in any case, light upon the concrete and personal presentation of the P in the GJ.

7.2. Concluding remarks

Methodologically it has been possible to avoid the mistakes both of searching one single meaning of the P and and of initially focusing upon probable backgrounds and background figures. Rather, a respect for the ambiguity of the presentation of the P in the GJ and a subsequent investigation of the functions of the P led in turn to a possible background figure - the M. The proposal of a background is, thus, the *result* of a chain of arguments instead of being the *presupposition* upon which conclusions concerning the P's functions and meaning were built. The probability of the proposed background is, then, apart from the historical problem of the M, dependent on the validity of the argumentation used.

Within the multidimensional model emphasis has been placed on the didactic aspect of the P's activity. This emphasis upon the didactics has consequences for the understanding of revelation, interpretation, tradition, succession, and authority, some of the most important issues and problems in the GJ. The idea of the P, then, is not only central to the GJ's message but becomes important also to that process through which the GJ became codified in writing. Thus, the special character of the GJ in comparison with the synoptics and the special presentation of the Spirit as the P in the GJ seem to be related. The particular role given the BD in the GJ can also be explained from this perspective.

The background of the P's basic didactic activity has been located in the synagogue. If this observation is correct it leads to the recognition of the important relation between worship and interpretation in the johannine community. Since the Spirit played a significant role in early christian worship, such a relation seems natural.

The fact that interpretation is the result of the P's activity in the context of worship might, finally, offer a means of building a bridge from the NT itself to its contemporary use. In other words, the P, in the context

of worship, could be seen as an important part of the contemporary hermeneutical discussion.[1] If one is to take the witness of the GJ seriously,
also from an historical point of view, one cannot overlook the functions
and the promise of the P. Hermeneutics, in a theological context, must
include the workings of the P as well as philosophical inquiry.

It would be an interesting research task to investigate if and, in that
case, how and to what extent the idea of the P has played a part in the
Church's intepretative work throughout history. It is obvious that the idea
of the Spirit has played an important role in this context, but it remains
unclear whether the Spirit, presented as the P in the GJ, has done so.
This task is, however, beyond the limits of this investigation.

[1] The reference to the P in contemporary hermeneutical reflection seems unduly rare.
One important exception is Vaticanum II. See Kothgasser, 1969. See also Feuillet, 1963.

Bibliography

Texts and translations

Biblia Hebraica..., ed. R. Kittel. 16th ed. by P. Kahle, A. Alt, O. Eissfeldt. Stuttgart 1971.

Biblia Hebraica Stuttgartensia..., ed. K. Elliger et W. Rudolph, Stuttgart 1968-76.

Die Weisheit des Jesus Sirach, hebräisch und deutsch, ed. R. Smend. Berlin 1906.

The Bible in Aramaic I-IV, ed. A. Sperber. Leiden 1959-1973.

Thargum Jonathan ben Usiel zum Pentateuch, ed. M. Ginsburger. Berlin 1903.

Targum Jonathan ben Uziel on the Pentateuch, ed. D. Rieder. Jerusalem 1974.

Das Fragmententhargum, ed. M. Ginsburger. Berlin 1899.

Targum Onkelos I-II, ed. A. Berliner. Berlin, Frankfurt, London 1884.

Neophyti 1..., ed. A. Diez Macho. I-IV. Madrid, Barcelona 1969-1974.

The Targums..., trans. J.W. Ethridge. I-II. London 1862-1865.

The Targum of Isaiah, ed. J.F. Stenning. Oxford 1949.

Septuaginta...I-II, ed. A. Rahlfs. 7th ed. Stuttgart 1962.

Novum Testamentum Graece, ed. E. Nestle, K. Aland. 26th ed. Stuttgart 1979.

Pseudepigrapha Veteris Testamenti Graece, ed. A.M. Denis and M. de Jonge. I-III. Leiden 1964-1970.

The Apocrypha and Pseudepigrapha of the Old Testament in English, ed. R.H. Charles. Oxford 1913.

The Old Testament Pseudepigrapha I, ed. J.H. Charlesworth. London 1983.

Jüdische Schriften aus hellenistisch-römischer Zeit, ed. W.G. Kümmel, C. Habicht, O. Kaiser, O. Plöger, J. Schreiner. Gütersloh 1973- .

The Assumption of Moses..., ed. R.H. Charles. London 1897.

Apocalypse syriaque de Baruch I-II, ed. P. Bogaert. Paris 1969.

The Ethiopic Version of the Book of Enoch..., ed. R.H. Charles. Oxford 1906.

The Books of Enoch. ed. J. Milik with the collaboration of M. Black. Oxford 1976.

Die Esra-Apokalypse I-II, ed. B. Violet, Leipzig 1910-1924.

Pseudo-Philon, Les Antiquites Bibliques, I (Introd., text, ed. D.J. Harrington, trans. J. Cazeaux). Paris 1976.

Discoveries in the Judean Desert 1-5, ed. D. Barthelemy..., Oxford 1955-68.

Die Texte aus Qumran, hebräisch und deutsch..., ed. E. Lohse. München 1964.

Philonis Alexandrini opera quae supersunt I-VII, ed. L. Cohn, P. Wendland. Berlin 1896-1930.

Philo... I-X, Suppl. I-II, ed. F.H. Colson, G.H. Whitaker, R. Marcus (The Loeb Classical Library). London, Cambridge, Mass. 1929-1962.

Josephus... I-IX, ed. H.St.J. Thackeray, R. Marcus, L. Feldman (The Loeb Classical Library). London, Cambridge, Mass. 1926-1965.

Die Mischna. Text, Übersetzung und ausführliche Erklärung..., ed. G. Beer, D. Holtzmann, S. Krauss... Giessen, Berlin 1912.

Mishnayoth, ed. P. Blackman. 2nd ed. New York 1964.

Tosephta, ed. M.S. Zuckermandel. Pasewalk, Trier 1879-1882.

The Tosefta..., ed. S. Lieberman. New York 1955.

Der babylonische Talmud... I-IX, ed. L. Goldschmidt. Berlin, Leipzig, Haag 1897-1934.

The Babylonian Talmud translated into English I-XXXV, ed. I. Epstein. London 1935-1948.

Midrash Rabba, ed. H. Freedman, London 1939.

Sifre zu Numeri..., ed. K.G. Kuhn I-IX. Stuttgart 1933-1959.

Die apostolischen Väter... I, ed. K. Bihlmeyer, Zweite Aufl., Tübingen 1956.

Hermas Le Pasteur, ed. R. Joly. Paris 1958.

Literature

Arndt, W. and Gingrich, F.W., 1957. *A Greek-English Lexicon* of the New Testament and Other Christian Literature. Chicago.

Asting, R., 1931. 'Parakleten i Johannesevangeliet', *Teologi og Kirkeliv,* Avhandlinger til den exegetiske forening 'Syvstjernens' 60-årsjubileum, Oslo, 85-98.

Aune, D.E., 1983. *Prophecy in Early Christianity and the Ancient Mediterranean World.* Grand Rapids, Michigan.

Aune, D.E., 1972. *The Cultic Setting of Realized Eschatology in Early Christianity.* (Supplements to Novum Testamentum.28). Leiden.

Bacher, W., 1913. *Die Proömien der alten jüdischen Homilie.* Leipzig.

Bacher, W., 1899. *Die älteste Terminologie der jüdischen Schriftauslegung.* Leipzig.

Bacher, W., 1906. 'Targum', *Jewish Encyclopedia,* New York and London, Vol.12, 57-63.

Bacher, W., 1914. *Tradition und Tradenten in den Schulen Palästinas und Babyloniens.* Leipzig.

Bacon, B.W., 1933. *The Gospel of the Hellenists.* New York.

Bacon, B.W., 1917. 'The "other" Comforter', *Expositor* 1917, 274-282.

Bammel, E., 1973. 'Jesus und der Paraklet in Johannes 16', *'Christ and Spirit'* in honour of CFD Moule, Cambridge, 199-217.

Barrett, C.K., 1978. *The Gospel according to John.* Second edition. London.

Barrett, C.K., 1975. *The Gospel of John and Judaism.* London.

Barrett, C.K., 1947. *The Holy Spirit and the Gospel Tradition.* London.

Barrett, C.K., 1950. 'The Holy Spirit in the Fourth Gospel', *Journal of Theological Studies 1,* 1-15.

Bauckham, R., 1983. 'The Liber Antiquitatum Biblicarum of Pseudo-Philo and the Gospels as "Midrash", *Gospel Perspectives,* Studies in Midrash and Historiography, ed. by R.T. France and D. Wenham., Sheffield, Vol.III, 33-76.

Bauer, W., 1925. *Das Johannesevamgelium,* 2.Aufl, Tübingen.

Bauer, W., 1958. *Griechisch-Deutsches Wörterbuch* zu den Schriften des Neuen Testaments und die übrigen urchristlichen Litteratur, Fünfte, verbesserte und stark vermehrte Auflage, Berlin 1958.

Becker, J., 1979. *Das Evangelium nach Johannes.* Kapitel 1-10. Gütersloh.

Becker, J., 1981. *Das Evangelium nach Johannes.* Kapitel 11-21. Gütersloh.

Becker, J., 1970(a). 'Die Abschiedsreden Jesu im Johannesevangelium', *Zeitschrift für die neutestamentliche Wissenschaft* 61, 215-246.

Becker, J., 1970(b). *Untersuchungen zur Entstehungsgeschichte der zwölf Patriarchen.* (Arbeiten zur Geschichte des antiken Judentums und des Urchristentums Band VIII.). Leiden.

Behm, J., 1967. 'παράκλητος', *Theological Dictionary of the New Testament* Grand Rapids, Michigan, V, 800-814.

Bergman, J., 1979. 'Discours D'Adieu - Testament - Discours Posthume', *Sagesse et Religion,* Colloque de Strasbourg. Paris.

Berrouard, M-F., 1949. 'Le paraclet, defenseur du Christ devant la conscience du croyant (Jn XVI,8-11)', *Revue des Sciences Philosophiques et Théologiques* 33, 361-389.

Betz, O., 1963. *Der Paraklet.* Leiden/Köln.

Billerbeck, P., 1922ff. See Strack, H.L.

Bjerkelund, C.J., 1967. *Parakalô.* Form,·Funktion und Sinn der parakalô-Sätze in den paulinischen Briefen. Oslo.

Blank, J., 1964. *Krisis.* Untersuchungen zur johanneischen Christologie und Eschatologie. Freiburg i.B.

Blinzler, J., 1965. *Johannes und die Synoptiker.* Ein Forschungsbericht. Stuttgart.

Bloch, R., 1954. 'Écriture et Tradition dans le judaïsme. Aperçus sur l'origine du Midrash', *Cahiers Sioniens* 8, 9-34.

Bloch, R., 1957. 'Midrash', *Supplément au Dictionnaire de la Bible,* Paris, V, 1263-1280.

Boice, J.M., 1970. *Witness and Revelation in the Gospel of John.* Grand Rapids, Michigan.

Boismard, M-E., 1959. 'Les citations targumiques du quatrième évangile', *Revue Biblique* LXVI, 374-378.

Bonnard. P., 1980. *Anamnesis:* recherches sur le Noveau Testament. Genève.

Bonnet, J., 1982. *Le "midrash" dans l'Evangile de Saint Jean.* St Etienne.

Borgen, P., 1965. *Bread from Heaven.* Leiden.

Borgen, P., 1968. 'God's Agent in the Fourth Gospel', *Religions in Antiquity,* Essays in Memory of E.R. Goodenough, ed. J. Neusner, Leiden, 136-148.

Borgen, P., 1969-70. 'Observations of the targumic character of the Prologue of John', *New Testament Studies 16, 288-295.*

Boring, M.E., 1978. 'The influence of christian prophecy on the johannine portrayal of the Paraclete and Jesus', *New Testament Studies* 25, 113-123.

Bornkamm, G., 1949. 'Der Paraklet im Johannesevangelium', *Festschrift für R. Bultmann,* Stuttgart-Köln, 12-35.

Bowker, J., 1969. *The Targums and rabbinic Literature.* Cambridge.

Brown, R.E., 1979. *The Community of the Beloved Disciple.* New York.

Brown, R.E., 1982. *The Epistles of John.* New York.

Brown, R.E., 1966-70. *The Gospel according to John* I-II. New York.

Brown, R.E., 1967. 'The Paraclete in the fourth Gospel', *New Testament Studies* 13, 113-132.

Brox, N., 1969. *Die Pastoralbriefe.* Regensburg.

Bultmann, R., 1950. *Das Johannesevangelium.* 11. Aufl. Göttingen.

Bultmann, R., 1972. *The History of the Synoptic Tradition.* Revised Version. Oxford.

Büchsel, F., 1926. *Der Geist Gottes im Neuen Testament.* Gütersloh.

Büchsel, F., 1964. 'ἐλέγχω', *Theological Dictionary of the New Testament* Grand Rapids, Michigan, II, 473-476.

Bühner, J-A., 1982. 'Denkstrukturen im Johannesevangelium', *Theologische Beiträge 13, 224-231.*

Carrez, M., 1981. 'Les promesses du Paraclet', *Église et Théologie* 12, 323-332.

Carson, D.A., 1979. 'The function of the paraclete in John 16:7-11', *Journal of Biblical Literature* 98, 547-566.

Carson, D.A., 1982. 'Understanding Misunderstandings in the Fourth Gospel', *Tyndale Bulletin* 33, 59-91.

Casurella, D., 1983. *The Johannine Paraclete in the Church Fathers.* (Beiträge zur Geschichte der biblischen Exegese 25.). Tübingen.

Chilton, B., 1980. 'John vii 34 and Targum Isaiah lii 13', *Novum Testamentum* 22, 176-178.

Chilton, B., 1983. 'Varieties and Tendencies of Midrash: Rabbinic Interpretations of Isaiah 24:23', *Gospel Perspectives*, Studies in Midrash and Historiography, ed. by R.T. France and D. Wenham, Sheffield, Vol.III, 9-32.

Conzelmann, H., 1981. *Der erste Brief an die Korinther.* 2. Aufl. Göttingen.

Corell, A., 1950. *Eskatologi och kyrka i Johannesevangeliet.* Stockholm.

Cothenet, É., 1972. 'L'Esprit de prophétie dans le "corpus" johannique', *Supplément au Dictionnaire de la Bible,* Paris, VIII, 1316-1331.

Cothenet, É., 1977. 'Les prophètes chrétiens comme exégètes charismatiques de l'écriture', *Prophetic Vocation in the New Testament and Today,* ed. by J. Panagopoulos, Leiden, 77-107.

Cullmann, O., 1948. 'Der johanneische Gebrauch doppeldeutiger Ausdrücke als Schlüssel zum Verständniss des vierten Evangeliums', *Theologische Zeitschrift* 4, 360-372.

Cullmann, O., 1945. 'Die Pluralität der Evangelien als theologisches Problem im Altertum', *Theologische Zeitschrift* 1, 23-42.

Cullmann, O., 1976. *The Johannine Circle.* London.

Cullmann, O., 1962. *Urchristentum und Gottesdienst.* 4. Aufl. Zürich.

Culpepper, R.A., 1983. *Anatomy of the Fourth Gospel.* Philadelphia.

Culpepper, R.A., 1975. *The Johannine School.* (SBL Dissertation Series 26.). Missoula, Montana.

Dahl, N.A., 1948. 'Anamnesis: Memoire et Commemoration dans le christianisme primitif', *Studia Theologica* 1, 69-95.

Daube, D., 1953. 'Alexandrian Methods of Interpretation and the Rabbis', *Festschrift H Lewald,* 27-44. Basel.

Dauer, A., 1968. 'Das Wort des Gekreuzigten an seine Mutter und "der Jünger den er liebte" ', *Biblische Zeitschrift* 12, 80-93. (Part I in 11, 1967, 222-239.).

Dautzenberg, G., 1975. *Urchristliche Prophetie.* Stuttgart-Berlin-Köln-Mainz.

Davies, J-G., 1953. 'The primary meaning of παράκλητος', *Journal of theological studies 4, 35-38.*

Dibelius, M. - Conzelmann, H., 1972. *The Pastoral Epistles.* Philadelphia.

Dodd, C.H., 1953. *The Interpretation of the Fourth Gospel.* Cambridge.

Dugmore, C.W., 1964. *The Influence of the Synagogue upon the Divine Office.* Westminster.

Dumais, M., 1976. *Le langage de l'Évangelisation.* L'annonce missionaire en milieu juif (Actes 13, 16-41). Paris-Montréal.

Dunn, J.D.G., 1983. 'Let John be John', *Das Evangelium und die Evangelien,* hrsg. P. Stuhlmacher, Tübingen, 309-399.

Dunn, J.D.G., 1977-78. 'Prophetic 'I'-sayings and the Jesustradition: The

Importance of Testing Prophetic Utterances within Early Christianity', *New Testament Studies* 24, 175-198.

Elbogen, I., 1913. *Der jüdische Gottesdienst in seiner geschichtlichen Entwicklung.* Leipzig.

Ellis, E.E., 1970. 'The Role of the Christian Prophet in Acts', *Apostolic History and the Gospel,* eds. W.W. Grasque and R.P. Martin, Exeter, 55-67.

Fascher, E., 1927. *Propheten.* Eine sprach- und religionsgeschichtliche Untersuchung. Giessen.

Feuillet, A., 1963. 'De munere doctrinali a paraclito in ecclesia expleto iuxta evangelium sancti Ioannis', *De scriptura et traditione,* Romae, 115-136.

Forestell, J.T., 1975. 'Jesus and the Paraclete in the Gospel of John', *Word and Spirit* (Essays in honour of D.M. Stanley), Willowdal/Canada, 151-197.

Forestell, J.T., 1979. *Targumic Traditions and the New Testament.* Ann Arbor, Michigan.

France, R.T., 1983. 'Jewish Historiography, Midrash and the Gospels', *Gospel Perspectives,* Studies in Midrash and Historiography, Sheffield, Vol.III, 99-127.

Freed, E.D., 1965. *Old Testament Quotations in the Gospel of John.* Leiden.

Gerhardsson, B., 1961. *Memory and Manuscript.* Oral Tradition and Written Transmission in Rabbinic Judaism and Early Christianity. Lund, Copenhagen.

Goulder, M., 1974. *Midrash and Lection in Matthew.* London.

Grant, R.M., 1966. *The Apostolic Fathers* (A New Translation and Commentary), Vol.4. London-Toronto.

Grayston, K., 1979. 'A Problem of Translation. The Meaning of Parakaleo, Paraklesis in the New Testament', *Scripture Bulletin* XI, 27-31.

Grayston, K., 1981. 'The Meaning of PARAKLETOS', *Journal for the Study of the New Testament* 13, 67-82.

Grudem, W.A., 1982. *The Gift of Prophecy in 1 Corinthians.* Washington, D.C.

Gryglewicz, F., 1979. 'Die Aussagen über den Heiligen Geist im vierten Evangelium, Überlieferung und Redaktion; *Studien zum Neuen Testament und seiner Umwelt* 4, 45-53.

Guilding, A., 1960. *The fourth Gospel and jewish worship.* Oxford.

Gunther, J.J., 1981. 'The relation of the Beloved Disciple to the Twelwe', *Theologische Zeitschrift* 37, 129-148.

Gaechter, P., 1963. *Das Matthäusevangelium.* Innsbruck-Wien-München.

Gächter, P., 1934. 'Der formale Aufbau der Abschiedsrede Jesu', *Zeitschrift für Katholische Theologie* 58, 155-207.

Gächter, P., 1936(a). 'Strophen im Johannesevangelium', *Zeitschrift für Katolische Theologie* 60, 9-120.

Gächter, P., 1936(b). 'Die Dolmetscher der Apostel', *Zeitschrift für Katholische Theologie* 60, 161-187.

Haacker, K., 1972. *Die Stiftung des Heils:* Untersuchungen zur Struktur der johanneischen Theologie. (Arbeiten zur Theologie. Series 1. Vol.97). Stuttgart.

Haenchen, E., 1980. *Das Johannesevangelium.* Tübingen.

Hanson, A.T., 1983. *The Living Utterances of God.* London.

Hanson, A.T., 1980. *The NT Interpretation of Scripture.* London.

von Harnack, A., 1927. 'Christus praesens - Vicarius Christi', *Sitzungsberichte der Preussischen Akademie der Wissenschaften,* Berlin, 415-446.

Hartman, L, 1984. 'An attempt at a Text-Centered Exegesis of John 21', *Studia Theologica* 38, 29—45.

Hartman, L., 1979. *Asking for a Meaning.* (Coniectanea Biblica, N.T. Series 12.). Uppsala.

Hartman, L., 1963-64. 'Davids Son. Apropå Acta 13, 16-41', *Svensk Exegetisk Årsbok* 28-29, 117-134.

Hartman, L., 1966. *Prophecy Interpreted.* (Coniectanea Biblica N.T. Series 1.). Lund.

Harvey, A.E., 1976. *Jesus on Trial.* A Study in the Fourth Gospel. London.

Hawkin, D.J., 1977. 'The Function of the Beloved-Disciple-Motif in the Johannine Redaction', *Laval théologique et philosophique* 33, 135-150.

Hawthorne, G.F., 1975. 'Christian Prophets and the Sayings of Jesus: Evidence of and Criteria for', *SBL Seminar Papers,* Missoula, Montana, Vol.2, 105-129.

Hegstad. H., 1977. *Synagogen, sted for skriftlesning og utleggelse på sabbaten.* Trondheim. (Microfiche).

Hengel, M., 1984. *Die Evangelienüberschriften.* (Sitzungsberichte der Heidelberger Akademie der Wissenschaften 3.). Heidelberg.

Hermann, A., 1956. 'Dolmetschen im Altertum', *Beiträge zur Geschichte des Dolmetschens,* von K. Thieme, A Hermann und E Glässer, München, 25-59.

Hill, D., 1977. 'Christian Prophets as Teachers or Instructors in the Church', *Prophetic Vocation in the New Testament and Today,* ed. by J Panagopoulos, Leiden, 108-130.

Hill, D., 1979. *New Testament Prophecy.* London.

Hill, D., 1974. 'On the evidence for the creative role of christian prophets', *New Testament Studies* 20, 262-274.

Holwerda, D.L., 1959. *The Holy Spirit and Eschatology in the Gospel of John.* Kampen.

Hruby, K., 1971. *Die Synagoge.* Geschichtliche Entwicklung einer Institution. Zürich.

Isaacs, M.E., 1983. 'The Prophetic Spirit in the Fourth Gospel', *The Heythrop Journal* 24, 391-407.

Jeremias, J., 1981. *Die Briefe an Timotheus und Titus.* Göttingen.

Johansson, N., 1940. *Parakletoi.* Vorstellungen von Fürsprechern für die Menschen vor Gott in der alttestamentlichen Religion, im Spätjudentum und Urchristentum. Lund.

Johnston, G., 1970. *The Spirit-Paraclete in the Gospel of John.* Cambridge.

de Jonge, M., 1979. 'The Beloved Disciple and the Date of the Gospel of John', *Text and Interpretation:* Studies in the New Testament presented to Matthew Black, ed. E. Best and R McL. Wilson. Cambridge, 99-114.

Joüon, P., 1938. 'La verbe ἀναγγέλλω dans Saint Jean', *Recherches de Science Religieuse* 28, 234-235.

Kahle, P., 1959. *The Cairo Geniza.* Second ed. Oxford.

Kelly, J.N.D., 1963. *A commentary on the pastoral Epistles.* London.

Klein, M.L., 1982. 'Associative and Complementary Translation in the Targum', *Eretz-Israel,* Archeological, Historical and Geographical Studies Vol 16, ed. B.A. Levine - A. Malamat, Jerusalem, 134-140.

Klein, M.L., 1976. 'Converse Translation: A Targumic Technique', *Biblica* 57, 515-537.

Kothgasser, A.M., 1971 and 1972. 'Die Lehr, Erinnerungs-, Bezeugungs- und Einführungsfunktion des johanneischen Geist-Parakleten gegenüber der Christusoffenbarung', *Salesianum* 33, 557-598, and 34, 3-51.

Kothgasser, A.M., 1969. 'Dogmenentwicklung und die Funktion des Geist-Parakleten nach den Aussagen des zweiten vatikanischen Konzils', *Salesianum* 31, 379-460.

Kragerud, A., 1959. *Der Lieblingsjünger im Johannesevangelium.* Oslo.

Krauss, S., 1922. *Synagogale Altertümer.* Berlin-Wien.

Kuhl, J., 1967. *Die Sendung Jesu und die Kirche nach dem Johannes-Evangelium.* St Augustin.

Kuhn, K.G., 1969. 'The Lords Supper and the Communal Meal at Qumran', *The Scrolls and the New Testament,* ed. by K. Stendahl, New York, 65-93.

Kümmel, W.G., 1972. *Introduction to the New Testament.* London.

Kysar, R., 1975. *The Fourth Evangelist and His Gospel:* An examination of Contemporary Scholarship. Minneapolis, Minnesota.

Langbrandtner, W., 1977. *Weltferner Gott oder der Gott der Liebe:* Der Ketzerstreit in der johanneischen Kirche:eine exegetisch-religionsgeschichtliche Untersuchung mit Berücksichtigung der koptisch-gnostischen Texte aus Nag-Hammadi. Frankfurt a.M. - Bern.

de La Potterie, I., 1977. 'Parole et esprit dans S. Jean', *Bibliotheca Ephemeridum Theologicarum Lovaniensium* 44, 177-201.

de La Potterie, I. - Lyonnet, S., 1965. *La vie selon l'Esprit condition du chretien*. Paris.

Leaney, A.R.C., 1972. 'The Historical Background and Theological Meaning of the Paraclete', *Duke Divinity School Review* 37, 146-159.

Le Déaut, R., 1971(a). 'Apropos a Definition of Midrash', *Interpretation* 25, 259-281.

Le Déaut, R., 1963. *La nuit paschale*. Rome.

Le Déaut, R., 1968. 'Le substrat araméen des évangiles: scolies en marge de l'Aramaic Approach de Matthew Black', *Biblica* 49, 388-399.

Le Déaut, R., 1965. *Liturgie juive et Nouveau Testament*. Rome.

Le Déaut, R., 1974. 'Targumic Literature and New Testament Interpretation', *Biblical Theology Bulletin* 4, 243-289.

Le Déaut, R., 1971(b). 'Un phénomène spontané de l'hermeneutique juive ancienne: le targumisme', *Biblica* 52, 505-525.

Leipoldt, J. - Morenz, S., 1953. *Heilige Schriften*. Leipzig.

Lemonnyer, A., 'L'Esprit-Saint Paraclet', *Revue des Sciences Philosophiques et Théologiques* 16, 293-307.

Lentzen-Deis, F., 1970. *Die Taufe Jesu nach den Synoptikern*. Frankfurt am Main.

Liddell, H.G. - Scott, R., 1968. *A Greek-English Lexicon*. Oxford.

Lindars, B., 1972. *The Gospel of John*. London.

Lindars, B., 1970. '$\delta\iota\varkappa\alpha\iota\sigma\acute{\upsilon}\nu\eta$ in Jn 16.8 and 10', *Mélanges Bibliques* en hommage au B. Rigaux, Gembloux, 275-285.

Locher, G.W., 1966. 'Der Geist als Paraklet', *Evangelische Theologie* 26, 565-579.

Lorenzen, T., 1971. *Der Lieblingsjünger im Johannesevangelium*. Stuttgart.

Malatesta, E., 1978. *Interiority and Covenant*. Rome.

Malatesta, E., 1973. 'The Spirit Paraclete in the Fourth Gospel', *Biblica* 54, 539-550.

Mann, J., 1940f. *The Bible as read and preached in the old synagogue,* I and II, ed. I. Sonne, Cincinatti 1940 and 1966.

Martyn, J.L., 1979. *History and Theology in the Fourth Gospel*. Second Edition, Revised and Enlarged. Abingdon, Nashville.

Martyn, J.L., 1978. *The Gospel of John in Christian History*. New York-Ramsey-Toronto.

Maybaum, S., 1901. *Die ältesten Phasen in der Entwicklung der jüdischen Predigt*. Berlin.

Meyer, G., 1974. *Index Philonis*. Berlin-New York.

Maynard, A.H., 1984. 'The Role of Peter in the Fourth Gospel', *New Testament Studies* 30, 531-548.

McNamara, M., 1972. *Targum and Testament*. Shannon.

McNamara, M., 1966. *The New Testament and the palestinian targum to the pentateuch.* Rome.

Meeks, W., 1967. *The Prophet-King.* Leiden

Merkel, H., 1978. *Die Pluralität der Evangelien als theologisches und exegetisches Problem in der alten Kirche.* Bern - Frankfurt am Main - Las Vegas.

Mettinger, T., 1971. *Salomonis State Officials* (Coniectanea Biblica O.T. Series 5.). Lund

Michaelis, W., 1967. 'ὁδός etc.', *Theological Dictionary of the New Testament,* Grand Rapids, Michigan, V, 42-114.

Michaelis, W., 1947. 'Zur Herkunft des johanneischen Paraklet-Titels', *Coniectanea Neotestamentica* 11, Uppsala, 147-162.

Michaels, J.R., 1975. 'The Johannine Words of Jesus and Christian Prophecy', *Society of Biblical Literature* 1975, Seminar Papers, ed. by G. McRae, Missoula, Montana, Vol.2, 233-264.

Michel, O., 1060. *Der Brief an die Hebräer.* 11. Aufl. Göttingen.

Michel, O., 1967. 'μιμνήσκομαι etc.', *Theological Dictionary of the New Testament,* Grand Rapids, Michigan, IV, 675-683.

Miguens, M., 1963. *El Paraclito* (Studi Biblici Francescani Analecta). Jerusalem.

Miller, M., 1971. 'Targum, Midrash and the Use of the Old Testament in the New Testament', *Journal for the Study of Judaism* 2, 29-82.

Minear, P.S., 1968. *I saw a New Earth.* Washington/Cleveland.

Minear, P.S., 1977. 'The Beloved Disciple in the Gospel of John - Some Clues and Conjectures', *Novum Testamentum* 19, 105-123.

Minear, P.S., 1983. 'The original functions of John 21', *Journal of Biblical Literature* 102, 85-98.

Moore, G.F., 1927ff. *Judaism* I-III, 1927-30. Cambridge.

Moreton, M.B., 1980. 'The Beloved Disciple again', *International Congress on Biblical Studies* 6, ed. by E.A. Livingstone, Sheffield, Vol.2, 215-218.

Morgenthaler, R., 1958. *Statistik des Neutestamentlichen Wortschatzes.* Zürich - Frankfurt am Main.

Morris, L., 1983. 'The Gospels and the Jewish Lectionaries', *Gospel Perspectives,* Studies in Midrash and Historiography, ed. by R.T. France and D. Wenham, Sheffield, Vol.III, 129-156.

Morris, L., 1964. *The New Testament and the Jewish Lectionaries.* London.

Moule, C.F.D., 1967. *The Phenomenon of the New Testament.* London.

Mowinckel, S., 1933. 'Die Vorstellungen des Spätjudentums vom heiligen Geist als Fürsprecher und der johanneische Paraklet', *Zeitschrift für die neutestamentliche Wissenschaft* 32, 97-130.

Müller, U.B., 1974. 'Die Parakletenvorstellung im Johannesevangelium', *Zeitschrift für Theologie und Kirche* 71, 31-78.

Müller, U.B., 1975. *Prophetie und Predigt im Neuen Testament.* Gütersloh.

Mussner, F., 1961. 'Die johanneischen Parakletsprüche und die apostolische Tradition', *Biblische Zeitschrift* 5, 56-70.

Neirynck, F., 1975. 'The 'Other Disciple' in Jn 18,15-16', *Ephemerides Theologicae Lovanienses,* Louvain - Leuven, 113-141.

Neusner, J., 1960. 'History and Midrash', *Judaism* 9, 47-54.

Neusner, J., 1983. *Midrash in Context.* Philadelphia.

Nissilä, K., 1979. *Das Hohepriestermotiv im Hebräerbrief.* Helsinki.

Nickels, P., 1967. *Targums and Testament,* A Bibliography together with a New Testament index. Rome.

Olsson, B., 1974. *Structure and Meaning in the Fourth Gospel* (Coniectanea Biblica N.T. Series 6.). Lund.

Otto, H-P., 1969. *Funktion und Bedeutung des Lieblingsjüngers im Johanesevangelium* (Heidelberger Zulassungsarbeit zum Theologischen Staatsexamen). (Not printed and not available according to the university library in Uppsala).

Painter, J., 1975. *John: Witness and Theologian.* London.

Painter, J., 1981. 'The Farewell Discourses and the History of Johannine Christianity', *New Testament Studies* 27, 525-543.

Pamment, M., 1983. 'The Fourth Gospel's Beloved Disciple', *The Expository Times* 94, 363-367.

Patte, D., 1975. *Early Jewish Hermeneutic in Palestine.* Missoula, Montana.

Perrot, C., 1973. *La lecture de la bible dans la synagogue.* Hildesheim.

Porsch, F., 1974. *Pneuma und Wort,* Ein exegetischer Beitrag zur Pneumatologie des Johannesevangeliums.Frankfurt.

Preiss, T., 1954. 'Justification in Johannine Thought', *Life and Christ* (Studies in Biblical Theology 13), Chicago, 9-31.

Raney, W.H., 1933. *The Relation of the Fourth Gospel to the Christian Cultus.* Giessen.

Reim, G., 1983(a). 'Johannesevangelium und Synagogengottesdienst - eine Beobachtung', *Biblische Zeitschrift* 27, 101.

Reim, G., 1974. *Studien zum alttestamentlichen Hintergrund des Johannesevangeliums.* Cambridge.

Reim, G., 1983(b). 'Targum und Johannesevangelium', *Biblische Zeitschrift* 27, 1-13.

Rengstorf, K.H., 1964. 'διδάσκω etc.', *Theological Dictionary of the New Testament,* Grand Rapids, Michigan, II, 135-165.

Ricca, P., 1966. *Die Eschatologie des vierten Evangeliums.* Zürich.

Richard, E., 1985. 'Expressions of Double Meaning and their Function in the Gospel of John', *New Testament Studies* 31, 96-112.

Riesenfeld, H., 1972. 'A probable background to the johannine paraclete',

Ex orbe religionum, Studia Geo Widengren..., ed. J.Bergman, Leiden, 266-274.

Roloff, J., 1968-69. 'Der Johanneische 'Lieblingsjünger' und der Lehrer der Gerechtigkeit', *New Testament Studies* 15, 129-151.

Rowley, H.H., 1967. *Worship in Ancient Israel,* Its Forms and Meaning. London.

Sasse, H., 1925. 'Der Paraklet im Johannesevangelium', *Zeitschrift für die neutestamentliche Wissenschaft* 24, 260-277.

Schelkle, K.H., 1961. *Die Petrusbriefe. Der Jakobusbrief.* Freiburg - Basel - Wien.

Schlatter, A., 1898. *Die Kirche Jerusalems.* Gütersloh.

Schlatter, A., 1932. *Die Theologie des Judentums nach dem Bericht des Josephus.* Gütersloh.

Schlier, H., 1973. 'Der heilige Geist als Interpret nach dem Johannes-evangelium', *Intenationale Katolische Zeitschrift* 2, 97-108.

Schlier, H., 1964. 'Zum Begriff des Geistes nach dem Johannesevange-lium', *Besinnung auf das Neue Testament* II, Freiburg i.B., 264-271.

Schmitz, O., 1967. '$\pi\alpha\varrho\alpha\varkappa\alpha\lambda\acute{\epsilon}\omega$ and $\pi\alpha\varrho\acute{\alpha}\varkappa\lambda\eta\sigma\iota\varsigma$ in the NT', *Theological Dictionary of the New Testament,* Grand Rapids, Michigan, V, 793-799.

Schnackenburg, R., 1965ff. *Das Johannesevangelium,* Teil I-IV, Freiburg - Basel - Wien 1965-84.

Schnackenburg, R., 1970. 'Der Jünger, den Jesus liebte', *Evangelisch-Kato-lischer Kommentar zum Neuen Testament,* Vorarbeiten 2, Zürich - Köln - Neu-kirchen, 97-117.

Schnackenburg, R., 1977. 'Die johanneische Gemeinde und ihre Geister-fahrung', *Festschrift für H. Schürmann,* hrsg. R. Schnackenburg, J. Ernst und J. Wanke, Leipzig, 277-306.

Schneider, J., 1978. *Das Evangelium nach Johannes.* 2. Aufl. Berlin.

Schniewind, J., 1964. '$\mathring{\alpha}\gamma\gamma\epsilon\lambda\acute{\iota}\alpha$ etc.', *Theological Dictionary of the New Testa-ment,* Grand Rapids, Michigan, I, 56-73.

Schulz, S., 1972. *Das Evangelium nach Johannes.* Göttingen.

Schulz, S., 1957. *Untersuchungen zur Menschensohn-Christologie im Johannes-evangelium.* Göttingen.

Schwarz, G., 1982. 'Gen.1:1; 2:2a und Joh.1:1a, 3a - ein Vergleich', *Zeit-schrift für die neutestamentliche Wissenschaft* 73, 136-137.

Schäfer, J.P., 1970. 'Die Termini "Heiliger Geist" und "Geist der Prop-hetie" in den Targumim und das Verhältnis der Targumim zu einander', *Vetus Testamentum* 20, 304-314.

Schäfer, P., 1972. *Die Vorstellung vom heiligen Geist in der rabbinischen Literatur.* München.

Seeligmann, I.L., 1953. 'Voraussetzungen der Midrashexegese', *Supple-*

ments to *Vetus Testamentum Congress Volume,* Copenhagen, 150-181.

Shafaat, A., 'Geber of the Qumran Scrolls and the Spirit-Paraclete of the Gospel of John', *New Testament Studies* 27, 263-269.

Snaith, N.H., 1945-46. 'The Meaning of "The Paraclete" ', *The Expository Times* 57, 47-50.

Strack, H.L., Billerbeck, P., 1922ff. *Kommentar zum Neuen Testament aus Talmud und Midrash* I-IV (1922-1928), V-VI (1959). München.

Strathmann, H., 1967. 'μάϱτυς etc.', *Theological Dictionary of the New Testament,* Grand Rapids, Michigan, IV, 474-514.

Stauffer, E., 1963. 'Der Methurgeman des Petrus', *Neutestamentliche Aufsätze,* Festschrift für Prof. J. Schmid zum 70. Geburtstag, ed. J.Blinzler, O. Kuss, F. Mussner, Regensburg,283-293.

Stuhlmacher, P., 1983. 'Zum Thema: Das Evangelium und die Evangelien', *Das Evangelium und die Evangelien,* herausgegeben von P. Stuhlmacher, Tübingen, 1-26.

Thyen, H., 1977. 'Entwicklungen innerhalb der joh. Theologie und Kirche von Joh.21 und der Lieblingsjünger des Evangeliums', *Bibliotheca Ephemeridum Theologicarum Lovaniensium* 44, 259-299.

Thyen, H., 1971. 'Johannes 13 und die "Kirchliche Redaktion" des vierten Evangeliums', *Tradition und Glaube,* Das frühe Christentum in seiner Umwelt, Festschrift K.G. Kuhn, Göttingen, 343-356.

Thüsing, W., 1960. *Die Erhöhung und Verherrlichung Jesu im Johannesevangelium.* Münster.

Trites, A.A., 1977. *The New Testament Concept of Witness.* Cambridge.

van Unnik, W.C., 1979. 'A Greek Characteristic of Prophecy in the Fourth Gospel', *Text and Interpretation,* Studies in the New Testament presented to M. Black, ed. by E. Best and R. McL. Wilson, Cambridge, 211-229.

Vermes, G., 1970. 'Bible and Midrash: Early Old Testament Exegesis', *The Cambridge History of the Bible* I, ed. by P.R. Ackroyd and C.F. Evans, Cambridge, 199-231.

Vermes, G., 1961. *Scripture and Tradition in Judaism.* Leiden.

Watty, W.W., 1979. 'The Significance of Anonymity in the Fourth Gospel', *The Expository Times* 90, 209-212.

Weingreen, J., 1976. *From Bible to Mishna.* Manchester.

Whitacre, R.A., 1982. *Johannine Polemic,* The Role of Tradition and Theology. Chico, California.

Wilckens, U., 1980. 'Der Paraklet und die Kirche', *Kirche,* Festschrift für Günther Bornkamm zum 75. Geburtstag, hrsg von D. Lührmann und G. Strecker, Tübingen, 185-203.

Windisch, H., 1927. 'Die fünf johanneischen Parakletsprüche', *Festschrift für A Jülicher*, Tübingen, 110-137.

Woll, D.B., 1981. *Johannine Christianity in Conflict:* Authority, Rank and Succession in the First Farewell Discourse (SBL Dissertation Series 60.). Missoula, Montana.

Wright, A.G., 1967. *The literary genre Midrash*. New York.

York, A.D., 1974. 'The Dating of Targumic Literature', *Journal for the Study of Judaism* 4, 49-62.

York, A.D., 1979. 'The Targum in the Synagogue and in the School', *Journal for the Study of Judaism* 10, 74-86.

Young, F.W., 1955. 'A Study of the Relation of Isaiah to the Fourth Gospel', *Zeitschrift für die neutestamentliche Wissenschaft* 46, 215-233.

Zeitlin, S., 1953. 'Midrash: A Historical Study', *The Jewish Quarterly Review* 44, 21-36.

Zunz, (L)., 1892. *Die gottesdienstlichen Vorträge der Juden*. Frankfurt a.M.

Index of Authors

Index of Passages (selection)